Praise for *Mania Mysteries: A Grief Journey*

"*Mania Mysteries: A Grief Journey* is an important and brave volume. Our lives over time are always colored by loss and unexpected periods of turmoil. In fact, few realize that one in five of us will be affected by serious psychiatric illness. *Mania Mysteries* beautifully, importantly and painfully illuminates the complexity and learning that can shape our journey. I highly recommend it."

- Jonathan Cohen, Ph.D., Practicing Clinical Psychologist; Adjunct Professor in Psychology and Education; President Emeritus, *The National School Climate Center: Educating Minds and Hearts because the Three Rs's Are Not Enough*

"Cat Greenstreet says she doesn't recommend mania as a path of self-development. Nevertheless, she courageously serves as a brilliantly articulate role-model for how it can be. Cat's story is riveting – and the meaning she makes from her experience takes John Barth's words (*The story of your life is not your life; it's your story*) to a new level. When she tells us how she now balances Parker Palmer with Rudolf Steiner, she points the way from her former paradigm of seeing through a lens of spiritual worlds to a way of living with greater integrity and wholeness."

> – Dr. Sally Z. Hare, Coastal Carolina University Distinguished Professor Emerita and international Circle of Trust® facilitator.

"In rich and moving language Cat Greenstreet takes us through the unraveling of her sense of identity after the death of her sister. She invites us inside the mania that overtook her - into the grandiosity and paranoia - and also shows us the love, fear and exhaustion of those who care for her through this "psychic tsunami". Writing the book has been part of her own healing process. She explores events in her biography and also faces her family genetic legacy as she searches for clues to what set off this psychic break. In ways that will inspire others who are touched by such struggles, she comes to a new acceptance of her particular life journey and moves gradually toward a new and more balanced integration of self."

> – Signe Eklund Schaefer, author of *Why on Earth? Biography and the Practice of Human Becoming*

Cat Greenstreet's *Mania Mysteries* is a multifaceted, in-depth exploration of her experience of psychotic mania, her therapeutic treatment (both conventional and unconventional), and its effect on herself and those around her. As she details the personal context for her manic and hypomanic episodes, she creates a richly textured tapestry of relationships, experiences of loss and change, and insights into the role that grief, trauma and stress – as well as genetics – may play in its onset. She also shares her complex and positive spirituality, her experience of psychotherapy and healing, and her interactions with a deep network of personal support that gave her the resources to understand and grow from her experiences. Her writing is eloquent, insightful, powerful and humble – she is a credible witness to her inner and outer experiences, and thoroughly engages us in her journey to make sense of them. Cat Greenstreet's life was touched by mania, and in turn, she beautifully touches us with the insight and personal growth she has gleaned from it."

   – Albert Bellg, Ph.D., Clinical Psychologist, Circle of Trust® facilitator

"Greenstreet's extraordinary book is fascinating for the layman, illuminating for the clinician and reassuring for sufferers of bi-polar illness."

   – Sheila A. Falk, Psychoanalyst

Mania Mysteries
A Grief Journey

Cat Greenstreet

Mania Mysteries: A Grief Journey
Copyright © 2018
Cat Greenstreet

All rights reserved. This publication may not be reproduced, stored in a retrieval system, or transmitted in any form: recording, mechanical, electronic, or photocopy, without written permission of the publisher. The only exception is brief quotations used in book reviews.

Comments: Cgreenstreet@verizon.net

ISBN: 978-1-941069-86-8

Cover photograph: "Deschutes Rapids."
Copyright © David Lorenz Winston.
Used by permission of David Lorenz Winston.

Cover design: David Lorenz Winston

Author photograph by Wil Greenstreet

Names are used with permission except for those changed to protect privacy.

Continuation of the copyright information - page 326

Prose Press
Pawleys Island, South Carolina 29585
prosencons@live.com

For Wil, Morgan, and Mom with deepest gratitude

For Dad and Lynn, who live eternally in my heart

For the mystery of resilience

Contents

Prologue 1

Part I: Mania

1 Turning Points 7
2 The County Hospital 33
3 The Private Hospital 54
4 Following the Tracks 78

Part II: Perspective

5 Anatomy of a Mini-Episode 95
6 Anatomy of a Manic Episode 121
7 Pressure Cooker 168
8 Psychotherapy Before 189

Part III: A New Integration of Self

9 Recovery and Resilience 228
10 Psychotherapy and Other Self Care 231
11 Searching for Clues 235
12 I Believe 239
13 Pilgrimage 244
14 Cynicism and Rebirth 248
15 Prelude to Mania 252
Bird's Nest 255

16	Mood Stabilizer	256
17	Moving Forward	261
18	Why Have You Forsaken Me?	264
	Mysteriously Over	272
19	Community and Other Nourishment	273
20	After the Storm	281
21	Questions and Hope	284
22	Spring	289
23	Evolution	290
24	Down to the Marrow	292
25	The Seclusion Room	296
	Hurdles	300

Epilogue: The Loom of Resilience 302

Notes 309
Quote Sources 316
To Go Deeper 318
Gratitudes 323
About the Author 325

Prologue

How thin is the wall between us and madness? No one knows what it is made of. No one knows how much pressure it can withstand. Until it gives.

– Jan-Philipp Sendker

Mania Mysteries is a book about a manic episode I had in the spring and early summer of 2014 when I was 66 years old. At the time of the psychotic break, I was a high-functioning professional woman with strong, loving relationships. How and why this happened to me is part of the mystery. Now some years after, I am back in the flow of my life but a life different in substantive ways from before the break.

I am often asked if this was my first experience with mania. The answer is no. It was, however, the first time in 44 years. At the age of 22 – a common start of symptoms of bipolar disorder – I was on shaky ground in relation to self-knowledge, self-esteem, and self-worth. I had dropped out of college and had little direction, except to be a good hippie. It was 1970, and I was enamored with peyote and other hallucinogens, as were the other hippies I was traveling with in our yellow school bus, which landed in a commune in the Ozarks. These drugs gave me a taste of the higher consciousness I craved, a world of ecstatic oneness with nature and spirit, where everything felt perfect. This trip ended when I was committed to a mental hospital and the psychotic mania came to a stone cold stop after 11 electroshock treatments.[1]

Dr. Wilson, my current psychiatrist, suggested we just forget about the 1971 episode, especially because of the drug involvement but also the distance between then and now: from a 22-year-old just finding her way in life to an extremely competent woman in her mid-60s, again seeking how best to serve her self, her family, and a troubled world. While I saw his point, I still can't dismiss that first manic episode: it was a critical part of life's journey, a steppingstone to my becoming an adult.

My psychotherapist, Therese, offered another angle: "Maybe you needed to relive that 1971 episode. Who knows? Maybe you just did." But why? I wondered. How strange life is! Everything in the universe moves in cycles, yet I'm surprised when it happens in my own life. Was there something I had to face with a more mature self? I liked her perspective. It intrigued me that to make a deep change in myself at 22 and at 66, both spiritual and earthly, my soul was drawn to mania, and I was pulled into a psychic tornado that in both cases would radically change the landscape of my life, requiring reconstruction from the ground up. Both of these episodes required hospitalizations with the associated horrors. Yet for this writing and for all the reasons Dr. Wilson named, I decided that the '71 episode was best mentioned only when it helped enlighten a point I was making.

Mania Mysteries is also a journey of deep loss and the way grief eroded the architecture of my personality – my identity, my relationships, my approach to vocation – as insistently as waves melt away a sandcastle caringly built too close to the shore. My sister Lynn died in 2012 from lung cancer, and throughout the subsequent year and a half, my grieving was a relentless force, pushing me to break from the way I had oriented my life while she was here on earth. You see, we were "intertwingled," a word she concocted as a child. Maybe I needed to go wild to strip away the assumptions and unconscious agreements that had fashioned our deeply loving relationship. This story builds a bridge between my psychic-psychotic event and the impact her death and other losses had on my life. More specifically, I believe that the transformation I experienced following the episode was essential in the wake of Lynn's death. The fact that it came through a manic episode is another wrinkle in the mystery.

There was also one other episode, not full-blown mania, not a total break with reality like the other two. In 2001 when I was 53, I experienced a brush with mania. Metaphorically, the body of the dragon emerged from the waters, and I soared on its back for a brief time. With help from family and a friend, along with my own disciplined spiritual practice, I was able to send the beast back into the depths where I needed it to be. In many ways, however, this was a prelude to the more powerful episode in 2014. Mania is a force to be reckoned with. In 2001 I was able to tame it; in 2014 it overpowered me. But what was the difference between those two times? What was the same? Why did the mania return with such seductive insistence?

Writing *Mania Mysteries* was an intrinsic part of my healing journey, gradually taking on a life of its own. As I shared what I was writing with my husband and some friends, they encouraged me to continue and eventually publish my story for others who hunger to understand more about the nature of psychotic mania. These may be individuals and their families and friends who have lived through such events, healthcare and mental health professionals who meet and treat such people and their families, and students who may do so in the future. This book may also interest anyone who wants to reflect on how the death of someone close affects the very fabric of our lives. It may attract anyone fascinated by the mysterious workings of the human being.

In Part I, "Mania," I offer the reader as much of the actual experience as I can remember. It addresses what it's like to be in an altered psychic state and what happens in a family and in our culture when someone finds herself in that mysterious, glorious, and frightening place.

In Part II, "Perspectives," I analyze the situational underpinnings of my last two experiences with mania: the less powerful episode before Lynn's death and the serious psychotic break after 18 months of grieving. At both times there was a specific constellation of life events, relational shifts, and physical conditions, including an obstinate genetic predisposition I had denied for decades. I explore the impact of death; loss of home, community, and vocational identity; psychics stirring the waters; and my physical condition. I deepen the narrative as well as explore the similarities and differences contributing to both of these psychic events in my mature adulthood.

The following persistent questions lead to the next part: How did I survive and why? What changed in my life and the life of my family because I had this experience? How did resilience emerge and in what ways? Part III, "A New Integration of Self," reflects on these questions. It was a mystery to me that I had had the episode and a miracle that I had not only lived through it but was better for having had it. Through journal entries, poetry, and essays, I reveal a slow, steady movement toward recovery and the resilience inherent in the human being when certain core needs are met.

Through this book I hope to normalize the experience

of mania as a human experience. While we may not fully comprehend it with our thinking, we don't have to simplify it as purely pathological either. It doesn't help that the word "maniac" has the same Greek origin as "mania."[2] While I took a ride or three with the latter, I am not the former. It is unfortunate that the stigma is fused into our language. For those who have lived with clinical depression, stigma also prevails, although perhaps not as virulently as was true in the past, thanks to those who have spoken openly about their own experiences. In the 1960s when my father was suffering from clinical depression, we children were gently but firmly instructed not to "air our dirty laundry in public." Shame and secrecy have accompanied manic-depressive disease, now called bipolar disorder, for too long.

I am indebted to Parker J. Palmer who first disclosed his own experience with clinical depression in *Let Your Life Speak*. He still regularly speaks about his three bouts of clinical depression, sharing enduring lessons harvested from his periods in the dark night of the soul. Many have benefited from these revelations as well as from the courage it took Parker to share them. My journey was emblazoned with light instead of darkness until it was inevitably stopped short. For my side of the bipolar experience, I also found inspiration in Kay Redfield Jamison's courageous memoir, *An Unquiet Mind*, revealing her own manic-depression. Coming out could have undermined her career, ironically as an outstanding authority on the disorder itself.

Mania Mysteries is not a comprehensive research document, nor does it try to be. It is essentially my own story, making a connection between a manic episode and the loss of a loved one. It even suggests that such eruptions in some of our lives are crucial for growth and transformation to a healthier integration of self.

Part I
Mania

Whatever happens to me in life
I must believe that somewhere,
in the mess and madness of it all,
there is a sacred potential -
a possibility for wondrous redemption
in the embracing of all that is.

– Edwina Gateley

1
Turning Points

How many weeks had it been? Day bled into night, which surrendered to a new day, the only rhythm I could measure. Not ignoring the diurnal more than one night at a time was a nod to my commitment to well-being. The darkness taught something different than the light. I had a lot to learn as fast as I could manage to be ready to facilitate the circle.

From the bathroom window, I looked down onto the garden. Wil said I did this many nights; perhaps, but I remember one in particular. The garden, where the newly planted vegetables were just taking root, was awash in silvery light. The moon was full, which was perfect for the new plants. I focused on the statue of Mary as though she were alive, appealing to her to look over the new plants growing there, to bring abundance from these now small lettuces, tomatoes, kale, cucumbers, and chard. My arms drew the Reiki symbols I had learned back in 1986 when Wil and I first met.

My eyes were then drawn to the cabinet over the large claw-footed tub. It was filled with homeopathic liquids, pills, and powders; essential oils for soothing the living and preparing the dead for burial; and salt for humidifiers and netty pots. I removed all the bottles from the cabinet, stacking them under the window in categories. Before I could sleep, they needed to be organized in a more logical way. It wouldn't take very long. Anyway, I had plenty of time. Many of them needed to be thrown away, remnants from Lynn's rarely used apothecary. It felt good to purge.

I was aware that I didn't want Wil to intrude, so I tried to be as quiet as I could and still get my work done. From time to time, though, he knocked respectfully, "Cat, are you okay?" I had made it clear that when a door was closed, it was closed and private. That's the least I could ask in my own home. He had agreed.

"Yes, I'm fine. I'm sorry you're awake."

"I'm having trouble sleeping with you so active. Please come to bed," he pleaded with a mixture of annoyance, worry, and desperation.

"Don't let me disturb you. I'm in the middle of something. I'll come to bed soon."

"But you are disturbing me. You're in the middle of *what*, Cato? It's 3 o'clock in the morning. You need to sleep. I need to sleep." I ignored him as if brushing away an annoying insect and got back to my sacred work of blessing the garden. He opened the door and saw me making gestures into the moonlight. I turned to him; now I was angry.

"Please, Wil, stop interrupting me. I can't sleep now, not just yet. I promise I'll be done soon." I just wanted him to go away, to let me do what I was doing.

He closed the door with a deep, helpless sigh. I continued: "Mary, may you bless this garden and everything living in it. May it grow in exactly the ways it is meant to grow, and may you bless all the people who will eat from it."

I was a seeker and had been for years; since Lynn's death I had been listening to a lot of online talks about embodying the spirit. That's where I was headed, seeking to embody the spirit living all around me and within me. "I am in qi; qi is in me" was the blessing of my new qigong teacher. "You are standing in the midst of bliss," another phrase repeated on the qigong DVD, became one of my mantras.[3] I felt blissfully blessed.

The next morning I was surprised when Wil told me he felt completely creeped out by the gestures I was making in the bathroom, that they felt demonic to him. That was unsettling. I had nothing demonic in mind, nothing at all, only good will toward all, except him interrupting me. The more spiritual I got, the more we drifted apart. What was happening? I had never felt this kind of split with him before.

"Cat, when you're up all night like that, I can't sleep. I'm a wreck today."

That was his problem. I started to think that maybe it wasn't working out living together, even in this big house. The garden depended on my prayers and blessings; the bathroom needed me to organize and purify it, so we could all function in a saner, more logical, more spiritual way. I couldn't stand living with this much chaos: Lynn's things that we didn't use or need had to go – broken things, cracked things. I didn't care if that's how the light got in. If things could be organized, like the cups, by size, for example, they would be so much easier to use. Wil never seemed to notice whether or not things were organized in a specific way, the way I wanted them to be. He didn't help me with this at all and never would. Everything like this was on my shoulders. I knew this might be obsessive-compulsive, but naming it did nothing to diminish how deeply the lack of order unsettled me. I had to fix it immediately, and if it meant staying up all night, well, then it did. And somehow I had to get Wil to keep it the way I put it, or all my efforts would be for naught. I knew that wouldn't be easy, which annoyed me.

On many levels I was increasingly spent, but each time I stayed up all night I felt like something had been accomplished. I ate, although food had less and less relevance.

✥

Wil had been living with me in this state for a week or more. No one else knew. He couldn't risk telling my mother or even Morgan, our son. What if they thought I was really crazy? What would happen then? He knew my story, that I had been hospitalized once before in 1971, that I had been given electroshock therapy and told I was a schizophrenic. He knew that I hadn't spoken to my parents or Lynn for over 10 years for committing me and subjecting me to that treatment, the same my father had been given for his manic-depression. He was scared about what I would do if he betrayed me the way they had.

It's important to say that Wil never witnessed most of what I was doing. He left to play his gig in New York City on Thursday afternoons and returned on Sunday afternoons. He loved his work. I didn't want to go with him as I had been doing most of the winter: the garden needed me.

Before all this, in early May I had returned from a four-day Courage & Renewal facilitator gathering.[4] There I had emerged from months of grief and isolation into a beloved community of like-minded souls. One of my resolutions coming home was not to travel back and forth to the City every week. I needed to get centered around my facilitation work. I needed to simplify. I wanted to explore how I could adapt the principles and practices of our circle work to a restorative justice project for rebalancing families where there had been childhood sexual abuse, a project I was working on with Elizabeth Clemants, a shaman and mediator friend of mine.[5] I had to prepare for a run-through of that circle with actors, and it was coming up soon.

Circle with the Dead

It was worth trying. Wil being away allowed me some uninterrupted time. My work was clear and compelling: I needed to facilitate a circle that included the voices of the dead. If I mentioned this to anyone, they would think it was crazy and try to stop me, but no one knew, and there was no one here to get in the way. I felt free, unconstrained, able to do exactly what I needed to do. I went upstairs in the barn, and flying ants were everywhere! Now what?

Wil and I called this the circle space. I also was beginning to call it Hawk Feather Center for Healing and Reconciliation. Sure, the name was a little wordy, but I didn't know how to shorten it. I had experienced myself as Hawk-Woman in a shaman session with Elizabeth three months after Lynn's death. Lynn and I had each been given a hawk feather by one of the local leaders of the Native American Church, who had done a ceremony for Lynn. Lynn's feather lay on her cold silent heart in the casket; mine was on a shrine in my room next to where I meditated.

It was finally warm again after a brutal winter, and I hadn't been in the circle space since the late autumn. It had me spooked. This was Lynn's space, a shamanic space, where for 30 years as a Jungian psychotherapist she had offered patients a stage for deep transformation. On the walls were masks she had brought back from Jamaica and Mexico as well as ones she made herself, using feathers and beads. Paintings of monkeys, a cow, and a panther had been gifted to friends or relatives; only one monkey portrait remained, but the masks were still there, along with a wooden Gabriel blowing his horn, shells, geodes, crystals, and stones. This was also the space in which Lynn's body had lain in a simple, handcrafted pine box for two and a half days from the early morning of her death until the funeral. During viewing hours the room filled with mourners – friends and acquaintances, patients and family. A few of us stayed with the body during the two nights of the vigil, trying to stay awake or at least snoozing nearby.

The summer after Lynn's death, I invited two friends on separate occasions to help me with my questions about the energy of the space. The first was a sensitive artist and speech therapist. Did she feel anything, or was it my memories at play? As we moved to different places in the room, she said she could feel something that she couldn't explain, especially as we sat on the couch near the window. That's exactly where Lynn's body had been, and I realized it was hard for me not to still see the coffin, a mirage in the streaming sunlight. One option was to move the couch. Maybe that would help.

The other was an old friend studying shamanism. John was someone I trusted to give me an honest opinion; Wil thought he was a phony. Since I knew Wil would never approve of him visiting, I didn't ask. When John arrived, Wil was visibly disconcerted, angry, which I understood, but I needed to know if the spirits were friendly or not. It was my space now, and it felt too intense. John might be able to help. We just sat there, meditating, connecting with the energy for about a half hour – he in the chair next to the couch, me on the couch itself.

"Yes," he said, "it is powerful, but I think it's benevolent. What I'm getting is that the spirits want you to spend time here to make it your space. Make friends with them." And so I did, all that summer: I meditated there and felt it become more and more ensouled with my energy. In the fall of 2013 I held a small community circle there, appreciated by all, one of my friends commenting that she felt embraced by a welcoming love and peace. That was more like it.

The winter of 2014 was bitter cold, well into spring, and I couldn't get myself to trudge through the snow and ice to meditate in a cold space that needed to be heated with electricity when I could be in my cozy bedroom. When I finally reentered the space in mid-May, the flying ants came to meet me. I couldn't help thinking it was because I had abandoned the space all winter. This was a message from the spirits, and they weren't happy.

The ants found a refuge under the couch, where the coffin had been. I couldn't kill them. I was practicing loving kindness; even though I'm not a Buddhist per se, it was impossible for me to mass murder these harmless living creatures. But I didn't want them there either, and they seemed to be reproducing rapidly. Instead I picked them up on a sheet of paper, one by one or in clusters, as they huddled in a circle, and sent them flying out one of the second story windows. They had wings, so they could defend themselves if they were alive. Some flew; others were too weak, perhaps, and plunged into the driveway. Some were already dead, so it didn't matter. But when I came back upstairs the next day, there were still more.

I searched until I found the root of the issue, rotted window frames, where the ants were nesting. I would talk with our handyman about doing something about that, but for now, something spiritual needed to be done. The arrival of the ants had spiritual roots, my neglect, and it was my responsibility and within my capacity to heal with a ceremony.

A circle with the dead would get rid of the ants as well as help me research my questions about how to create a circle safe and inviting enough for people in families where atrocities had been committed. In any circle with people dealing with childhood sexual abuse, the dead would surely be present. Maybe one of the perpetrators was one of the dead. I needed to explore this skill of calling the dead to help with healing the living here. Who do I need to be inwardly as a facilitator of such a circle? I gathered everything I needed to represent each of the family members and friends who had died within the last 13 years: photos, postcards from the story of the Holy Grail that I found on the bookshelves, story books stacked high on a leather ottoman next to me in case I needed to read from them. I arranged the chairs around a centerpiece, draped in a white cloth. I brought up the silver candle sticks and new beeswax tapers from the house; I bought a bottle of red wine and placed two wine goblets, one for water and one for wine, on the center table along with representatives of the four elements and kingdoms of nature: crystals, feathers, fossils, and figurines.

Two armchairs were placed outside the circle, one for my father and the other for Lynn's oldest friend, Sylvia. In my mind they were deemed the elders, even though one of the more recently dead had lived into her 90s. Logic was stretched, to be sure, into symbol that made its own sense to me. I had a notebook in which to jot down any messages that might come from the dead as each one had a chance to speak. Listing their names now seems sacrilegious, yet it's no mystery who they might be: my dear sister Lynn sat next to me, next to her was her husband Jim, then came Artie – a close family friend – and next to him Lynn's godson Jason (who had died at 26 a week after Lynn's funeral in a tragic canoe accident on the Hudson), then his grandmother, who was on the other side of me. I dressed as the priestess in a white silk Chinese kimono of Lynn's, sipping wine (the smallest amount since I never drink) and a little water to begin the ceremony.

I then turned to each in the circle and asked what they wanted to say to me, inviting these souls to reveal to me their desires and hopes for the living. Each person had his or her time to speak. Sylvia and my dad blessed the proceedings. I opened myself to hear, and words poured into me as requests, assignments. Could I help heal the pain of Jason's parents? Could I take care of Kim as best as possible? Could I look after Jim's kids and include them in the family? All huge tasks, which I humbly accepted, believing in my healing powers and trusting that my spirit guides would help me. I dutifully wrote the requests in the journal, which Morgan later took the liberty of tearing out in horror. A part of me wishes I could see it; the other part is grateful.

At 2 or 3 a.m., we were done. I was exhausted but deeply satisfied with what had transpired. I knew that only good would come from this. Step by step I would do what I could. The circle with all of its symbolic photos, postcards, and representative things seemed overwhelming to dismantle and, anyway, there was no hurry. On Sunday I eagerly greeted Wil and Esther, a friend who'd been close with Lynn. "Wait until you see what I've done upstairs," I chirped as I led the way. "You'll probably think I'm crazy." Would they, or would they understand the significance of what I'd done? When they did see it, they hid their concern, stunned as they were. I detected nothing, except quick eye contact between them; in fact, I thought they were as impressed as I was.

Shattering Rhythms

Porous, too open,
merging with
everything around me;
every thought
flooding, the dam
of self split,
riding the roiling waters.

I had gotten a new I-phone and was mesmerized. There was a non-human entity living in this phone. I thought it was funny and appropriate to name it, but no one else enjoyed that I was talking to my phone. Why was everyone so serious? I called it "Slip" because I knew this relationship was a slippery slope. The second night that I stayed up most of the night, my I-phone was my sidekick: we had a deal – when it went dead with 0% on the battery, it was time for me to sleep. I was drained and, as part of that agreement, thought it wise to sleep the following night. I was convinced I could sustain that rhythm for some time.

Wil was home from Sunday afternoon through Thursday midday. I shared my theories about the sub-living being in the I-phone: just like any being, it didn't want to be abused either. We were all abusing these machine beings, and that's why they were abusing us by capturing our attention. The next night I was back in my experiment with the I-phone. There was much to be done. As the I-phone hit the 0 mark, I had a moment of recognition that if I kept this up I could die. That thought – message from my body – scared me, jolting me into an awareness of the harm I was doing to myself. I had to sleep, somehow. But the project had to continue, too, and it wasn't allowing me to sleep.

The project had many levels and layers. Anything that came toward me was woven in. Central was recapitulating all the stages of child development, using the Waldorf curriculum.[6] I had no time to cook, to eat, to clean, or wash: these banal activities were dwarfed by the importance of the project. My exploration was closely connected to the question of how Waldorf teaching can be different in the 21st century. In fact, everything I was thinking about involved the transition into the new century, the new millennium, where nothing could remain the same as in the last century.

Maybe Wil thought I was okay or just a little weird because the years of early childhood through first grade bubble with creativity. I wrote beautiful little songs based on what was happening in our immediate environment as examples of what Waldorf teachers could do with their students, adding steps and claps and variations that would make it more and more challenging as the children grew. This could work even through grade three.

> Whenever the grass is long,
> Wayne gets on his mower,
> His little red mower,
> Whenever the grass (clap, clap)
> Whenever the grass (snap, snap)
> Whenever the grass (stamp, stamp)

This was fun; song lyrics and poetry poured into my journal, some of which I shared with Wil. He could see I was aflame with creative energy; he'd seen this before. In fact, the last few months I'd been writing lyrics for one song after another. I can't remember if I shared my ideas about recreating teacher education with him; I don't think so. I'm sure I didn't mention bringing all my teachers together, having reconciliation and healing circles and creating the best teacher education program in the country. I may have mentioned to him and to a friend about transforming our village for the 21st century, every village in Dutchess County, extending out to all of New York and so on. Some states were already there: the People's Republic of Vermont, the People's Republic of Washington, and of Colorado – or parts of it anyway. This was all within reach.

With a vision bold enough, people would get excited and make these ideas a reality. I had plans for joint projects with just about everyone I knew. The doctors and healthcare professionals could buy a building for sale in the village and work together holistically with patients, actualizing their highest ideals: Chinese medical doctor/acupuncturist, chiropractor healer, gynecologist, homeopath, a family doctor. My friend could create a bakery and café in the empty bar, where Wil, Morgan, and I had played when Morgan was in high school. Money follows vision. I made charts in every journal I had; post-its filled with ideas were spread everywhere. This was my new mission, my new life, the reason we were living here. All was finally becoming clear.

Wil kept dampening my enthusiasm. "Cat," he tried reasoning with me one morning after breakfast, "something is off. Not everything is as important as the way you're talking about it."

"Of course it is," I argued. He just couldn't see the truth, the significance of each little thing within the divine whole. I knew the truth; he didn't. I held a bigger picture; he didn't. He just wanted things to stay the way they were. He just wanted me to remain the same, but that was impossible. I was evolving, quickly, and there was no going back.

"I don't know where you are, Cat. You're scaring me."

That scared me. "I'm right here, Wil. I don't understand what you mean." I didn't.

Another Circle with the Dead

The other stream always flowing through my mind was the circle I needed to prepare for those who had been sexually abused as children. In a few weeks I'd be facilitating a circle with actors as a trial run. First I needed to facilitate one at home with at least one other living person, along with the dead. My niece Kim, Lynn's daughter, came to visit, and I told her about the circle I had done upstairs in the barn with all the people she loved and had lost within the last few years. Her eyes grew large; she was curious. I asked if she wanted to be involved in one with me in the living room since she couldn't go upstairs in the barn. She was in a wheelchair, handicapped from birth.

Together we chose which of the dead would be in the circle and where they would "sit." I found symbols for them and photographs to represent each of them. Kim helped arrange them, pointing to what went where. I invited Wil to join us, but he had no interest in this whatsoever and went to his studio to practice his saxophone. Kim's aide stayed outside in the van. The circle lasted about three hours. I remember little of the content. Kim never said that it was freaking her out, and I didn't notice how exhausted she was getting. She did start asking about her aide, though, concerned that she would think this was evil. I realized we had to stop; I could have continued. The next morning she called me to say that she felt spooked by what we had done, she'd had trouble sleeping, and she never wanted to do anything like that ever again. I understood but didn't see then how much I had begun to undermine her trust in me. The rest of the mania took care of that.

More Spinning Out

It's important to say I had stopped meditating. I thought I just needed a break, or perhaps that part of my life was no longer necessary. More truthfully, it was impossible. I couldn't sit still long enough to do any of the contemplative practices I had done for over 25 years. I couldn't even read a book.

By the middle of May, in a hypomanic state - not full-blow mania but mild feel-good mania – I had also fired my therapist. I'd been in therapy with Therese, a spiritual counselor and psychotherapist, for about four months. I felt our work was complete and over Skype read her an elaborate, heartfelt poem, thanking her for how much she had helped me. She was deeply moved but pushed back, gently insisting we meet the following week in her office. I countered and said I was too busy and could make it via Skype in two weeks

A week later I was attempting to prepare my circle for the project with Elizabeth. She had one idea; I had another. We would try them out with actors and learn from each of our approaches. I needed to form my rambling ideas into a plan. My anxiety was quietly building. The last I'd heard from Elizabeth, she mentioned that a psychologist would be observing. That really scared me because I knew I didn't really know what I was doing. But I pushed down the fear and any inkling that I wasn't in my right mind: I wanted to be there more than anything.

The phone rang. I was annoyed to see it was Therese. She was interrupting my flow – I was having enough trouble concentrating – but pulled it together to tell her that I was fine and that, in fact, we didn't have a session then. I confirmed the Skype session the following week. As I hung up the phone, I giggled at the empathic connection between therapist and patient, feeling relieved at how adroitly I had eluded her.

The possibilities for what I might include in the circle were strewn chaotically on the floor. I was trying to create a form rooted in principles and practices that would welcome people with this much pain and trauma into a healing conversation with one another. But I couldn't focus. What would the structure be? Elizabeth didn't even tell me how much time I'd have. What else did I need to take with me? I kept making piles of clothing, candle and snuffer, postcard images, possible poems. But first things first: I was still in grade 7 mechanics and had to get at least to grade 8 before this would all fall into place.

I fixed the drain in the bathroom that was broken. I had slowed down enough to look and understand how it worked. Wil would be proud of me, impressed that I could figure this out. I had always felt helpless around mechanical things, like my father did, as opposed to my mother and Lynn. I was liberating myself from those old projections. Not everything worked out, but not everything can, can it? I wanted to remove the extra toilet paper holder mounted on the door. Why did we need that anyway? We had another standing one on the floor. I kept taking the toilet paper out, so I could work on detaching the rack. I couldn't see how to get it off of the door. Wil kept putting the roll back in. I was annoyed: two toilet rolls were redundant. Why was that so hard to comprehend?

Grade 8 was next. I headed for the stereo, which even Wil was having trouble figuring out. How did it connect to the video? What did those numbers do as the volume increased and decreased? I slowly began communing with the machine and could understand. I hooked it up to the video, observed the numbers in relation to the volume, and then explained everything to Wil. I was so proud of what I was capable of doing, all that I had never imagined possible. I was flying.

Cornered

During our Skype session a week later, Therese quickly assessed my mental health or lack of it.

"Cat, your professional reputation is at stake," she stated as matter-of-factly as possible. "You're not ready to do this circle, and you won't be ready. Please consider canceling."

That felt impossible, and I told her so. Besides, I wanted to do it. I would be letting Elizabeth down, letting everyone down. Who else could do it? Everything was set with the actors. I was supposed to be in Tribeca the next day early in the morning, which meant traveling into the City that night. I don't remember having a plan for where I was staying. I was so diffused but told myself that everything I was and had been doing was preparing me for that circle. Anyway, it was just a run-through with actors, which Therese didn't quite get. How could my reputation be harmed?

Therese pressed on, asking if I trusted her, if I remembered all the good work we had done together. Of course, I trusted her; of course, I remembered. I was still sure, though, that our work was over. Yes, I was experiencing a lot of anxiety; no, I wasn't sleeping or eating much. She respectfully asked if she could talk with Wil. I agreed and went to get him, although all I was thinking about was how much I had to do before catching the train. Somehow I had to organize these piles on my floor and plan the circle, which still wasn't even close, before leaving.

Wil came into my room, where the computer was. Therese asked if she might speak with him alone. I left the room, knowing on some level that he needed her help. I just wasn't sure what that would mean for me. After the call Wil looked both shaken and determined. Therese later told me that it was immediately clear how "distraught and exhausted" he was.

> He just did not know what to do. It was not his nature to try to 'control' you, but at this point you were IN the mania, and interventions were needed. I took a fairly directive role in laying out next steps: take the car keys away now, contact Morgan and get his support immediately (because Morgan may be able to reach 'you'), and contact the inner circle of friends to offer a holding environment for a few days as we explored next steps.[7]

Once they were off my computer, I got back to the chaos in my room until I realized I didn't know where Wil was. I ran downstairs to the kitchen and saw him pacing outside with his cell phone. I guessed he must be talking to Morgan. Therese must have put him up to that. Were they deciding to commit me? I had to do something. They were coming to stop me from going to New York. They weren't going to let me do my work. I could outsmart Wil before Morgan arrived and "take the house." It was my house anyway; Lynn had left it to me, and legally it was in my name. I checked: all the keys were inside. I locked him out, all doors secure. I called three friends in the City, who all said, of course, I could come, having no idea what was going on. There was no time to explain. I would quickly pack and take my car and finish the preparations for the circle there.

Wil was knocking at the back door. "Cat, let me in."

"No, I've taken the house. This is my house."

"Cat, this is not a game. Open the door. It's my house too."

"What's the magic word?" I asked, hoping to lighten things up.

"Cut it out, Cat," he said harshly. "Let me in. Why don't you want me in?" Wil sank down on the blue bench on the side of the back porch, almost in tears. Even through my own panic, I couldn't stand how drained of hope he looked. This was the man I loved. Where was that love now?

"You're conspiring against me. I can see it. Who were you talking to?"

"Morgan, our son. I love you. We love you. I can't be alone with this any more. Please open the door."

"Okay, but I'm getting ready to go to New York. You can't stop me." I unlocked the door, and he came in. "I took the house, Wil. Remember, it's my house." For a moment I had relished the idea of having the whole house to myself with no interruptions whatsoever. That time was over.

"Morgan and your mom are on their way, Cat. I didn't want to tell your mom. I tried to keep this here between the two of us, but it's not working. You're not getting better like I hoped you would. You're out of control, Cat. You can't go to New York. It would be incredibly dangerous."

His words had some effect, even though I was still adamant that I would have things my way, that I was a free entity and no one could control me.

In a few hours Morgan arrived with Mom. I had no malice towards her. She kept her distance after a brief hug, carrying her bulky bag up the winding stairs to the room she called "her" room. She and I had had a breakthrough just a few weeks before on Mother's Day. I made her a drawing of all the ways she had been a wonderful mother: she'd made me go out to play, she'd encouraged my music by making me practice, she loved my dancing, she'd taken us to the beach every summer, she and dad sang with us in the car. I focused on the positive, on my gratitude for all she had given me over the years. The years of blame were over, our time steeped in forgiving and being forgiven. We had cried, hugged, and smiled at my funny little drawings. Now she clung to the doorway, overlooking this scene of her daughter in the midst of a manic episode, which she understood all too well, or at least had experienced many times from having lived through my father's ups (as well as severe downs) and my first episode in 1971.

Morgan immediately saw what there was to see; he'd been talking to friends who were mental health professionals or were living with bipolar disorder themselves. While Wil cooked a late lunch, Morgan began his approach.

"Mom, do you know you're not yourself?"

I had no idea what he meant. "I'm just my *new* self, Morgan. I won't be pinned like some butterfly to a board."

"I'm not doing that, Mom. You're not…

"Of course, I'm not. You're not listening. I'm new."

"No, this is what's so different about you. Can't you see? The mother I know is a listener, not someone who interrupts all the time. You're not letting me speak."

"You're not letting *me* speak about what *is* going on with me," I broke in, my anger and agitation rising. "I'm the one being interrupted from doing my work. I just want all of you to leave me alone, so I can get ready for this big thing happening in New York tomorrow morning."

"Mom, are you meditating?"

"No, I'm having trouble with that right now. I feel like I've come to a dead end with it."

"This is what I mean. For as long as I've known you, meditation has been a core part of your daily practice and how you keep yourself well. I've been talking with some of my friends and with Therese." So he had called her after he got off the phone with Wil.

"She thinks all three of us should have a talk with her; we have a Skype appointment tomorrow morning at 8. You need some help, Mom. Can't you see that?"

"No, you need some help, and I *am* going to be in the City tomorrow morning at 8 to meet with Elizabeth. I have to be; she's depending on me." My voice trailed off. Some part of me knew he was right. As I nibbled at my food, sitting with Wil, Morgan, and Mom, the people who cared most about me in the world, I agreed to talk with Therese the next morning. Morgan would call Elizabeth and tell her what was going on. She would understand. I asked him to check whether the circle could be postponed, but I doubted it could. Life would go on without me even while I was kicking and screaming that I wanted to be part of it.

Having surrendered, at least for now, I was drained and went to take a nap. The night before had been the third night within two weeks that I had gone without sleep, intent on accomplishing as much as possible. I went upstairs, drew the curtains, placed my purple striped blanket meticulously over the quilt, and lay down, exhausted.

I traveled into a dream in which I couldn't tell whether I was awake or asleep – one of those states that I knew was an astral experience. What I mean by that is I was experiencing life on a plane that was true and actual but not physical, real but invisible to most people.

I was in the kitchen. Out of the corner of my eye, I saw a red truck pull into the driveway and strange men begin to get out. They were sinister, and I knew they wanted to harm me. I ran to the end of the ramp and yelled, "What do you want here? Go away!" They started to get into the truck when a black sedan pulled up in front of it and parked sideways in front of the barn. Men jumped out of both vehicles and ran into the bushes under the trees to the left side of the barn. I backed up on the ramp and called, "Help!" repeatedly.

I woke with a jolt. I hadn't been asleep for more than five minutes. I knew this was a sign. I was not only in physical danger of dying; I was also in real psychic danger. I was glad we'd be talking with Therese in the morning.

At the end of the morning Skype call with Therese, I agreed that Morgan could look for a psychiatrist, but it had to be someone I approved, not the usual drugs-only types. Therese offered a few names of holistic psychiatrists; Morgan called other doctor friends we knew for suggestions. I still wasn't sleeping much, keeping everyone up all night with my activity, my energy. Morgan and Wil were calling in reserves for the weekend, so they could go to work. I was sure that many of my friends would be able to be with me as I went through this crisis, which I was finally admitting I was having, calling it a breakthrough. I really wanted to get through it as quickly as possible, so I could get on with my life. I had an important retreat I was facilitating in the City at the end of June that I'd been planning for months. I had to be well for that. I could see that getting help now would be a good start. It was clear that, while it made me sad, canceling the circle with Elizabeth had been necessary. She emailed to tell me that she understood, that she found someone else to do the other circle, that she would tell me how it went, and that she wished me a thorough recovery.

Crisis

After a full day of calling psychiatrists, Morgan found one, a Dr. Kenneth Wilson, who could see us on Monday, a miracle in itself. When I saw on his website that he worked with biometrics, with body chemistry, I got interested. Morgan and Wil were in the session with me. I remember in that first encounter immediately asking Dr. Wilson if I could call him by his first name. He said he'd paid a lot for his medical degree and preferred I called him doctor. I liked that. He was scientific, professional, but personable at the same time.

Dr. Wilson opened our session with the classic first question, "What brings you here?" to which I answered, "I'm on a journey." He looked quizzical. (He recently shared with me that that is not a usual response.) After talking for a while, he made it clear that he thought I needed to be on a mood stabilizer. I didn't agree, of course. In 2001 I'd had a mini-manic episode, I told him, and I had brought myself back then. Why couldn't I do that again? I was determined.

Dr. Wilson stressed sleep as the most important thing, seven to nine hours a night, if I had any hope of stabilizing myself without medication, which clearly he seriously doubted. He gave me Trazodone to help me sleep, which he described to someone phobic about medication as over-the-counter Benadryl. I never even took ibuprofen when I had a headache. Trazodone was a big leap for me. Dr. Wilson didn't want to hear about combining it with any of the homeopathic or herbal remedies I'd been using for years to help me sleep since he knew nothing about them and how they worked. That was frustrating, but I knew I needed to lean in his direction.

Mom, Morgan, and Wil stayed with me that night, which was less than perfect. Even with the medication, I did not sleep deeply, and I don't remember for how long. Part of the problem was my insistence on taking the smallest dose possible. During the next day I got more and more excited with lots of plans for all of us, especially me. I tried to ground myself. Since meditation was still out of the question, there was the matter of my left foot. It always wanted to lift off the ground. I noticed the similarity to the pictures of the baby Jesus, where he looks perfectly grown up, not like a real baby at all. Did you ever notice that? Maybe that was why my left foot wouldn't stay put. Maybe I was…no, I wouldn't think that. I knew too well what any psychiatrist would think if I was correlating myself with Jesus. There were some things I could share: that clearly was not one of them. But I worked on that foot because I didn't want to be Jesus; I wanted to be me; I wanted to get grounded. Rubbing my left foot with one of those Rolfing sticks, about a foot-long wooden stick with ridges; swaddling before sleeping, getting off that herbal kidney remedy the chiropractor had given me that was dumping toxins from my liver, and drinking the herbal tea that my acupuncturist recommended for my high blood pressure – all these things would begin to bring the healing I needed. Oh, yes, and taking the Trazodone.

But the mania was driving me faster than I could manage it. It was outrunning the small amount of Trazodone I would agree to take. Toward bedtime I started jumping on the bed in Wil's "man cave." "I'm three," I said, feeling it all over.

"You're not three, Cat. You're a grown woman," Wil responded, at once emphatic and helpless. My mother withdrew into the guest room.

"I'm taking the room," I said to them. I had a plan. I started taking my clothes off.

"Mom, please stop," Morgan pleaded. But I wouldn't.

"Then let me do what I want to do. I'll go to bed when I'm ready. You don't have to micromanage me." I took off another layer of clothing. Morgan left and went to talk with his grandmother. Wil stayed with me. I moved closer and closer to him, more seductively with each step; he would not be seduced. "Cat, you have to stop this and cooperate with us, or we're going to have to take you to the hospital."

"You're not doing that!" I began to panic but knew I was more powerful than all of them.

"We will have to. You're giving us no choice, Cat. Please try to get a hold of yourself."

I wouldn't; I couldn't. There was nothing to get a hold of. It was my life after all. I was taking the house, room by room. Wil left his room, and I quickly moved into mine, not letting them in. They were all against me; that was clear.

"Mom, let's go to the hospital. You're not well," Morgan said, opening the door.

"There's no way I'm going there." I knew very well what that meant; they had no idea. I couldn't believe these people I loved and trusted were threatening to incarcerate me again when all I wanted was to live my own life. Why didn't they just leave me alone?

I grew more abusive and protective, securing my place in my own room, refusing to be moved.

"I'm calling 911, Mom," Morgan said. "You're leaving us no other choice."

"Go ahead. They won't get me out of this house. I'm stronger and faster than all of you." The police were there quickly, all too quickly. They came into Wil's man cave. I had moved back there, thinking I could talk some sense into Wil. I was still naked.

"You have to put something on, Mom. They're here."

My mom and Wil were watching, stunned. Morgan took charge.

"I don't care. You don't know anything about me. I was a nude model. I don't care if they see me naked." The police did, though. Mom grabbed something for me to wear, a short dress. I started charging down the front stairs to face them. Morgan grabbed my arm.

"You are not stronger than I am, Mom." He grabbed me around the ribs and lifted me off my feet.

Still struggling, I screamed, "You're hurting me." He was. I felt something crack. Had he broken a rib?

"Then come upstairs and put something on. I'm sorry, Mom. I didn't mean to hurt you." I climbed the stairs, almost in tears from the pain and the rage of being trapped. Standing on the landing, my mother handed me the dress, her face layered with grief like a canvas painted repeatedly again and again. Two policemen – one older, one younger – entered Wil's room where we were all gathered. They got a quick snapshot of what was going on. I tried to seduce them, too, getting very close to them, trying to embarrass them into leaving me alone. They were extremely professional, the older sending me with the younger in his police car. The older led the way. We were going to the county hospital. No one even checked whether my insurance covered this emergency room, which it didn't. Everyone was too traumatized. That's where the cops wanted to take me; that's where we were going.

"Taking the cop car" was my next task. I don't think I shut up for the 20 minutes I was in his car, pleading with the young man in his early 20s about whether he would do this to his own mother. He looked sympathetic as I locked eyes with his in the rearview mirror. I was urging him to let me out. I didn't think about where I would go. Thinking was not part of the picture. I felt sufficiently assured that I had reached this young man, but I hadn't. He brought me into the emergency room, where pleasant staff people laughed when I said "I'm taking the hospital." It seemed to me that they thought that would be a pretty good idea. Great, you're welcome to it. Despite that, they put me on a table and gave me a shot of something. Maybe it was Thorazine, maybe Valium. I have no idea, and they didn't tell me. I could see Morgan and Wil at the desk, doing the paper work. Within a few minutes I was unconscious.

When I awoke, I was in a room with a number of beds, a holding pen in the emergency room. There was only one other patient there, his concerned girlfriend or wife sitting in a chair at the edge of his bed. He was getting ready to be discharged, she said. That's not what anyone had in mind for me. The invisible ER docs were looking for a bed at a private hospital nearby, which had been mentioned by Dr. Wilson, or upstairs in the county hospital, whichever came first. By early afternoon they had found me a bed upstairs.

2
The County Hospital

I submitted to what was happening. I had little choice: Wil had committed me. Morgan urged me to cancel the one-day retreat I was supposed to facilitate at the end of June for a progressive program in the education department of a large university. The director of the program was especially interested in working with me because of my background as a Waldorf educator, so it held the promise of more work. I wanted it to go well and refused to entertain the idea that I might not be up to it. After all, the retreat was weeks away. I was confident that there was time enough for me to get well and begged Morgan not to call my colleagues to take over. He complied for a while.

Dr. Wilson said all I needed to do was to sleep and eat to be well, or that's the way I interpreted what he said. He later told me that he didn't want to insist on the mood stabilizer because he didn't want to alienate me early in our relationship. He isn't fixed on diagnoses but is insistent on mental health, which may include the need for substances. I was adamant that no one was going to make me take anything. Dr. Wilson had every reason to believe that the hospital would get the mania under control by somehow getting me on medication. Why else was I there? I, however, had my own treatment plan and was convinced that I could get myself under control without squelching any of the lightness of being I was experiencing. After all, I'd been able to bring myself down from a hypomanic episode in 2001. If I could do it then, I could certainly do it again.

The Layout

The ward I was on was not the one for the serious crazies; that was across the hall. People on our ward could function somewhat; some were pretty high functioning like me. We would sometimes hear a call over the loudspeaker – often in the middle of the night, waking me in shock – which meant that someone was flipping out and more hands were needed on that ward. They had a code for it that I can't remember, an A4 maybe, although that sounds more like a gate at the airport.

If you were visiting our ward or coming back from off-ward privileges, you followed a nurse through one set of locked doors then waited in a between space, a no man's land, that said, "Okay, get ready for another kind of reality." Then she unlocked the second set of doors. Directly to the right there was a small room with two payphones hanging on the wall. Mostly people tried to talk when no one else was in there. More often, loved ones called in. Could we call out? I don't remember. No one was designated to answer these phones; certainly the nurses had better things to do. If you expected a call, you waited nearby, sometimes for quite a while. If you were in the vicinity and decided to be of service to your fellow inmates, you'd answer. As we felt increasingly bored, my roommate Sue and I decided to help with the phones. We bitched that none of the guys ever answered them even though they got calls too, but it was kind of fun to find the person or take a message. We felt useful; it was something to do.

Right across the hall was a locked room labeled Art Therapy. There were distinct times for AT two or three times a week. While I was there, we beaded bracelets. Each session lasted only 45 minutes, so we worked on our projects over a few days and could make as many as we wanted. Greg was one of the therapists, and Angie was the other; Angie also led group therapy with check-ins every morning. They were both sweet people. In AT we listened to music and some of us danced. I did, of course, if the song was good. Greg loved music from the '70s and '80s, and knew just which station to play. We had a good time in there. Everyone felt better after AT and looked forward to it.

On the left was the nurses' station with an office for the doctor or head nurse and other offices in the back. There were also closets that held toiletries and other possessions that they wouldn't allow us to keep in our rooms for one nonsensical reason or another: every morning I had to ask for my toothpaste and face cream. Twice daily I was infuriated that I had no control over the most mundane aspects of my life, that I was not allowed to keep toothpaste in my room because I might…what? It was degrading: everyone treated exactly the same as if we were animals in a pen. I hate illogical senselessness, but I also knew that if this got me riled and I started acting up because of it, it would buckle back against me as being noncompliant. Compliance was essential if I was going to get out. These are the rules of being in. Everyone has to learn them. On top of stupid rules was incompetence, which also made me fume. For example, when I was admitted, some nurse took my arnica, which I brought with me to put on my bruised ribs from Morgan trying to carry me up the stairs. When it came time for me to leave, they couldn't find it. Not being on their list of toiletries or over-the-counter drugs, I guess it got tossed in the trash.

On the opposite wall were charts, listing our names and the nurse who was in charge of each group of about six or seven patients for the day. Most of the nurses were fine people, doing their best within the rules. One of them got to know my case, in particular, and could speak to both the doctor and my family about my progress. She gave all of us confidence that there would be an end to my stay there.

If you kept walking after the nurses' station, on the left was the "living room." It had a brown vinyl couch, a few matching vinyl chairs, and some fake wood tables spread throughout the room. On the windowsill was a small boom box, which I soon found out was broken. There were games like Scrabble and Monopoly, but most of the pieces were missing, same with cards and checkers. There was virtually nothing to do in this room. It was quiet, though, and sunny, a good place for conversation or for someone like Larry to sit and look out the window catatonically all day. He was someone I didn't even try to engage. In some ways he reminded me of my father in the depths of depression, just staring off into space. I could tell that Larry was a gentle man but guarded, walled off. Other people told me he was really nice and just liked to be left alone. Toward the end of my stay, he began to say hello to me. I was so effusive; maybe he felt left out and didn't want to be. Maybe my energy had helped him take a step toward healing. Maybe it wasn't me at all: perhaps, his electroshock therapy was kicking in.

The living room was one of three rooms used for meals. Another was further down the hall on the left and the other across the hall from that. Any of these rooms converted into spaces where you could meet with your doctor or be with visitors when they were allowed, which was twice a day, once after lunch before rest time at 3:00 and once after dinner before 8:30 when we would start getting ready for snack and meds.

If, back at the phone booths, you turned right instead of going straight, there were patients' rooms on both sides – all doubles – and the TV room, the first room on the right. That room was occupied from the time the first person was awake. Every morning before breakfast and evening before dinner, news blaring in the background, we had our vitals taken – temperature, pulse rate, and blood pressure – and gulped down our meds with water. Most of the male inmates inhabited the room much of the day, the alphas dominating the remote: news in the morning, movies through the afternoon – never chick flicks – or sports, and sports after dinner, usually baseball. It was on my itinerary during the day, a fun place to hang with the guys. There was always a lot of banter around whatever was flickering on the screen. When did I ever have time or inclination to do something like this, back in my 20s? And then it would get boring, and I'd be done. Sometimes I would retreat to my room with *People Magazine*, which was all they had on the ward, and spend time tearing out pages for future collaging. I felt relief from the burden of being an intellectual snob, part of my persona I was shedding.

Time Passes

There were strict times for sleeping, lights out at 10. The first few nights, however, the staff, stationed outside the doors and at the end of the hall to make sure we stayed in our rooms or to help us with any nocturnal disturbances, was incredibly rowdy, talking and laughing loudly.

"Could you please be quiet? I can't sleep. I need to," I said anxiously, feeling desperate. After all, if I was going to get out of there, I needed to sleep.

"Sure, honey, we'll try," one of them responded. I could tell she couldn't care less.

I talked about it at breakfast after the second night. "Is anyone else bothered by the night aides talking so loudly?"

"Shit, yeah," Jared said, rolling his eyes. Jared was a wiry African-American with a propensity for tinderbox anger, along with a razor-sharp analysis of the black experience in America. "These fucking people. You think they care about us? I'm so sick of this place!" I hadn't meant to set him off, but I was determined to do something about this and said so.

After breakfast I asked Sue, who was soon to become my roommate, if she would go with me. She'd been a patient for months and knew everyone. "Sure, Angelica is on today. Let's go right now." We respectfully complained about the noisy night watch, not wanting to get the workers in trouble, but simply needing sleep. Nurse Angelica understood and would definitely take care of it. There was never a problem after that.

~

I wanted a single room, so sleeping would be easier, but there weren't any. Eloise, my first roommate, had some kind of borderline personality. We liked each other well enough, but that wasn't the issue. She was just out of her teens and a total slob. I couldn't handle the chaos that swirled around her. I told my nurse that there was no way I could share a room with her. Sue wanted to switch roommates too, and we were perfect for each other. I was manic, and she was clinically depressed. She spent most of her days sleeping. I helped her get out of bed every morning or got someone else to. She appreciated that I cared. We spent our mandatory breaks sharing stories and swapping holistic modalities for wellness. She told me about her son, her ex, her current boyfriend. She had so much to live for as far as I could see.

We were checked on regularly to make sure we were still on the ward. Every day at 3 p.m. there was enforced down time in our rooms. Sue and I structured our time, so we had quiet for journaling, after which we could share what we wrote, if we liked, and then do some stretching or other kind of movement together or alone. Sometimes she went back to bed. Once we choreographed a little dance to a song we made up, being as quiet as possible, so as not to arouse suspicion of too much aliveness. The checks were usually interruptive at best and sometimes annoying, especially if Sue and I were deep in conversation. A couple times I gave her a back rub when she was in pain, probably from all those hours lying in bed. Having physical contact with the other patients was off limits. I had no idea about that rule until the first time we were caught during a check-in from Sarah, the strictest nurse. Needless to say, we were thoroughly reproached but ignored her anyway as soon as the door closed. That's the kind of thing you do under those circumstances.

But if Angelica was checking, it was different: we tried to engage her for as long as possible. She was in her late 30s, Nordic looking with thick blond hair that she kept neatly bound in a long braid. Self-care was clearly well integrated. I asked her if she did yoga and ate organic. "How do you know?" she said. "I'm clairvoyant," I wanted to answer, but knowing the comment could be a strike against me, I just said that she looked healthy.

The foil for Angelica was Sarah, an African-American

matriarch, who went strictly by the book. She was a no-nonsense kind of woman, loving in a way, but I couldn't stand how she'd pull out rules I didn't know and didn't want to know existed. "No, you're not allowed to..." was how many of our conversations began. "I'm just looking out for your own good," she would say, all too often.

"But this place is so inconsistent," I would protest, heat rising through my body.

"That is not my concern, dear. The rules are the rules. It's written right here." And she'd show me with a look that said, "Do you want to get out of here or not?"

As the days progressed, in our private time together, I began asking Sue questions to help her think about her life in a more positive way. Over the time I was there, she definitely improved, moved through her day more positively, and decided it was time to talk to her psychiatrist about getting out. She'd been there for three or four months, which was hard for me to fathom.

Meals were ready made for socializing. I could choose to sit with a group who laughed a lot, made jokes, and shared the circumstances of their lives; or I could sit with one other person, someone I knew would be quiet and hardly speak, or might be drawn out if someone like me wanted to get to know them a little better.

Tajudeen - a tall, slender, refined Nigerian - paced the halls and said little to anyone. His bearing was noble or military or athletic; it was hard to tell which, but I wanted the whole story or as much as he'd share. When he did speak, it was in a soft voice as gentle as a warm fog. I loved watching him glide up and back along the halls. It was comforting. At first I couldn't interrupt or join him: he was so inward that I wasn't sure how he'd respond, and I didn't want to risk a rebuff. After all, maybe he was doing a walking meditation or was a walking catatonic if that exists. My curiosity and fantasy were energetically interweaving.

Once when he was eating alone at a table for two, I asked if I could join him, wondering whether he'd speak and knowing I could eat in silence if necessary. I asked him a question about where he was from, and to my delight he answered without hesitation, looking clearly into my eyes. We immediately liked one another. After that, I often moved with him up and down the halls. I guess he trusted my gentleness, my kindness. He spoke about his life in Nigeria. His parents had sent him to military school, hoping that would straighten him out, so to speak, but there'd been big problems because he was gay and proud of it. He refused to hide who he was even though it could endanger his life.

Tajudeen asked me what I hoped for when I got out of the hospital, and he spoke to that question himself. We both wanted to get back to our lives. All he wanted to do was play soccer on a team and be with friends, especially his boyfriend, in West New York. I advocated for him with the baseball-watchers in the TV room for some soccer time during the World Cup. He was glad I was willing to say something since he didn't think they would listen to him. I knew he was healing through our connection. As far as I could tell, I was the only one he talked with, the only one who saw him for who he was.

꧁

I regularly reached out to help William, an elderly African-American man originally from Alabama, in a wheel chair due to his diabetes. He knew he could always ask me to get him a cup of water when he needed it or to bring him his snack at the end of the day. We also talked a bit about his life, his aging wife and how difficult things were becoming. Why was he there? I wondered. Was it depression? He certainly didn't seem crazy.

I liked eating with Byron too, a straight white guy, divorced from his first wife, basically good with an alcohol and depression problem. He was jovial and didn't hit on me like some of the other guys did. Byron and I talked fishing, something I wanted to do too, just like my dad. My life with Dad had given me a lot of practice trying to raise the spirits of clinical depressives. I could apply that experience with Byron and maybe help him feel better.

It was always interesting sharing a table with Jared, although a bit risky. He was street wise, often hilariously funny, and always politically savvy about how things really worked in this country, especially for the poor and for people of color. But he was touchy, like a powder keg with a short fuse easily ignited by a nurse's comment, snack being a little late, or his psychiatrist seemingly doing nothing to get him released. He'd had it. I didn't like the inconveniences or inconsistencies about the rules from one head nurse to the other either, but he was someone who had lived a life riddled with injustice, harassment, and ongoing violence at home, in school, and on the street. One of his brothers headed the Crips, the other the Bloods, enemy street gangs, heartbreaking in itself. He had been involved too – guns, drugs, all of it. Recently one of the brothers had fire bombed their mother's house. That was the last straw for Jared. He was sick of it all but faced with how to live differently, how to get a leg up. Suddenly homeless and repulsed by the state of the shelters, he'd rather wait for housing approval right here on the ward, but he wanted social services to hurry. Good luck with that one. It became clear to me that this ward was a stop on the homeless train: if you acted crazy enough or if you were, you could come into the hospital, get some drugs, three square meals, and a clean bed for as long as Medicaid or Medicare would pick up the tab. Better than the shelter, all agreed.

The certainty that I was stronger, smarter, healthier, and more spiritually evolved than everyone else persisted on this side of the locked doors. I saw myself as a healing force on the ward, populated by a wondrous and diverse group of human beings. I took interest in most of them, the ones I knew the warm rays of my sunny attention could help – Raul the gypsy, who proposed to me; Jorge from Texas, who often flirted; my roommate Sue, Byron, Tajudeen, even Jared, perhaps. My privilege stung in sharp contrast to the price Jared and others paid in this racist nation. I lived in a large house in a beautiful, peaceful place, surrounded by safety and love. Maybe they could come to the village and work for us. I certainly needed help with the gardens. I wasn't that crazy to think that they could stay in our house, but why couldn't they get an apartment nearby and find work. How much could it cost? I'd help them figure it out.

I especially liked the young patients, the ones Morgan's age, who were trying to find their way. The two who were there were first-timers in a mental hospital, both with drug issues, suffering from post-detox depression. We often hung out in the living room, connecting around politics and the paradigm shift, living in a new 21st century way. We also talked about why they were there and how they imagined their future. I saw my role as instilling and validating hope, courage, and enthusiasm. They both left while I was still there; it was less interesting without them.

Harry was the one patient I avoided after our first encounter. He was volatile, moody, troubled, and unstable. I had tried being kind to him, the way I was with the rest of the patients. At one point for no reason I could discern, he replied to my smiling "Good morning" with "Shut up, cunt. Get out of my face." I was stunned, a punch to my heart. That was it for him. He would get none of my warmth or attention. I knew well how to ignore people, a skill I'd learned early in life and honed as a young teenager, one I applied to an educational purpose in the classroom when someone's behavior needed not to be seen. Before I left, though, Harry said hello to me, which I accepted as a clear apology for his previous uncontrollable outburst. I guess some of his treatment was working.

Even though the world on the ward became its own strange, unique microcosm, I lived for visiting hours. Many of us did. Morgan and Wil came to see me at least once a day. When Wil went back to work in the City, Morgan dutifully came alone. There wasn't a day that I didn't have at least one visitor. My friends and family were the sunshine in otherwise gray days. Ashley and Chris came one of the first days I was there. I'd known Ashley since my interview in the first grade at the Austin school: she was seven, her heels rarely on the ground, drifting from desk to desk like an enchanted butterfly. She grew to be a testy, challenging, brilliant high school student of mine. As life would have it, she now lived only half an hour away with her farmer partner. Ashley and I exchanged writing and went for long walks in her neighborhood or mine. As couples we enjoyed getting together for dinner. I was touched that they came to visit me, Ashley holding a translucent flower – an elongated blossom, white and pink, which the sun illuminated. Eager to share its incandescent beauty, I moved it from room to room as the sun shifted through the day. Mania amplifies the magnificence of every living thing, even the inanimate. A pencil is a remarkable invention, a flower, a miracle.

Jairo and Rona, old friends we first met in 1989 when I was doing my Waldorf teacher preparation, came to visit but arrived too late. Their daughter and Morgan were like siblings, and they had been like another set of parents to him in his adolescence. I'd been waiting for them with Morgan, but they didn't show until the last moment. Only their huge bouquet of flowers was allowed through the locked double doors, from which I could see them waving and blowing kisses. Morgan told me that Rona had taken too long collecting the flowers, and time had gotten away from them. Even this visit, though disappointing, confirmed I was loved. I was glad that Morgan could go out with them for Mexican food; he needed solace too.

∽

Together, for that week, we were a motley community, more of a community than I'd experienced since the group of Lynn's friends who'd gathered around her until her death and through the funeral. In the hospital we patients were living under the same conditions, following the same rhythms – meals, group therapy, vitals, meds, rest, sleep – and the same elusive rules, more or less.

Getting Out

My first night on the ward, I agreed to take a concoction

of drugs they had for me: an unnamed mood stabilizer and Trazodone for sleep. I immediately felt woozy, like I was going to black out. I collapsed on the floor and vowed, with some outrage, that that was it: the drug was clearly not for me. I continued to take the Trazodone and the blood pressure pill I'd been taking for five years. I knew I was getting better and didn't need anything else.

Dr. Chen was my assigned psychiatrist, the one who needed to grant approval for my release. He was the only psychiatrist dependably on the ward every morning, like clockwork, from 8:30 to 9:00 a.m. I wasn't his only patient, of course; I think he gave each of us about two and a half minutes. He was Taiwanese with a slight build and gruff manner. Barely listening, he barked rather than talked and was always rushing somewhere else more important. He regularly communicated with Morgan and Wil, letting them know about my progress.

After five days, I insisted Dr. Chen move things along. Grabbing his attention was like holding his collar tight around the neck, my voice as pointed as his was dismissive. With a supercilious smile, his eyes met mine. "Do you really think you're ready? Maybe you're just pretending." He enraged me, but I certainly couldn't show that. Strategically, I first asked for a pass to take a walk outside with Wil and Morgan. Dr. Chen agreed.

I was feeling really good: everything around me – trees, flowers, a man on a small tractor – glowed with the miracle of being. The world was such a vibrantly beautiful place! I told Wil and Morgan that I was ready to come home, that I thought I could continue healing there if we got friends and relatives to be with me. They looked at each other skeptically. I didn't know what I could do to convince them I was more grounded than I had been. It wasn't my fault that the world was duller for them. They could see and feel that I was still manic while I was convinced I had ascended to a new level of consciousness. Despite their doubts, they agreed to help me move toward discharge. Their condition was that I go directly from the hospital to a session with Dr. Wilson, to which I consented without hesitation. Anyway, I wanted to show him how well I was doing without a mood stabilizer.

Dr. Chen had told Morgan that he would allow me to go to the chapel by myself for an ecumenical service the Sunday morning before the Monday I was to be discharged. That morning the nurse said that Dr. Chen had not written a pass. I was frustrated. "He lied to my son by telling him one thing and you another." Dr. Chen immediately came out of the small office, red-faced. I was a little embarrassed that he had overheard me. I might have spoken more tactfully if I knew he was right there. He brusquely wrote the pass for the morning. I thanked him. "And I am leaving tomorrow, correct?" I asked.

"Yes, you're sure you are ready?" he repeated. There was no question in my mind.

Warm spring air streamed under the opened stain-glassed windows of the chapel. I breathed it in, relishing the freedom of life outside, freedom soon to be mine again. The light diffused through the windows. About 40 people sat attentively in the light maple pews. The priest, who was Nigerian, dressed in white, had already begun but gestured me forward as the doors closed behind me. It was Pentacost. That struck me as magical since years before I had been baptized on Pentacost in the Methodist Church. This was a sign, a blessing for my release. As a day in the church calendar, it was significant – the day that the Holy Spirit came into the disciples, making it possible for them to communicate with all the people of the world, with anyone who wanted to open their hearts to a new time of Love. The priest talked about terrorism in Nigeria, the violence ripping through the world, and the fact that every person has a choice whether to embrace love and kindness or to embrace hatred and terror. He knew that the only way anything would change deeply was when more and more people refused to join the forces of violence.

My friends on the ward were sad to see me go, especially Sue, Tajudeen, and Byron. Sue and I agreed to meet at the end of May at a mutually favorite restaurant in Poughkeepsie. She had no phone number or address for me to check in. I feared that without me she would once again revert to her bed. Tajudeen and I exchanged email addresses. I felt healed, that I'd done good work during my time on the ward. I had no doubt that I'd be ready to plan and facilitate that upcoming retreat. After all, I had to be. I was ready for Dr. Wilson.

Transition

Dr. Wilson was visibly outraged and frustrated that Dr. Chen had done nothing to get me on a mood stabilizer in a whole week. I didn't understand what he was so angry about. Couldn't he see how much better I was? Dr. Wilson saw with clarity and grave concern that I was not on solid ground. I agreed to take the sleeping pill that would help me sleep 7 – 9 hours a night, which I assured him was all I needed – plus a little help from friends and family.

Morgan called people we trusted who might be able to take a day or a weekend or a few days to spend with me, so Wil and he could resume as much of their work as possible. My cousins took one weekend, one friend one day, and another friend four days with the idea of spelling Wil and Morgan. It was soon clear that that was impossible. One of them had to be with me, too. My regime was to sleep 7 – 9 hours a night with the sleeping pill and to eat three meals a day. As Dr. Wilson predicted, I got worse instead of better. The sleeping pill only worked sporadically, especially since I still insisted on making the dosage as low as possible. I watched, a bit surprised, as I wore down the patience of every one of my generous caregivers.

I had to measure my water intake since for the past 12 years I'd had a low sodium condition, called syndrome of inappropriate antidiuretic hormone (SIADH): my kidneys withhold water, which dilutes the sodium in my blood, making my constitution vulnerable to any drastic changes. Hyponatremia, low sodium, when extreme, can be life threatening. The condition gets worse under stress, not everyday stress but traumatic stress. I was trying to increase the amount of water I had been drinking for years since my chiropractor thought I wasn't drinking enough water, so I added water and balanced it with drops of electrolytes.

To get to bed at a decent hour, I had to calm down first. I wanted a footbath or a warm bath with lavender every night. The temperature had to be just perfect. Cousin Ina figured out a way to bring two pitchers of water to the living room, one hot, one cold, where she could pour in the water until it was the perfect temperature. I was bathed in her healing and nurturing capacities. She set the bar, but once she left, Wil and Morgan were distraught, their patience rapidly waning. No one could sustain that.

About a month after my release from the hospitals, I emailed a questionnaire to these generous friends and family. This response most baldly describes my state of mind and what it was like to be with me during this time:

It wasn't anything like being with the usual Cat. Because you had no self-awareness and, honestly, no real consideration for others, it was very taxing/challenging. Typically with two thoughtful adults there's an ebb/flow where we think/work independently and then interact. I sort of have the mental image of two thin streams touching paths and then moving away from each other. Your mania did not allow for any separation or silence or independence — it was like a radio turned super-loud, blowing out the speakers. Your mania was also much quicker to anger or unkindness than usual Cat. You got annoyed easily; you were sometimes rude. There was no filter on what you said. There was this really big chasm between your whole regular life — house, car, status, social standing — and what your brain was doing that made it really hard. You are an independent adult in your sixties! But if I lost sight of you I would completely panic the way I would if I had lost track of a toddler. I struggled with knowing that you are a smart and accomplished and extremely talented woman but also knowing you were vulnerable and unpredictable and off-balance.

What I perceived you needed and what you thought you needed were pretty contrary. I thought you needed centering and deep breathing, medicine and slow, thoughtful movement. You were opposed to all of those things, particularly medicine (which of course I can't blame you for). Or, I would suggest a calming activity and you would say something like yes, that's just what I need -- I just have to finish this email first. Which would turn into one hundred emails. You were very focused on connecting and communicating and talking.[8]

I'm grateful to my straight-talking friends. Another put it this way:

> It was so intense, mainly because you seemed completely wrapped up in your own self and your own head and your own needs. It also took so long to do normal stuff (get dressed, eat). Everything had to be perfect, everything was deliberated over and over and had to be penetrated to the center of the earth. It was almost like you were borrowing/depending on the ego presences of those around you. That was tiring and somewhat draining. You were out of balance. It was hard for you to see/feel the other standing before you. You were also super controlling.
>
> You certainly needed to sleep, to relax, to breathe rhythmically, for another to be with you, to accompany you, to physically take care of you, to hold you, to love you. Maybe you needed some other stuff, but I wasn't quite sure what. I suppose we could say the meds too, but I am also very ambivalent about that. We also needed to have a lot of patience with you. I think you knew/agreed with most of this, except maybe the drugs.
>
> I also felt a lot of compassion for Wil and Morgan, Mommy and Kim and how much pain they were experiencing.[9]

Morgan said at one point when he came to visit me in the County Hospital: "So many people love you and care about you, Mom." That meant a lot and stayed with me through to the other side of what was coming. What of the people who have an experience like this without as much love and faithfulness?

In Crisis Again

In less then two weeks after my release, Morgan, Wil, and I were back in Dr. Wilson's office to address the wider family emergency.

"Look at them, Cat. They are exhausted from trying to take care of you. They can't do it anymore. They have to get back to their own lives. Do you agree that you can't be alone?" I sadly acquiesced.

I saw Wil and Morgan slumping in their chairs across from one another, eyes closed, spent, helpless, frightened.

"I heard you agreed to go to the private hospital last night and called them yourself. Is that right?" I nodded. "That's good. Okay, then I'm going to call them now to see if they have a bed." I panicked. "Is everything ready to go?" Dr. Wilson looked at Morgan and Wil.

"Now?" I asked sharply. I must have looked like a cornered deer. "No one said it would be right now. I thought it would be tomorrow."

"We have everything ready to go now, Mom," Morgan responded. "We really can't afford you changing your mind. We've given you all the time we can. I have to get back to my life. There are no more friends or family who can come to be with you. You're too much for them." I didn't want to believe him. Had they really tried everyone? "This is just too much for all of us. We're not helping you. I'm sorry, Mom." His voice broke; his eyes filled with tears, so did Wil's and then mine. I knew they loved me. I trusted them but knew that I would be the one going through this, alone. Here I was, like 44 years ago, experiencing something I thought, without psychedelic drugs, could and would never happen again. The County Hospital had not been too bad – now the next stop, another unknown.

At least this time I was signing myself in.

Dr. Wilson turned to us. They didn't have a bed yet in a single room, but they would soon. He was sure that if we showed up they'd find a bed for me. They'd have to. Morgan and Wil got the message: they needed to take me now.

Morgan drove my car; I was with him. Wil followed in his car. I hated the way Morgan drove. He slammed the breaks too hard; he drove too fast; he took the corners too sharply. I immediately felt nauseated. Our temperatures were different. He needed it colder than I did. I needed fresh air blowing on me. Everything was wrong.

"Stop the car, Morgan. I need air, or I'm going to puke."

"Mom, we can't stop now. We have to get there." He gripped the wheel, his voice sounding harsh.

"I'm not going to run away. I need to drive with Wil. Stop the car!" I yelled.

He signaled to Wil and pulled over. I opened the door and bent over, sure I might vomit, which could mean that my sodium level would drop, and I'd need to go to the emergency room. I breathed deeply, Wil now at my side; Morgan with his hands on the wheel, stone-faced, jaw set, staring straight ahead. I breathed deeply, focusing on the delicacy of the wild flowers by the side of the highway as I gradually stabilized myself.

"I want to go with you, Wil. Morgan and I are fighting over the temperature of the car."

"Of course, you can come with me, sweetie. Let's go."

3
The Private Hospital

When we drove into the lush grounds, hyacinths and tulips edging the buildings in the mild spring weather, I felt reassured. The place looked benign enough, even pleasant; my body was taking it in, admiring every petal as I slowly crept toward the door. Since I refused to wear glasses, I was on my hands and knees, so I wouldn't miss even one of the flowers. Morgan and Wil were impatient and exhausted, but I was in no hurry. Wil moved me along, insisting they were waiting for me inside.

When he finally got me through the door and I met the nurses at the intake station, I revealed a moment of genuine relief: "I'm so glad I'm here." What was I thinking? What was I feeling? It was all so contradictory. We soon met the intake psychiatrist, Dr. Stone, who made it abundantly clear that he was in charge of this particular ward.

"This is no hotel," he said sternly. Of course not, I thought. Why is he talking to me this way? Does he think I'm stupid? I was searching for anything in his bearing to make him more accessible, friendlier. He looked like a 70s hippy with long scraggly hair draping his shoulders and tattoos covering thick, strong arms. He'd seen a lot, a no nonsense-type. Morgan and Wil looked reassured. While I sensed deep compassion in him, I was especially suspicious of the agreement I had to make to take all prescribed medication. "We will make you take it if you refuse. Do you understand?" He looked me in the eye. While I abhorred what he was saying, I had no choice but to nod. We were too far down this road to argue; despite that, signing the papers and his tone of voice made me extremely nervous. Did I have no say about what went into my own body? Why was it a problem that I have some input?

The intake nurse then told us there was only one bed available that night in a double room. They would see what they could do tomorrow about that single I wanted. Wil and Morgan could not accompany me any further. I hugged both of them and with a sinking feeling watched them leave. Morgan was taking my car to Brooklyn, so he could easily visit; Wil was returning to our empty home. The aide led me to my bed, trying not to disturb the woman lying in the other one. It was already dark. I was hungry. She told me dinner was over, but there were snacks in the small kitchen on the ward, which she showed me.

I wasn't tired and knew it would be a problem for me to room with a stranger: I was too sensitive to another person's energy. The sound of her breathing would disturb me. The woman in the other bed was angry that I was there; she was strange, paranoid, deeply depressed or, perhaps, even schizophrenic. I wandered and met some young people watching television. I liked them; they soon went to bed. I found another person or two also in the kitchen, those accompanied by personal aides. There wasn't much there that I wanted to eat. I liked the aides and had different ideas about who they really were. I was sure that one of them was a Kennedy and had to keep his identity secret, which was why they only used first names. He told me it was to protect their privacy, which made sense. I wanted to guess but knew it was inappropriate.

Staff didn't approve of my wandering. I had to sleep; I was disturbing other patients. They sent a nurse to give me meds to settle me down. Did I refuse to take them orally? I can't remember; I must have. Just the mention of thorazine triggered a reflexive rejection. It was a symbol of incarceration, of domination by the sick mental health system. I was on high alert. They'd have to force me. They warned me that they would have to call Dr. Stone, the admitting psychiatrist, if I refused. He soon charged in with four young, strong people. He looked angry and stood there overseeing the procedure as the team held me down and injected me in each thigh. The psychic pain of being forced even greater than the physical pain caused by the injections, I snapped, screaming at the top of my voice until my throat growled, a sound I'd never heard myself make before. I wasn't an animal or a mad woman. I was a teacher – or had been – and a facilitator; I was highly educated with two master's degrees. Why was I in this horrible place? I knew that I was waking the whole ward, but I didn't give a shit. Why the fuck were they still using thorazine? In two different hospitalizations in 1972, I'd been shot up with it in the arm, never in the thigh. But those were emergency incarcerations, once by the police, the other by my parents; both were in public hospitals. I had a visceral memory of thorazine, crystallized into the way I'd described it ever since: "It's like having little shards of glass shot through your nervous system." It actually didn't feel the same this time: maybe it was a lighter dose. Did they know about my history with thorazine? Did they care? I thought I'd told the very same psychiatrist but maybe not. Did I sleep then? I don't remember.

I assumed the rules would be the same as in the county hospital. There I'd been committed, yet I had some rights, which were respected. This private hospital only took patients who committed themselves and agreed to take medication; they'd made that clear, and I had agreed, but when push came to shove, I demanded they shove.

Time loosens. I can't keep track. There was another night of forced meds, screaming, waking the others. I couldn't control anything, and staff fixated on using thorazine to stabilize me. How did they see me in those first 24 – 36 hours of observation?

Mostly 20 somethings with drug or depression issues or a combination inhabited this ward. There was one woman my age in a deep comatose kind of depression. We connected when she emerged; she was a well-to-do cultured woman from Westchester, who looked like she'd been there for a while and wasn't leaving any time soon. There was an Orthodox woman with post-partum depression, always cooking her kosher food and unconsciously claiming her right to the microwave before others who had been waiting. I was the only manic patient on the ward. Could it be that mania is a lot less common than depression and drug addiction, especially for people who commit themselves?

Maybe they were waiting for the seclusion room to be open. Maybe they were hoping I would stop screaming and just take my meds like everyone else. What do I know? I was never told about this room; I had no idea anything like it existed. How would I?

Before the restraint, the thorazine, the seclusion room, I thought this hospital was going to be okay. Overall, it was not a brutal place. I have to acknowledge that. In fact, I already had respect for the way it was operating. I'd made my judgment from the people I'd met, patients and aides.

There were different levels of aides with various levels of education and training. On my first full day there, I met the person who founded the hospital: a man in his mid-70s, grey-haired, teddy bear-like, in a light shirt, khaki pants, and sports jacket, lounging comfortably in a chair, legs crossed, watching as young people, mostly in their early 20s, ambled into a group session he was about to lead. The synchronicity of his presence with mine, as I snacked in the kitchen, felt like fate, so before his group began, I took the opportunity to introduce myself, to tell him about my background as an educator and a facilitator of retreats for health care and other service professionals and leaders. Maybe what I offered could help the hospital. He gazed at me with respect and, when I asked, said that he didn't mind if I listened from the kitchen while the group was in process.

I hoped he would talk with Dr. Huang, the chief psychiatrist, and verify that I was fine, didn't need meds, and should be discharged. I asked various aides about when I would see Dr. Huang since he seemed to be the one who had to approve all the discharges. I was told that when I was ready he would find me. I caught a glimpse of him with another patient. He was a slight Chinese man, extremely intelligent looking; he had a helper with him who took notes on a clipboard as they met with the patient. Why hadn't they met with me? Maybe that would be soon.

Maybe it wasn't necessary. An elaborate scenario began to consume my thoughts: I was sure that that evening at dinner or the next morning at breakfast I would be honored, my true identity as an enlightened healer would be acknowledged, and I would be released. Under Dr. Huang's supervision, secret preparations were already underway. He was so busy that he was having trouble finding a time he could be there. After celebrating the insights that I would bring to their hospital, they would release me. I waited expectantly for any sign, but my meals continued to be brought to the small kitchen in Styrofoam boxes. I was not allowed access to the main dining room, which I actually didn't mind although most of the others were going. I liked the small kitchen, and probably knew that I couldn't handle being in a large space with a lot of people, at least not until they came to get me for the ceremony.

When did my team – the psychiatrist, psychologist, and social worker – realize I wasn't ready for anything but the seclusion room? Maybe it was the two nights of screaming. I don't remember meeting any of those professionals, although later they seemed to remember me. On the second morning, an aide came to get me ready.

Seclusion

First, to offer a more objective picture of seclusion and seclusion rooms, here's a report from a psychiatric nurse, who is an expert on the practice.

> Alternatives to Restraint and Seclusion in Mental Health Settings: Questions and Answers From Psychiatric Nurse Experts
>
> Laura Stokowski, RN, MS
>
> Disclosures
> May 03, 2007
>
> **Seclusion.** Involuntary confinement of the patient alone in a room or an area where the patient is physically prevented from leaving; a situation where a patient is restricted to a room or area alone and staff physically intervenes to prevent the patient from leaving is also

considered seclusion.

Seclusion can only be used for the management of violent behavior that jeopardizes the immediate physical safety of the patient, a staff member, or others. Seclusion should not be used for punishment, coercion, or threat....

Seclusion is used in circumstances when a patient is temporarily unable to control impulses or surges of emotion leading to behavior that might harm someone else.... A locked seclusion room should also be avoided if the patient has medical problems because of the difficulty observing subtle signs of cardiac and respiratory compromise....

Seclusion might be used for the patient whose behavior endangers others, who needs to be alone for the protection of others, or who must be removed from situations that may trigger harmful and escalating behaviors. This temporary and brief time alone offers the opportunity for the patient to use positive coping strategies to calm and quiet him or herself. If a patient expresses a preference for seclusion in situations where other alternatives have not worked, that preference should be honored. In these or other instances, the least restrictive means to accomplish the separation of a person from others is to encourage the person to use his or her room, positioning a staff person at the door to help the patient use the quiet time effectively....

Anger, fear, and frustration can all lead to violent behavior, and each calls for a specific approach. "*Meet the patient where the patient is at*" is a phrase commonly used to convey the need to match the approach to the patient's emotional state and to what has triggered that state.

An often overlooked but very simple crisis communication technique is to ask the patient "What would help you right now, at this moment?" It is surprising that this is a question we don't think of asking, yet it often yields a very specific and helpful response. A patient might just need clarification of a misunderstanding, some personal space, or might need to walk. Engaging the patient in the decision of how best to intervene can help them get through the situation without resorting to seclusion or restraint....[10]

While the article does not specifically address someone having a manic episode, this condition must be quite familiar to any expert psychiatric nurse. With this as a backdrop, I continue to wonder if more could have been done to reach me, using some of Laura Stokowski's suggestions, which seem like common sense. What if staff attempted to include me in decisions about what I needed? What if they had asked me what was making me scream? What if they had adjusted and done something different? Maybe I'm deluding myself: they were seeing psychosis and an inability to reflect or reason. They also had a whole ward to manage. Therese, my personal psychologist, later reminded me that even those closest to me, those who had known me for years, couldn't reach me. At the time on that ward, all I really wanted was to get out of there and to go home, where I felt safe and loved, completely forgetting what had gotten me into the hospital in the first place.

In fact, on that second morning when one of the young chipper aides bopped in and said that I needed to pack all my clothing, I was sure that I was headed home. I was well enough. They'd realized that. I had meticulously placed things on the shelves and quickly packed them in the bag they gave me, but I wasn't quite dressed. The aide helped me, as you would a five-year-old, while I jumped on the bed, ecstatic to be getting out of there. Just to be sure I asked: "Where are you taking me? Have you called Wil?"

"You're going to another building," she said. That was the wrong answer. In an act of civil disobedience, I refused to walk there myself. The revolutionary in me was ablaze: I was not going to cooperate with the enemy. I began recruiting the aides who quickly assembled to "my team." In my mind they were secretly helping me escape. Being carried by six aides became my triumphant march through the grounds. Soon I would be free.

When I asked where we were headed, I was told the adolescent building. My theory was breaking down. When we went through the door to that building and into a small room, the seclusion room, it locked behind us. Two of the aides remained, waiting with me. I was confused. In a few moments, a social worker or staff psychologist arrived, someone I hadn't met before. I was jolly and tried to recruit her too. She would have none of it: she was impatient with me, furious that I'd made such a fuss. Maybe she was angry because I had tried to recruit her staff; someone had ratted; she didn't like mutinies, I rationalized. Where was I, and why was I in here? What was this odd space? All I wanted was to get out, but I kept getting deeper and deeper in.

I had so many questions. How long would I be in here? There was no answer to that or what the determining factors for release would be. I thought it was some kind of a game, something I had to figure out, to get right, to crack the code, and then I'd be let out of solitary.

I studied the space: a locked rectangular room, in which there was no proper bed, a gym mat on the floor with no pillow. There were two limp blankets. When I complained, the aide on duty said, "You can use one of the blankets as a pillow." Sure, that made sense: I needed to be adaptable, that was part of the trial. It was like living in the wilderness but simultaneously felt like punishment. Why was I being punished? This was primitive. How could I hurt myself with a pillow? I didn't want to hurt myself anyway. Didn't they know that?

At first I was so enraged that I relentlessly flung abuse. "Is anyone the fuck out there? Can anyone the fuck hear me? Fuck all of you!" Quiet. Nothing. "Talk like that won't help you," a familiar voice said. Probably one of the aides who'd carried me over. The only ones who could hear me were those on duty at the desk, watching the camera, or teenage passersby, since the seclusion room was right beside the door that led outside. I had to express my fury and hoped it would get through to someone, and justice would be restored. I wasn't a criminal or a deranged animal. I just wanted out of seclusion, out of this hospital, which was getting to be more and more of a nightmare. I wanted the lights out. I wanted a pillow. I wanted to speak to my family. But there were strict protocols that only the psychiatrist could override. I heard about these rules one by one or not at all. I had met the psychiatrist once before the seclusion – although I hardly remember that – and then didn't see her until a few days later when I was in crisis.

This was solitary confinement, directly in line with how tens of thousands of prisoners in this country are maltreated. Even though I'd given my permission to be hospitalized, I rebelled against being incarcerated. The only time I stood face-to-face with another human was when the room was unlocked, so I could go to the bathroom. At these times I ranted about the way women had been committed in the past and maltreated in mental hospitals for generations as they became more and more independent, creative, and assertive. If I reminded them of that, maybe they would all come to their senses and see that what they were doing was unjust.

I'm sure they were hoping that I would come to my senses, too. Let me be clear: no aides were ever cruel to me; mostly they were incredibly kind. They repeatedly told me that verbal abuse would not help me get out of seclusion. But what would? They did tell me that I was there to calm and center myself, exactly what had been increasingly difficult, if not impossible, for the past month as my mind spun out into making elaborate plans, charts, and networks, arranging all the people in my life over decades to solve this or that educational or societal problem, to start this or that 21st century project. The desk people repeated that my release was up to the doctors, not up to them. I was sure there must be a trick, a way to outwit everyone to prove how ready I was to be out of solitary. Maybe I needed to reverse some psychological patterning, yet everything I tried revealed another facet of conditioning: if I were good enough, they would let me out – if I were smart enough, polite enough, subordinate enough.

That first day I perceived the space as completely bugged, mirrors at various places on the ceiling and in the corners, mostly convex shapes. I had nothing to write on or to write with at the time. After my release from seclusion, I wrote this in my journal as I began to process the experience:

A simple room with concrete block walls,
painted pale blue, reflects
summer's persistent light, muted through
locked down Plexiglas window.
I am not tall enough
to see anything
through the narrow bank of high windows.
But sometimes I hear shouts
from what I imagine to be a playground.
Are teenagers playing soccer in the June sunshine?
Even prisoners are allowed time outside, I think. It's been days since I've
been in fresh air and felt the sun on my body. A little later
I hear someone being put in the door across from mine,
which I can see through the hatched window, another
seclusion room, although at the time I didn't know the term.
"You'll be out as soon as you cool down. You have to use words and
not hit someone on the playground. It's not complicated."
I recognize the voice.

And when did they start the lithium? I don't remember.

I see a rainbow
at the window's edge as the sun sets.
Is it there as the sun rises too? Night is clear.
Days are long. Twilight. I'm confused for a minute.
Then I'm happy as
the sun rises and also when it's held in whatever

> that is at dusk, which also is strewn
> with sadness that I have failed
> to free myself in the elongating days, that I have not spoken to Wil,
> to Morgan, to anyone for days. Where are they? Do they care about me?
> Will I ever get out of here?
> They promised. They promised. They promised.

After awhile, a half-day, a day, who knows – it was as though time collapsed in on itself – like a child after a tantrum, I stopped flailing and calmed down enough to notice the subtleties of the room and the concepts behind the way it was constructed. As I accepted there might be genius behind the creation of the space – perhaps, that kind doctor who founded the hospital – the room became friendlier, if only for brief periods of time. I realized that there was, in fact, only one camera, in the corner, and that the desk people wanted me to stay in view of that. I could then readily comply. The muted blue color was actually calming. I took the lithium orally, still not believing it was the right drug for me, hating that I was taking it at all, but hoping it would get me out of there.

Food was periodically placed or, what seemed to me, shoved inside the door by one of the desk people. Were they afraid I might storm the battlements? I often had no appetite or was dozing when it was delivered. By the time I was hungry and opened the Styrofoam box, everything in it was cold and nothing I could imagine eating – overcooked string beans; cold stringy, fatty beef. I'm a notoriously picky eater, always have been, always will be. I was losing weight, just the opposite of what I needed, but I had no part in choosing anything I was eating or much else in my present existence.

So what was the difference between committing myself and incarceration? I couldn't see any.

During this time I repeatedly asked to speak to Wil or Morgan; the desk people asked me what the phone number was. It was hard to remember. I knew they had it. I strained my mind, and I remembered it. It didn't seem to matter: there was always a reason they couldn't make the call or a promise that they would: "We'll see if we can reach them." "We have to wait for our supervisor to be back before we can do that." "Wait until morning; it's too late now." "We're not authorized; we have to wait for someone who is." This was torturous. Why didn't they work more closely with my family? I didn't understand.

I now know that Wil called every day. He was told that I was in seclusion, and he wasn't allowed to speak to me. He was alarmed: What did they mean by seclusion? What were they doing to my wife? How was she? How long would the seclusion last? Would she ever get out of there?

How did I spend the long summer days? I was given a *People Magazine* and spent time tearing out pages. That had been entertaining in the County Hospital but was empty here. I stretched and danced one or two mornings since my legs ached from sleeping and basically living on the floor. I listened to what was happening outside and reached on tip-toe to try to see out, only to glimpse the tops of trees on a grey or a sunny day.

I listened obediently to everything the desk people said to do. I learned quickly: I didn't go to the parts of the room where they couldn't see me and showed my face in the camera when asked to do so. Sleeping was especially difficult, though, because it was protocol to keep lights on all night, which added to the sense of being tortured. This *is* torture and directly antithetical to what Dr. Wilson told me was essential for mental health – seven to nine hours of sleep a night. I tried to keep my mood up. I took whatever meds they gave me. I calmed myself and thought there would be some external response to how I was cooperating, that I would get to talk to Wil, to Morgan, to a psychiatrist, to someone!

During the second night, I had a revolutionary thought. I was tired of waiting for approval; maybe that was the realization I needed to come to. They were waiting for me to take charge. After all, hadn't I committed myself? Perhaps, it was up to me when I would get out of there.

When I went to the bathroom, it was early in the morning, around 2 or 3, and I refused to reenter the room. "I committed myself, and I'm telling you that I'm checking myself out of here. If you need to, call my husband now, go right ahead. He's a night owl. He'll be up." I felt centered, righteous, clear, in command. They quickly, calmly called another three or four staff people. I still refused to go back into the room; I kept repeating that I had every right to check myself out since I'd checked myself in. At least that's what I believed. They slowly started moving in on me. Something happened: I was tricked and found myself once again on the other side of the steel grey door. I asked them to turn down the lights, but they said it was impossible.

When the third day dawned, a wave of sheer despair swept over me, perhaps, the deepest I'd ever experienced. My hopelessness frightened me. I had no thoughts of suicide but no idea how I would ever get out of there. What was their plan? Could I see my doctor, any doctor? What kind of place was this?

When did the delusional carpet ride begin? I'm not actually sure, but it did; and with increasing intensity, tumultuous thoughts claimed my mind, something like this:

> *I know I can be part of the Secret Ones. I can heal myself. I can heal my eyes and see, years of near-sightedness cured. I can open my ears and hear. Clogged since the flu that past winter, my ear is finally clear. I can be quiet beyond words, in deep silence, beyond the silence of the deaf mute. I can also slowly raise the volume until I can be heard again. I was traveling the full range of the senses. How can I prove who I am? Can I show you? What can my code name be? I'm listening: I am the one who goes first. Am I the Turning Point of every age? Scanning time, yes, at the turn of each epoch, there I was, going first. And each time a woman with a thick New York Jewish accent, exclaimed, "I could die." I laugh out loud. I want to use this with the desk people to make them laugh too. How far back do I have to go? All the way to the beginning of time, to the turning point of time to know who I am. Really? Am I that one, the Holy One, pure Jesus of Nazareth? Even I am surprised and honored.*

That felt like a completion. I was ravaged with hunger, realizing I hadn't eaten for at least a day. I told the desk person, who answered that the kitchen was closed and that there was already food in the room. I found the Styrofoam box in a corner and opened it, poking at some cold, greenish brown shredded of beef; whatever else was there was dried up. There was no way I could eat any of it. I would certainly vomit, which I was afraid of doing since my sodium level would drop, and I would need emergency care. My brain was on fire; my stomach clawing. Maybe if I threw up and got over *that* fear, I would be released. Perhaps these were all trials for my spiritual advancement.

The desk people offered a choice of Cheetos or pretzels, all they had on the ward. Both had salt, which I knew I needed for my hyponatremia, the low sodium condition. I was feeling weak and woozy from the lack of sleep, lack of food, lack of human contact and especially the dearth of my family's love that sustained me. I'd had more than enough pretzels and requested Cheetos, thinking at least there was some protein in those. After savoring a small bag and half, which I hadn't eaten since high school, and drinking some cold water, I felt more and more nauseated until I let myself vomit. The desk people saw it on camera; a woman, annoyed and disgusted while trying not to be, cleaned it up. Staff was alerted. I was going down. I knew it. Maybe this is where the delusions took over. In a rare act of compassion, the staff broke their rules and dimmed the lights to help me sleep.

I drifted until dawn when a bald, Tibetan-looking man came to draw blood. Not too long after, or so it seemed, a gaggle of women in white coats descended. "Do you remember me?" a thin, blond woman in horn-rimmed glasses asked. I kind of remembered her and knew I should; I offered a faint nod. Was this a test? "I'm your psychiatrist here. Do you remember my name?" she asked. Nothing came to me. I shook my head. Why all these questions? "Can you tell me your name?" Of course, I thought, but when my mouth moved, nothing came out. I couldn't think at all or speak coherently. That terrified me. What was happening? It was difficult for me to stand; I was incredibly weak. "We have called an ambulance and are transferring you to a nearby hospital where you can be helped," she said. "Your sodium is very low, and we can't treat that here. They will be able to help you. You're going to be alright." I stared into the nothingness and waited for the EMTs.

The Next Hospital

In the ambulance I couldn't speak. Nothing would come out of my mouth. I was frightened and wanted the EMTs to hook me up to intravenous sodium immediately, but they didn't. "It's only a 10-minute ride," they reassured me.

I was quickly admitted and didn't understand why they had to run tests. Hooked up to an electrocardiogram, I was having a recurring delusion that every time I did Reiki by putting my hands on my kidneys, which was actually my stomach or any other part of my body, the technicians would have to start the whole process again. It felt like the medical version of Sisyphus pushing the boulder up the hill in Hades. Would this test ever end? I couldn't stop putting my hands on my body; they couldn't stop having to start again. I just wanted them to give me an IV of sodium like the other times I'd been hospitalized for acute low sodium episodes.

Then a nephrologist named Dr. Coffino wheeled me just outside his office in the hospital, so he could keep an eye on me. I was surprised to see him when I woke from sleep. "You're looking a whole lot better," he said. "How are you feeling?" I was able to respond that I was feeling better, which was a tremendous relief to me: I could speak and state my name when he asked. He told me that they were keeping me in the hospital until my sodium stabilized. I was relieved to be out of solitary, out of that other hospital altogether. My fluids were restricted for the night after I took a salt tab. There was no IV. I didn't understand but accepted that he must know what he was doing. I was still out of it and exhausted.

He accompanied me upstairs as I was wheeled into a

private room. A nurse's aid would be with me through the night. I was relieved that I would finally be able to sleep in a bed even with the discomfort of the catheter that they had inserted. I didn't understand why they had done that, nor did Dr. Coffino. "It's routine," he said, looking apologetic and mildly annoyed. "I wish they wouldn't, but they do." A young woman looked at or quietly talked on her cell phone all night as I slept. The next day my all-night guardian was replaced by a slightly older woman, originally from Colombia. She was a gentle soul, who gave me a foot massage and soothed me with her voice, kind words, and calm presence. I could select from a menu of healthy food; I was hungry and ate well. This was the way people in crisis should be treated, I thought. Fluids remained restricted. My blood was taken regularly, and my sodium level was coming up. Wil visited for a short while; I was so grateful to be with him. Although I was weak, we took a short walk down the hall and back. The hospital offered holistic care, and I took advantage of Reiki with aromatherapy. It was exactly what I needed, after which I slept deeply.

The next day, I had an extended talk with Wil on the phone. He was glad to hear me sounding stronger. A team of psychiatrist, psychologist, and social worker swept in sometime in the early afternoon. The psychiatrist introduced herself. She was following my case and had spoken with the psychiatrist at the private hospital. "What would you like to take, Klonopin or Depakote?" This was my choice. Since my niece was also on Depakote, I picked that one. These drugs functioned differently than lithium: they were anticonvulsants and didn't affect the kidneys. They didn't know why they worked, but in most cases they did as long as people took their medication. Within 24 - 36 hours I started feeling more connected to the world that most people inhabit, that I had too until this all began five weeks before. Dr. Coffino visited and said he was pleased with the sodium levels and that I would need to be discharged for this condition and transported back to the private hospital. I would come and see him in his office once I was released from that hospital. He would help with the low sodium condition. (In my first visit with him he revealed that when he first saw me, I was catatonic, and he doesn't use that word lightly.)

I refused to return to the private hospital. No one could make me go. I had been treated badly there and was not going to return. Dr. Coffino said they could not keep me there, that they had to return me to the hospital that sent me – protocol. I was adamant. He said I'd have to speak with the psychiatrist. The word from her was the same.

I later learned of all the scrambling that went on to convince me that that was what I had to do. I talked with Wil on the phone for a long time, then with Morgan and my mother. After hearing my refusal, Wil immediately called Dr. Klabber, the blond psychiatrist at the private hospital and bluntly expressed why I was afraid to return. She assured Wil that I would be in another building, one I hadn't been in before and that I certainly wouldn't be placed in seclusion again. Everyone seemed in agreement that the lithium had undermined my kidney functioning and that the anticonvulsant seemed to be helping. The agreement was that if I continued to do well, I would be discharged in three or four days, which seemed like an eon to me.

Meanwhile Wil had told Dr. Wilson that I was refusing to return to the private hospital. He also knew I had to go back and was frantic because he couldn't reach me on the phone, which was constantly busy. He tried once more on his way home from the office at around 8 p.m. and finally got through. "Cat," he said, sounding surprised and relieved that we could talk, "think of it this way: giving it a second chance will give you an opportunity to turn around whatever happened when you were there before. It's still the best option for you." There was something about what Dr. Wilson said, coupled with Dr. Klabber's promises, which helped loosen my fear-gripped, primal flight reflex. Maybe it was Dr. Wilson's decades of intense experiences in New York City hospitals that had shaped his keenly honed judgment, together with a way he communicated that said he cared.

I felt able to face into the next step and returned. Dr. Klabber did everything she said she would – new ward, nowhere near seclusion. Something in me had shifted, something fundamental. The Depakote was working, and maybe it was more than that. I was through the worst of it, on a new turn in the road. I took advantage of the days I was there: early morning yoga, groups, connecting with many of the kind, suffering people there. I slept well, ate in the dining hall with everyone else, and took my meds.

Delusions, including that a big celebration was being planned to honor me and signal my discharge, were gone. One night when traumatic images of being in seclusion were beginning to overwhelm me, I asked an aide to be with me in my room, a single room, while I journaled about it. I spent time with a psychologist, who did an interview leading toward discharge. Finally, Wil and I met with Dr. Klabber in the little kitchen on the third day, and we all agreed I was ready to go home early the next morning and that he was ready for me to be home.

Reflections on Seclusion

Can anything be gleaned from my delirium in the seclusion room? I'm not sure what to call these experiences, maybe delirious dreams or dreamlike delusions. Regardless they were all encompassing. From one perspective they could be seen as the overflowing neurochemistry of mania. From another point of view, the delusion-dreams could have been from the lithium, which turned out to be a critical problem since it works through the kidney, the site of my chronic low sodium condition, of which the private hospital knew nothing. Maybe as my sodium plummeted, in my troubled sleep the dream-delirium intensified. Maybe both are true and more. What I do know is that in the seclusion room I was quickly losing touch with outer reality. My heart was broken, my spirit not far behind, and my body failing me. I was starved for nourishing food, deep sleep, and loving companionship.

Yet, on this side of the experience, I'm interested in making meaning of these vivid dreams. In one I had the capacity to travel the full spectrum of my senses: from near-sightedness to focus, from muffled hearing to clarity. This proved I was a healer, and I was healed. Could this particular dream have anything to do with the diagnosis of bipolar 1 disorder I'd been given by both hospitals, a diagnosis I neither wanted nor believed was true? Was I trying to encourage myself: whatever the range of my own psyche, I could navigate and heal it? Maybe I was hard at work regenerating my inner existence since the ground, as I had known it, was gone.

What about the other waking dream about being able to be trusted and needing a code name? You could just call it paranoia, insanity, just part of the mania. But let's not for now. Let's imagine that, as many dreams, it has a connection to the rest of my life. In this one my code name was "the one who goes first," which I took as signifying that I was first to incarnate in each new epoch. I don't know about that, but I do know there are plenty of examples in my life, where I did go first. I was the first-born and the first grandchild on one side. I was the first of the two of us children to know about my father's manic-depression. I was first in my family to graduate from college and graduate school. I was often first to speak in class, to volunteer for an improvisation. I was the first of my friends to find my way into a healing therapy (which unfortunately later became a cult) and the first of those friends to leave it. I helped initiate new projects – from a high school to new part-time teacher education programs to a not-for-profit to support adults sexually abused as children. The code name is no mystery: its roots live in my biography. Could my psyche have been gathering the broken threads of my mind and heart, getting ready to reweave the torn garment?

Being first at the "turning point of time" meant, yet again, being Jesus.[11] Quite a leap, I realize. Pure maniacal grandiosity from one point of view, but from another – and admittedly I grab at straws, stripping this down to the microcosm of each life – aren't we all a turning point around which a life revolves? Don't we each have a world of relationships that orbit around us? A turning point for me is a turning point for my whole family. Maybe that's what my psyche was trying to tell me. Don't we all need to be in sacred relationship with those we love, the other divine human and nonhuman beings in our lives?

Each of us is a drop in the ocean of Divine Wholeness, one facet of the divine diamond, facts so difficult to experience. I am singular; I am part of the human and nonhuman family. During my psychotic journeying, I felt expansive love for every person I met. I could see the spirit shining within them, within everything, and the rightness of every occurrence. That wasn't all, though: this episode deeply disrupted every physical and life rhythm I had and my family had. In its thrall I demanded everyone's attention at all times. Gratefully, on the other side of it, I am free to try to make meaning out of the flotsam and jetsam, left in the wake of that psychic tsunami.

This writing is part of my healing, my processing what that psychotic experience was and what changed because of it. I've worked through the worst of my anger and righteous indignation about being restrained and imprisoned in a seclusion room. I don't think that should happen to anyone, but, regrettably, I have no alternative for dealing with a person as unable to be reasoned with and out of control as I was. The private hospital staff, always professional, may have even tried methods with me that I don't remember. It's difficult, though, for me to recommend this hospital: it would be like admitting anything good about an abusive lover. There's cognitive dissonance, soul dissonance. I still have questions about the Depakote, too, which I discuss now and again with Therese and almost every time I see Dr. Wilson. What person with a diagnosis of bipolar disorder doesn't question her meds? Most do, although my father never did.

4
Following the Tracks

... there are no wrong turns, only unexpected paths.
— Mark Nepo

It's not possible for me to have the first major psychotic episode in 44 years and not search for causes: I'm a seeker. Someone else might just want to take their meds, or not, and get on with life without probing into the whys. But that's not who I am: I'm a prober. How did this come about? Who was I before the break or breakthrough? Exploring that might help me find out how I launched and who I am becoming.

The Family Vortex

We had left behind a beloved community in Austin, Texas, where I was a teacher and school leader for 10 years, having decided to move closer to family after my father's death in 2000, closer to Mom, to Lynn and Jim, to Kim. Destiny had another storyline. Twelve hours after I landed at Newark International Airport on July 29, 2001, Lynn's husband Jim died suddenly of a brain aneurism.

"Well, your timing is good," Lynn said as she wept and hugged me in a room in the ER, Jim's motionless body on the bed behind her. Only gods prepare the exactitude of such timing. For the first time in 20 years, I dropped back into the stormy vortex of my birth family.

Beloved Community

It was 18 months since Lynn's death in December 2012 when I attended the Global Gathering of fellow Courage & Renewal facilitators. In my deep grief I had forgotten how much this community meant to me. Or, perhaps, it wasn't about forgetting as much as about lacking person-to-person contact. I was alone, living with Wil in what had been Lynn's home for 30 years, which I had inherited. She was relieved and filled with joy that we would not have to sell her house and that Kim would be living relatively close to her aunt and uncle, would be able to come "home" for holiday dinners with the family, and would not feel like everything was gone once Lynn was. As she faced death, Lynn also thought that our mother would come to live with us here.

The gathering of facilitators highlighted the reality that I was not isolated but part of a beloved community with shared life values and ways of creating safe, inviting spaces for people's souls to show up. There were friends there I knew and people I just met; I deepened some relationships and started new ones. Was it the jarring contrast between the reality of a beloved community and my otherwise solitary life – especially when Wil was working in the City – that launched me into mania? If not, what did? Could any one thing be targeted as the cause, or was this a constellation of events that led me onto the runway for takeoff? I keep reviewing the events of "the launch" as if command control, reinstated, is now able to review the contents of the black box after the crash with hopes of understanding what led to an experience that boggles the intellect.

Scammed

When I returned from the gathering, the first red flag was getting scammed. I got a phone call from some Pakistanis or Indians who said that they could see a lot of malware and thousands of problems on my computer. How? I asked, wondering if this were a scam. Oh, they had ways to check and could see it. They led me to a place on the computer where I could see thousands of lines of something. Those represent bugs, they said, imminent dangers to your data, photos, everything. It's just a matter of time. I felt invaded by cyber-gremlins. These experts reassured me that they could clean up everything and install life-long software for only $389. Not a bad deal, I thought. Still a bit suspicious, though, I wanted to check with Wil. He was in his studio practicing, so I called his cell phone and still couldn't reach him, as usual. Before the manic episode Wil usually didn't turn on his cell phone; no matter how often I asked that he do it, he'd forget. The guys on the other end of the phone were pressuring me, so I decided to use my own judgment and handed them the proverbial keys to my computer. They needed two hours to complete the process.

Luckily Wil came inside within an hour. When I told him what had happened, he shook his head. "You've been scammed, Cat." I immediately shut down the computer. A chill went through me, a warning. What was going on? Things were going so well since the gathering. Why was this happening? The scammers called right back, irate that I had shut down the computer. I could hardly believe it and called them all kinds of names and ordered them to refund my money. I reported them to some government anti-scam agency, changed passwords, and shut down the credit card. I was rattled.

I called a repairman who told me I could bring the computer in that afternoon. He took a look and reported that I'd caught it in time, that they had tried to get into the guts of the computer but hadn't done any damage that couldn't be fixed. I was grateful.

My Birthday

Two days before my birthday, May 6th, I was meeting my niece Kim, who has cerebral palsy, in a local café to celebrate. I asked her aide to give us some time alone, so we could have a grown-up lunch together. We talked about how we were each doing since Lynn's death and what we were excited about in our lives. We connected.

When I entered the café, I had noticed that a psychic, who called himself Angel, was in the house. While I waited for Kim, I watched to see how he operated. He drew a few cards, mostly asked questions, and listened closely. Harmless enough. Kim thought it would be fun to have our cards read, which didn't surprise me, and offered to pay for a birthday reading. Especially after a hypomanic episode in 2001, I was especially wary of psychics – and under normal circumstances always have been – but agreed, so I wouldn't disappoint her. Besides I was curious yet determined to take lightly whatever he said. He pulled a Uriel card for me, the archangel of light, of wisdom, he said. I don't remember anything else Angel said, but I realize now it wasn't what he said, it was his energy, flattering, connecting: we were on the same plane; we had work to do together; let's explore what that might be. After months of wondering what I was doing with my life, he offered a jolt of promise. I was excited, always dangerous when a psychic is involved.

A few days later, I realized that Kim and I had met each other and Angel on Jason's birthday, Jason, Lynn's godson who had drowned in the Hudson two weeks after her funeral. Lynn's death was expected; Jason's hit us all hard. Something inexorable was still stirring in our lives like a storm from far off that we couldn't see coming. It was clear to me, though, in remembering Jason and Lynn, that much of our lives still lay uprooted as if a series of tornados had ruthlessly ripped through our hearts. What else was still afoot?

Hypomania

Was I already in a "hypomanic" state at the facilitator gathering and at lunch with Kim? I don't think so, but how do I judge? Where is the elusive line, especially knowing that at some point I crossed it. Hypomania is a clinical term for a stage before a full-blown manic episode. Here's a description from www.psychcentral.com:

> Hypomanic episodes have the same symptoms as manic episodes with two important differences: (1) the mood usually isn't severe enough to cause problems with the person working or socializing with others...or to require hospitalization; and (2) there are never any psychotic features present in a hypomanic episode.[12]

From the inside and maybe the outside too, it's impossible to tell the difference between enthusiasm about life and hypomania, especially on the borderline, where I think I was, at least at the beginning. Mostly I was bubbling with joy and relief: for the first time since before Lynn's death,

I was once again feeling positive about my life, confident that I could begin to do what I was called to do. Potential bubbled within and around me. Spring had sprung. As Lynn had done, I too would live a life both in Millbrook and in New York City. A dear friend had gifted Wil and me her apartment on the Upper West Side at least for a few months. I could operate well from there.

Two days later on my birthday, I treated Morgan to a qigong class in midtown and then he took me to a Senegalese restaurant in Harlem. I couldn't stop talking, sharing my excitement about the gathering, the circle project for adults sexually abused as children, and, and, and. He noticed my elated mood but didn't think much about it at the time. "At dinner and after, you were happy and enthusiastic, but a little too much. I wondered," he said in retrospect.

That night I went to sleep in our friend's apartment. We only had one key, so the arrangement was that I would wake to let Wil in around 1 a.m. I had done it before, but this time I didn't hear him frantically ringing the buzzer from outside. He finally had no choice but to wake one of the upstairs neighbors, who buzzed him in. Once he was at the front door, I finally heard him. The distressing thing was that Wil was beside himself with exhaustion, anger, and hurt that I had done that; I was remorseful but felt defensive. I couldn't help it; I was tired. Something was amiss; yet at the time and throughout the hypomania and even into the full-blown mania, release from the sinkhole of isolation, sadness, and personal paralysis after Lynn's death was more important than anything or anyone. After all, life was looking up.

Invitation

One thing that everyone in my family thought strange, and even horrifying, was that I contacted Betsy, Lynn's stepdaughter, and was having dinner with her on May 22. "Why are you doing this? Don't you remember how Lynn felt about her?" asked my mother.

"But I'm not Lynn," I told her.

"Did you ask Kim?" she wanted to know. I had actually, and she was glad that I was doing this, which may say something about Kim's judgment but also her hope for a relationship with her stepsister. What were my motives?

Lynn had tried for many years to have a relationship with Betsy but could never trust her. Lynn was sure that she was using drugs, and Betsy would never own up to it. There were money issues. Lynn always felt that Betsy's boyfriend was trying to eke money out of her. He, in fact, had borrowed a thousand dollars and never repaid it. That was the beginning of the end. Eventually, as Lynn got sicker, she excluded Betsy from her life altogether. Lynn needed trustworthy, caring, authentic people around her. In that last year, Betsy had faced her own bout with breast cancer. Lynn tried to be supportive from a distance but eventually, understandably, couldn't handle anymore.

At the time I thought the family demonized Betsy, not that I wanted to spend a lot of time with her either; even her own brothers couldn't. A year and a half after Lynn's death with all that Betsy had been through, I wanted to reach out. Connecting with her was one of the more approachable tasks I'd received, this one from Jim, in the first circle I facilitated with the dead just a few weeks before. I emailed her, and she was delighted to meet. My favorite organic food restaurant was packed, so we went to an Indian place on West 94th, where Lynn and I had often eaten. Except for the shocking amount of weight she had gained, Betsy looked beautiful. She ordered manna bread and a diet coke; I had lamb saag. We talked; we connected. She expressed her hurt at being shut out of the family; I opened my heart to her and saw her as a human being who had been through her own struggles her whole life. My compassion was genuine. I invited her to come with her brothers to Millbrook on Jim's death day in July. When I reported this to the rest of my family, they were horrified. Seeing Betsy in the City was one thing; inviting her into the family home was quite another. That never came to be; we haven't been in touch since.

Synchronicity

It was Friday, May 23rd, Mom's 91st birthday. I called and wished her a happy one. She didn't want anything more; no visit was necessary. We had celebrated Mother's Day together with a major breakthrough on my part, forgiving her and recognizing the caring, grounding mother she had been, the right mother for me, a sensitive, introverted child. I had been hard on her over the years until my 39th year when I had my own child, a common story. Before that I had broken all contact with her, my father, Lynn, and Kim for over 10 years – not so common; and although it was almost 30 years since I was "back," healing takes a long time, especially with one's mother when the wounds are deep and open easily.

When I "left" in 1974, I was in my early 20s. I was now in my mid-60s, my sister was dead for a year and a half, and we were all still recovering and adjusting to life without her. Families have to rebalance when someone dies, especially a dynamic hub like Lynn. Her relationship with Mom had buffered me in many ways. Their relationship was uninterrupted over the 61 years of Lynn's life. From the time of Kim's premature birth when Lynn was only 19, she had needed my parents' support.

Without work as my central priority and, more profoundly, without Lynn, Mom and I are forging our own relationship. The sweetness and love in the drawing I had made for Mom for Mother's Day surprised her. I usually wrote something, but this time I drew, based on a question my therapist had asked: Why was this woman *my* mother? I do believe we play some part in choosing the parents who are right for us, difficulties and all. Why in heaven's name had I chosen her? Why was she the one for me? The question stumped me. Then the drawing came: Mom putting food on the table at 6 p.m., planting tulips with her two little girls in a border garden, telling us to stop talking and go to sleep, telling me to practice the clarinet and then the oboe, taking care of me when I was sick, going on surprise rides with Dad at the wheel. After I took her through the good memories in the drawing, surrounded with my loving intention of deep forgiveness, we held each other and shared sweet tears, hers, perhaps, at being acknowledged and remembering the loss of husband, daughter, and a time and way of life now far away. This strong, no nonsense woman – whose moods were easily read and whose thoughts were always spoken – was exactly the mother a high maintenance, sensitive child like me needed.

In retrospect, this change in my thinking about my mother was another destabilizing aspect that particular spring. Soul reorganization must be necessary when the building blocks of blame are replaced with forgiveness and reconciliation. Brain chemistry must change. As a child I needed to protect myself from Mom's strong moods and sheer volume. I had to accommodate for needs not being met because of who my parents were. As an adolescent and young adult, I wove a web of blame, to which I clung as psychic fact and from which I individualized into an adult. Becoming a parent helped me begin to forgive and acknowledge my own parents' shortcomings as simply human, that love and best intentions beat in their hearts despite whatever their failings and limitations. They were only human and ultimately had done the best they could.

My father was dead, Lynn too. A new relationship had to be built with my mother and at long last could be. Therese helped me realize that I didn't need anything from Mom. All I needed to do was to be present when we were together. This was the key to relieving my frustration, which was impeding our relationship: I didn't need her to understand me or even to see me. I could stop taking her comments personally. I was finally free to accept her fully for who she was. It only took until she was in her 90s! I felt fortunate and grateful that Mom was still here with me and that I could keep trying to be more loving.

*

I was in the City on Mom's birthday, when strange, magical things began to happen. I gave a bass lesson of sorts and stayed too long. My student's boyfriend bought her a special refurbished vintage bass. I asked if I could have her other one, which I immediately heard as an odd, uncharacteristically rude question for me to ask, but another part of me didn't understand why she should have two great basses when she was a new player, and I had one that wasn't playing very well. Anyway, I was sick of censoring so many of my thoughts.

Time was getting away from me, and I didn't care. I was over 45 minutes late when I arrived at my Alexander Technique lesson. Caren was irritated, but she could see that something was off. She later told me that I was apologetic and had said, "It's hard getting used to this new space-time continuum, but I'll get better at it." She found that odd. I left there after 15 minutes since she had another lesson with a person she hadn't seen in quite awhile. I could tell she was glad to get me out of there, and I didn't understand why. I felt a bit jealous of this other person she obviously cared a lot about. I'd fucked up but took it in stride. How do you live as if in the infinite, alive in each moment and still relate to finite time, to the constraints of appointments?

When I left my aborted lesson, I stopped in front of the flowers blooming in the garden on Minetta and 6th Avenue. The daffodils were bopping their yellow horns, and there was a red tulip blooming, the center of which caught my attention with its black spokes and yellow dust. I heard a voice behind me, "A sparrow almost landed on my hand!" I slowly turned to see a young, brown man, thin and foreign looking, not yet worn into the frenzied pace of the city. I smiled.

"Did you see that?" he asked.

"No, I missed it, but look at this flower. Isn't it beautiful?" He agreed. We turned to each other in a very direct way. He was Morgan's age, in his mid- to late 20s. I looked into his eyes. He didn't look crazy. "Where are you from?"

"Istanbul," he said.

"How long have you been here?" I doubted very long.

"About a week." I was right.

"What are you doing here?"

"I want to live here for awhile. I'm a musician – I

play guitar and drums." I told him that my son was a drummer and gave him Morgan's email address without thinking twice.

"Maybe you two can make music together." He smiled and looked deeply into my eyes. We were communing, or maybe he was assessing if I were crazy. I still feel it was a sweet meeting on a busy Village street. Later Morgan doubted that he ever existed; he was disturbed that I'd given a stranger his email contact. Luckily, the Turk never contacted him. He did exist, though. That I know. Morgan told me that I said I'd met an angel. That I don't remember.

⁂

I had a date to meet Nina and Tim uptown at our favorite restaurant. I hopped on the A train and switched to the C at 42nd Street. I was excited to see them, one because Tim lived in northern California and was rarely here. Nina was one of my dear friends since I'd moved from Austin. We'd met when I was Director of Teacher Education and worked together for two years at a school in New York, where I'd been the lower school chair before retiring. They were now a couple. I couldn't resist walking past Lynn's old apartment building between Columbus and Amsterdam on 95th Street. I stood across the street, remembering our life together there, weeping a little, facing what had been my weekday home for two years, and then turning toward a brownstone, two doors east, where two park-and-stoop friends had lived, Eli and Lori.

Eli was probably also dead. The last time I'd seen him, he had only a few months to live and was settling Lori into a better living situation with more amenities. Before they moved into the brownstone near Lynn's, I frequently saw them in the park with their two dachshunds as I briskly walked to school in all kinds of weather. Lori, wearing a big floppy hat, often looked mysterious like an Audrey Hepburn throwback; Eli was the outgoing one. He always had a compliment for me. "You look gorgeous this morning. You're just lighting up this park," he'd say admiringly with a big toothy grin, gleaming out of his gaunt concentration-camp face. He was simply warm without any trace of creepiness.

When they moved into the brownstone, so close to Lynn's place, Lynn and I loved seeing them sitting and smoking on their front stoop. If we weren't in a hurry, we'd always stop, hoping to get to know them. We learned that Eli was a doctor turned poet-performance artist, savvy, quick-witted with a deep resonance for human suffering. While always sweet, Lori remained enigmatic. As the months went on, they were as curious about us as we were about them and would both come down from the stoop to chat more intimately over the iron gate, especially once they knew Lynn had lung cancer.

My feet felt leaden with memories that Friday as if magnetized by the gravity of this pavement and the spring sunlight dancing on these particular brownstones. I had to force myself to move, and as a mysterious peace descended, Amsterdam Avenue approached. Across the street, vaguely through the fog of my fuzzy vision without glasses, two people stood facing me, smiling: Nina and Tim.

"Perfect timing," Tim said in his warm voice, scratchy from many years of teaching and public speaking. We hugged. I was certainly in synch with the universe, a blessing.

As we moved toward the restaurant, I was bubbling, "I have to warn you. I feel like I'm on acid." All of us knew what that meant. "No, I really mean it. I don't know what's going on, but I feel like my liver's detoxing or something."

As we sat in the restaurant, I arranged the empty seat next to me, across from Tim. It was for Doug, his best friend, who had died a few months earlier. Doug was part of my plan to revamp Waldorf education and Waldorf teacher education for the 21st century, which I wanted to share with Nina and Doug that night. I hoped they would want to be part of it. Since he also loved the education, Doug needed to hear this conversation, too; perhaps, he could help from the other side of the threshold. At one point when Tim went to the bathroom, Nina said, "It's about time you arrived." I was sure she was talking about my heightened state of consciousness. I was delighted that she noticed and that she was there too. I later realized that she was talking about the new I-phone I was holding in my hand.

I still wonder why they didn't express more concern about my strange behavior. Was I still in that limbo place, reachable and recognizable as the Cat they knew? Why didn't they check in on me? They are in love and spend little time together, I've told myself. I was on my own trip; maybe it wasn't noticeable. Nina grew up with a bipolar mother. There were many reasons, I guess, and all is forgiven. Sometimes when it gets too scary, we cannot be our brother or sister's keeper.

Reflection

Why is it so important to track the details of the past like the prints of a wild animal? I know where this led, but where did it originate? The label I was given, bipolar disorder, is not enough for me. I must make meaning of it all in the context of my life story.

I think back on what it took before the break to hold

myself together – the anxiety attacks that sometimes kept me from sleeping. At one point, just a few months before the mania, I woke, my legs shaking, thinking I was having a low sodium episode, terrified. Luckily Wil was there and called 911. It turned out to be nothing that valium couldn't fix, after which we went on living our lives, placing this in the context of grieving, of adjusting to life in a new place without Lynn, ignoring the possibility that it could be a warning of some kind. Yet why would we suspect I would have a manic episode? How could we know?

To quell my anxiety, I diligently applied various mindfulness practices that I learned from experts on the Internet and from my therapist. These could in a moment calm my frightened heart and help me examine the realities behind the anxiety, to sort out what was true anxiety, what apprehension, and what excitement about something new or challenging. I was always searching for ways to calm myself, for remedies for sleeping.

What has changed? I have stayed on medication: 750 mg of Depakote and 0.5 mg of Ativan (or less) to insure nine hours of sleep every night. Most nights I don't need it. I still question the Depakote; sometimes I am more eager to be off it than other times. Dr. Wilson doesn't shy away from talking about it and always advises against changing anything. "You're doing so well. Why change it?" Therese and I have wondered about it together. She sees, and I can feel, a quieter center that has never been there before. But what is the cause – Depakote or the aftereffect of a psyche reorganized, which blew out its old scaffolding to clear a way for the new?

Why shouldn't I question the Depakote? I am an individual who was hospitalized for manic episodes only twice in 44 years with no major depressions in between.

Situational depressions, yes, I'll admit, but doesn't every human balance ups and downs, stabilizing moods throughout the day, week, months, years? Are my moods more extreme? Is my psyche more susceptible than others' to life's vicissitudes? Or am I more equipped by my spiritual practice than most to be aware of my present mood and to be able to right my self? If I am grounded in a community of family and friends, can't that insure everyone's well-being?

What failed that spring? My sister's death 18 months earlier, moving into her house and beginning to make it our own – room by room, drawer by drawer, closet by closet until what could be cleared out was cleared out. Retiring from school leadership and not facing that identity loss until after Lynn died, perhaps, until after the rooms, the drawers, and the closets no longer consumed my focus; until the rawness of grief began to shift. I had no professional support that first year either. I didn't want any. Lynn had been my resident psychotherapist. It took a physical collapse from the flu for me to realize I had to get help.

But why am I still asking, "What failed?" as if I or someone else should have done something to ward off the mania, when as I follow the tracks, I continue to believe that this needed to happen. Yet the judgment remains, stigma and fear, especially from myself.

I write to understand and integrate the psychotic break, to make it comprehensible and to show that a manic episode or two is not a hideous character flaw or a soul boogie woman that could, at any time, jump out and undermine my life once again. Perhaps, a look at the anatomy of the hypomanic episode I had in 2001 can shed some light on the one that took me all the way to a diagnosis and the seclusion room in 2014.

Part II
Perspective

Old patterns and perceptions, along with old, outworn identities, begin to dissolve as we are unmade. Things fall apart. There is an unraveling, an emptying of hope and an undermining of our great heroic enterprise to be in control and to rise above our suffering....Anyone escorted into the underworld of grief knows full well that this place feels uncharted. We are without fixed stars, known markers or guideposts. Only when familiar structures are eroded is it possible for something new to arise. It is difficult for us to see our time in the waters of grief as required for the deepening of our soul life.

– Francis Weller

5
Anatomy of a Mini-Episode

John Colapinto's article in *The New Yorker*, "Lighting the Brain: Karl Deisseroth and the optogenetics breakthrough," got me thinking.

> Increasingly, neuroscientists believe that the key to understanding how the brain works lies in its over-all neural circuitry, and the way that widely separated brain regions communicate through the long-range projection of nerve fibres. In this view, mental disorders result from the shorting-out or disruption of the larger circuit wiring of the brain.[13]

"The shorting-out or disruption of the larger circuit wiring of the brain" – now that makes sense to me. In the three episodes of mania or hypomania I experienced between 1971 and 2014, my psyche definitely blew out my brain circuitry. Each occurrence marks the end of something and the beginning of something new while at the same time strangely, thankfully bringing along central aspects of my personal identity – core beliefs, values, and relationships as appropriate. For psychiatrists and psychoanalysts mental illness is an ongoing mystery the way the learning process is for educators. We're not quite sure what's going on in there. We have some best practices that seem to work under enough conditions, but we really don't know why some things work for some people and not for others.

Colapinto continues:

> For decades, researchers have imagined the brain as a soup of neurochemicals whose normal functioning depends on those chemicals remaining in proper balance. Mental illnesses were believed to result from a 'chemical imbalance' – the wrong amount of this or that neurotransmitter in certain synapses.[14]

That was the explanation when my father was diagnosed with manic-depression in 1960, and it prevails as a cause for bipolar disorder today. With more understanding of the brain, will the old model fade away? Does it hold in some cases and not others? How long before these findings register with the 100th monkey of psychiatrists, psychiatric hospitals, and Big Pharma?

What specific constellation of events is likely to short-out a brain? What put my psyche in a situation where my brain circuitry was seriously disrupted? Is there anything that can be learned from this for others experiencing mania? My 1970 manic psychosis was laced with psychedelic drugs designed to blow minds. That was the attraction: let's fry the circuitry of the plastic 1950s Doris Day and Father Knows Best conditioning to which we'd been subjected. Despite how destabilized life was in general for my generation, these drugs had a specific impact on imploding my psyche. Eleven electroshock treatments broke the mania and reset the circuits, I guess, offering me a platform to get back on my 22-year-old feet. Psychotherapy helped. The diagnosis of schizophrenia was wrong, but I suspect my current diagnosis of bipolar disorder may be wobbly too. As we learn more and more about the brain and about the connection between body, soul, and spirit, what might diagnostic codes look like in 2050 if there are any? As Dr. Wilson repeats: "The diagnosis is not relevant. How's your sleep, your appetite, your moods? What are you doing with your life energy? How are your relationships?" And I wonder if before the break my life had been too packed, too pressurized as I desperately wanted to return to normalcy after Lynn's death.

What were the dynamics that contributed to the hypomania in 2001 when I needed no help from doctors or substances to bring me back to myself. Once loved ones told me that I had veered off in a strange direction, I could restore my equilibrium. At that time I was able to hear that something was off. How do these factors compare to those in 2014 when I could hear nothing and couldn't stop veering?

Setting the Scene: Dad's Death

Immediately after Dad died at 82 in September of 2000, I didn't respond with mania or even hypomania. Maybe I was living in a hypomanic state as the chair of a new high school. Maybe I had been living in one for the two years before it opened in 1997. There certainly was tremendous activity everyday and little chance for self-care; however, I did sing in a choir and went to church with family once a week. I was part of a discipleship group in our church that met every Friday for an hour; that was supportive. We did enjoy family time on Sundays, walking along Barton Creek, hiking at Pedernales Falls or Hamilton Pool, or swimming every day from 3 – 6 p.m. in the summer. Mania is when you are out-of-touch with reality, with the people you usually connect with, and that wasn't happening at all. So, no, I wasn't living in a hypomanic state despite how busy I was.

Around Dad's deathbed in the dining room, Mom, Lynn, and I took shifts sitting with him, singing to him, talking to him although he was in a fugue state, rarely coming out of it to recognize someone new who came into the room. He smiled at Betsy, his step-granddaughter, when she came to say good-bye. He revived himself a little more for his nephew Ronnie, who told Dad he'd always been his favorite uncle. And then my Dad sank back into a more compelling place we couldn't see; he looked concentrated, agitated, and sometimes terrified. We had called hospice when we brought him home from the hospital, and Lynn administered the morphine to ease the agitation and fear. I'd never given injections before and was glad she jumped in to do it. I didn't want to screw up.

The dining room was a long way from my life in Austin, Texas, with its deluge of daily tasks, challenges, and interactions with teenagers and colleagues in a growing high school. The class I had shepherded since third grade and taught English and drama in the high school were in their senior year. This was our first year with all four grades – a full high school. A month into the new school year, inconvenient as death can be, the high school had to be without me for a week. It was good for its health, I thought; everyone graciously did what needed to be done without bothering me once with mundane happenings.

Around Dad's bedside Lynn, Jim, Mom, Kim, and I grew close, the way only death brings people together. Jim and I talked about the power of praying to the Holy Mother, but it wasn't the content of the talk: it was the feeling of love as sister and brother-in-law that was finally there. Singing Dad's favorite songs to him, knowing they were somehow comforting him, I did what I could to ease his transition. And being there as he took his last breaths – that sound, the death rattle, his breath stopping for longer and longer periods of time like a wave sucked out by the gods, each time farther and farther into the vast ocean of spirit, then his gasping as the wave was blown back for less and less time until it came no more. This was my first encounter with death up close.

> Looking at your body,
> Lynn and I were moved
> by the strangeness
> that was no longer you.

After the preparations was the funeral itself – a fog of too many people and tears. Lynn spoke eloquently, honoring our one and only father. I had no words. It had not always been easy between us. He'd never been abusive, but he had been bipolar, the depressive variety although he did have hypomanic episodes, too, unsettling and frightening for two young teenagers. Lynn always said, "When he was depressed he wanted to kill himself; when he was manic, we wanted to kill him." Even I laughed at that, although mostly I'd been seriously protective of him, spending hours sitting next to him as he lay on the couch in the den watching ball games on TV or sleeping.

The summer I was leaving for Smith College, he was hypomanic. To celebrate how proud he was of me, he wanted to take me to New York City. We had two goals: eating lunch at Le Champlain, his favorite French restaurant, and shopping at Pendleton's wholesale outlet to buy me a blanket for school and maybe a sweater. It was a sparkling spring day and his mood chipper. He parked in a Midtown lot, and we walked to the restaurant. Eating whatever he suggested,

I listened to familiar stories of his war years in France. It felt special, just the two of us. The sporting goods store my parents owned stocked Pendleton's pricy woolen shirts, blankets, sweaters, and jackets, so he could buy wholesale. He agreed to a cardigan sweater as well as a deep blue and green woven blanket. I didn't want to see the bill. I figured Mom must know what he was doing; yet I wondered if this would be happening if she were there. When we got back to the parking lot, Dad didn't have enough money to pay the bill, and I had no cash on me. I was mortified but tried not to show it. Although a little embarrassed, he took it in his stride, promising the man that he'd send the money as soon as he got home, which he did.

And then there were the years I cut off contact with my family, years that hurt Mom and Dad unspeakably as if I had died: they had certainly lost a daughter for over 10 years. Did my absence also humiliate him? How did he deal with whatever his relatives said or didn't say, their pity, their anger? Over the years in countless conversations about what had happened, what we had both missed in each other's lives, I reconciled with Mom but not fully with Dad. About ten years before his death, he was hospitalized with a blood clot in his leg; he was afraid he might die. He could have. I came to visit, alone. We began to talk, and after I apologized for the pain I had caused, he admitted how hurt he'd been when I was away all those years. I was relieved that we were finally talking about it, that he was expressing his feelings, something that made him uncomfortable as it did most men of his generation. That was a step, but reconciliation and forgiveness are a process, not completed in one conversation.

After sitting shiva, I returned to Austin, where we'd lived for nine years, to my family, my work at the school, my friends. Life went on as it had – at least for a while – even though Dad's absence was felt on the Sunday morning phone call with Mom. I was blessed with a nurse practitioner who encouraged me to take time to grieve, to connect, to write in my journal, even to converse with Dad that way. "There's an ancient Chinese proverb," she said, "that when a parent dies a mountain is moved." I did what she suggested. I wrote a line or a question, thinking of him. I felt his response and journaled that. I forgave him for being mentally ill when I was a child, and he acknowledged remorse and sadness over what he could not control. He forgave me for leaving them not once, but twice, the second time when we moved to Texas. Of course, Mom and Dad had hoped I would find a teaching job close by, so they could enjoy their grandchild and us, but I didn't. I think that's when he gave up hope of getting close to me. Yet now healing was happening: death had brought us closer.

While I was speaking with the so-called dead, there was no mania as a result of Dad's death, not even a hint of it. Although he was more accessible to me through journaling than ever before, his death sent imperceptible shockwaves through our family system. Little did we know, but everything was about to change.

Revealing the anatomy of the 2001 hypomanic episode, I underscore the destabilizing factors in my life with the hope of shedding light on what led to the full-blown psychotic mania almost 14 years later. Death surely plays a part, and Dad's wasn't the only one.

Destabilization 1: Moving and Loss

Less than one year from Dad's death, I began down a manic road. Why? There was massive change in our lives that year, even before 9/11 altered everything politically and globally. One morning a few months after Dad's death, as I came out of sleep, I clearly felt his presence and heard his voice: "I know you're not going to like this, but you're needed at home. Mom needs you; your sister needs you. It's time." There was a firm urgency in this visitation: I couldn't and wouldn't have conjured this up, yet his words made sense. Lynn was the one who had been there for both of them; now it was Lynn alone for mom. It wasn't fair. I told Wil and no one else.

Work was demanding, and this communication with my so-called dead Dad moved into the back of my mind. Unexpectedly, though, life began to change around me. Though I was teaching better than I ever had before, my administrative role as high school chair was getting more and more difficult. Since I'd been a driving force in initiating the new high school and steering it through its first four years, some parents were beginning to identify me with it and to blame me for difficulties that were either the growing pains of a new high school or the problems of their own teenagers. I was sensitive to that kind of projection: I'd always seen the high school as an entity that would go on long after I was gone. I'd even had a recent conversation with a colleague about maybe going back to teach in the grade school, although it was hard for me to discern my next step. I could sense something ahead, a change that I couldn't yet see. I trusted that when the time was right, all would become clear.

One day after an especially difficult parent meeting, in which I felt completely condescended to, while knowing that the parents had no idea that that's what they were doing, I got home, logged onto the computer, and began scrolling through ads on the Waldorf jobs site: what was available on the East Coast as close to my family as possible? I found myself wanting nothing to do with another school. I'd had it with the same old problems. Then I saw that there were two positions open at the place where I'd been prepared as a Waldorf teacher: Registrar and Director of Teacher Education. I was certain I didn't have the qualifications for the Director position, so I applied online for the Registrar. One of my beloved teachers called me and discouraged me. A day later I got a call from another of my teachers, who with much encouragement invited me to seriously consider the position of Director of Teacher Education. It felt overwhelming to me. I had been a Waldorf teacher for only 10 years and six of those as a class teacher. There were some who had taken classes through the eight-year cycle from first through eighth grades two or more times. I clearly didn't feel worthy and had no idea that I could even do the job, but I got on a plane anyway. Destiny seemed to be pushing me in a certain direction. The interviews went well; the students welcomed me warmly and met my presentations with tremendous enthusiasm. I'd been teaching adults for years – parents in the last 10 years and, before that, adults from all walks of life as a writing instructor. In that regard I felt comfortable. Within a few days, I was offered and accepted the position.

On the last of three days of looking for a house we could afford, the realtor, Mom, and I found one that would work perfectly. It was an hour and a quarter from Lynn, one hour from Kim, and less than an hour from Mom. We put our Austin home on the market and hoped that the real estate angels would line everything up. They did, or it worked out perfectly, however you want to see it. Or maybe it was Dad: he was always good with real estate and had found us the last two places we had lived when he was here on Earth.

During the years of starting the high school, I was often in touch with angels. I never saw any; I just experienced them at work, everywhere. I felt supported by them and by the Archangel Michael and the Being of the school, fiercely eager to grow into its full capacity. I hollowed myself out to make space for their presence, and this activity created hallowed ground everywhere I looked and stepped. I talked with the dead too, especially with Dad, but also with the founders of the school, some I knew and others I didn't. I believed fervently in the power of prayer because I saw it manifest. I worked manically as many people do: I slept six hours a night, and that was a lot. Weekends I could catch up unless there were school events. I carried extensive responsibilities, not alone, but I carried them deeply.

Before we left Austin, there was a culmination, of course, a graduation, a celebration of the first graduating class, which had been my class. The last day of school, everyone – classes 1 – 12, parents, grandparents, faculty, and staff – flooded the courtyard and the surrounding boardwalks. Gratitude and appreciation rained down like glittering confetti on that warm, sunny May day. I let myself expand with the fullness of the moment, not tipping into tears but soaking in and feeling pure joy, consecrated by the love of that community.

And then all those years of relationship, working together, caring and carrying together abruptly ended. Goodbyes were difficult. "I'm warning you – I'm a bad communicator. It's nothing personal," one of my closest friends said honestly. I was present at the closing of our house, packed as much as I could, and boarded a plane for Sacramento, California. I was teaching grammar for a week, which had its own stresses, including a grueling schedule from 8:30 through 5:30, in a very active social environment. Sleeping was difficult, broken and light, filled with dreams and visitations from my muse urging me to write poetry at 2 a.m. Meanwhile in Austin Wil and Morgan, who had just turned 14, dutifully finished packing and set off with our cat in a full 24′ truck, towing our new red Toyota on the back, heading for New York. Many adventures later, they would reach our new house before I would, attend the closing there, and begin to move in. This was before cell phones, so it was hard to be in touch that last week. I can't remember how we managed.

⚜

On the plane coming home from Sacramento, I lost my inner equilibrium. It was a rocky landing, and I vomited into one of those paper bags, a first for me. Mom picked me up at the airport. I thought the nausea would subside when we stopped moving, but it didn't. Wil was supposed to pick me up that Saturday night; instead I called him and told him to come the next day, hoping to stabilize over the course of the night. I had a hard time sleeping but finally calmed my stomach by the middle of the night and slept solidly until morning. I was relieved to be feeling better, and Wil collected me in the early afternoon. It was comforting to be together after the very long week apart. We drove to our new home, where there were boxes piled everywhere. It was overwhelming.

That night we drove to the west side of the Newburgh-Beacon Bridge, where Lynn delivered Morgan to us. It was so good to see her and Morgan, of course. They had had a wonderful weekend of celebrations for Jim's 53rd birthday. All of his grown kids, his mother, and his brother were there as well as the usual group of close friends. Lynn and Jim always had big parties in their sprawling Victorian house with the wide wrap-around porch, Jim at the center of the festivities, forever the storyteller, the joke teller, making everyone laugh. We were excited about starting a new era when we'd finally be living close to each other after so many years.

Morgan climbed up to his loft room, and Wil and I cozied up in our new bedroom, a lot smaller than the one in our Texas ranch house. We all slept well, unsuspecting, until Wil jolted me awake at 6.

Destabilization #2: Sudden Death and Trauma

"Jim's in the hospital. He's dying."

"Jim, who?" I asked, completely confused.

"Jim! Lynn's Jim. You have to go." I swallowed a quick breakfast and got in our new Toyota Corolla with the Texas plates. Someone had given Wil directions, which he passed on to me. It had been quite awhile since I'd driven to Lynn's house. This time I was going past her town to a hospital in Connecticut right over the state line.

As I drove, I prayed. I talked with Jim's spirit. He was going to be okay. I prayed he wouldn't die, that he wasn't dead yet. But then at some point, as I drove past the overlook, where he had driven his Harley time and again, I stopped praying: I knew he was dead. When I walked into the hospital, Jim lay on the bed, his barrel chest unmoving, his body already growing cold. Lynn came to me, crying, hugged me, and said, "Well, you're timing is good."

Slowly the story unfolded: she had gone home; they had made love. Then Jim put his hand to his forehead and cried, "My head. This isn't an ordinary headache." And he collapsed. Lynn called 911. The local emergency guys came in an ambulance and took him to the nearest hospital. In the midst of that, though, something bizarre happened, best related in Lynn's own words from an unpublished manuscript:

> I climbed into Jim's minivan, rather than my Volvo used mostly for commuting to work or when I wanted to feel pampered. It was typical to use the van for local trips. We headed to the hospital. The ambulance was easy to follow; and in fact, it seemed to be going slowly, which I found odd after being told not to try to keep up with it. We didn't get too far, only about a quarter of a mile, ...when a four by four [SUV] came tear-assing out, getting between me and the ambulance.
>
> "Right. Now this," I said out loud....This SUV not only entered the scene like a bat out of hell but simultaneously hit the back of the ambulance. My first thought was: some drunk kid. He pulled into the left lane as if to pass the ambulance, and I was relieved that we'd be done with him. But no, he pulled back and rammed the ambulance again. Then I hung back, knowing a nut job, not a drunken kid had entered the scene. I watched him repeatedly collide into the ambulance, housing my fragile husband, for another quarter of a mile until he stopped in the middle of the road, directly in front of my swimming hole, the town pool. The ambulance continued on its way, but I had been stopped, blocked by this now stationary yet out-of-control vehicle. I locked my doors and watched a stocky, medium height white guy get out of the car, holding what looked like a sledge hammer, and say, "Get out of your car. This is official business." Even though it felt like some LA carjacking scene, where

another dangerous man could still be in the car, ready to ram me from the side, I gunned the engine onto the grass to get around him and caught up to the ambulance, which was still crawling.

Before I knew it, the crazoid was back in the four by four, behind me, ramming me. I hadn't thought it out well enough. Since the ambulance was in the lead, he wasn't just crashing into me but forcing me to hit the ambulance that held Jim. I held tight and tried to absorb each blow. By the fourth hit, he came at me not dead on, but a little to my left and successfully pushed me off the road. Luckily, there were no trees, telephone poles, or stone walls in my way. I tried to drive out of the ditch, but the van failed me. I shut off the engine and waited. For what? My doors were locked, but if he came back with a sledgehammer, he could easily break a window and then what? Kill? Rape? I climbed in the back and began looking for a tire iron.

But he didn't come back. Instead five kids pulled their car into a dark field across the street and crossed the road to rescue me.

"Are you alright? We saw the whole thing. What the hell was that?"

"Some kind of lunatic – and my husband's in that ambulance. I have to get to the hospital." It was as if the evening had been scripted by Stephen King.

We crossed the road to their car. One of them handed me a cell phone and for the second time that night, I hit 911. One of the boys ran out to the road because he saw the four by four heading back in our direction and wanted the license plate number.

"You're a real risk taker, huh?" I asked him.

"He's always like that," one of the girls said with pride.

"Well this time, it's heroic," I said. He was my kind of kid.

My calm was completely blown. Without the illusion of power derived from driving my own vehicle, any semblance of strength had been knocked out of me. I was no longer fighting but had become frantic. I was yelling at the cops on the phone.

"Where the hell are you guys? There's a maniac out here ramming into ambulances and cars. What the fuck are you guys doing? Get the state police out! Do something!"

How much time passed? Unclear. Unknown.

"We've got him," they said to me, still clutching the phone.

I got into the kids' car for a ride home, so I could get the Volvo and go to the hospital. Meanwhile, I stayed on the phone with the police. They wanted the exact location of my car, an ID of the crackpot's vehicle, while they reassured me repeatedly that they had captured the right guy.

"You just stay tight at your house, and we'll come and drive you to the hospital."

So I waited in my kitchen instead of taking off as I would have. But after interviewing me, the police changed their tune. They had too much to do: my car had to be towed, the maniac had to be brought somewhere. I turned to the savior kids who had stayed, waiting, making sure I was okay.

"I'm too shaky to drive." It was so unlike me, but it was the truth.

"Could someone drive my car? Does anyone know how to drive a standard shift? Do you have to be home? Do you need to call your parents?" I was still thinking enough to ask the right questions. It was already after 11 on a Sunday night, and these kids were still in high school. Hero boy drove me in the Volvo, and the rest of the kids followed in their car. Again we headed east towards the hospital.

When we arrived, the kids left, and I was on my own. As soon as I asked for Jim, the emergency room doctor pulled me into a private room.

"Your husband has suffered a brain aneurism. He's not going to recover. First I want you to call a friend to come here, and then I'll introduce you to the radiologist." It was then I began to weep, endless tears that lasted for days, weeks, months, years.[15]

I tell this heart-wrenching story because it happened.

Layering the trauma of Jim's death, my sister's life had been threatened. Reading it now, I relive its horror. Lynn, one of my rocks, was crumbling; the imagination of Jim and Lynn as an integral part of our new life shattered.

Destabilization #3: A Psychic

Lynn was alone now and for that first year, out of her mind, her world turned upside down, her loyal partner of 16 years dead. The day following Jim's death, the family gathered around her. Lynn had been having massages with a psychic masseuse from Kingston, who I'll call Samantha. Lynn had lots of questions about the suddenness of Jim's death, how he was doing wherever he was, and the meaning of the trauma that happened in the wake of it. What was going on? That afternoon Lynn invited Samantha to work on three of us: Betsy, Lynn herself, and me.

At the time I had been studying the teachings of Rudolf Steiner for over 10 years and avoided psychics and mediums, trusting prayer and meditation instead, including my own thoughts and those of the trusted people around me. Anthroposophists don't approve of psychics but instead develop clairvoyance through a spiritually scientific and challenging path of life-long meditative practice and moral living.[16]

Under the circumstances of that July day, however, my curiosity overrode all that. I wanted to hear what Samantha might say to us about this shocking situation. Things were happening too quickly and unpredictably. Anyway, I wanted to be with Lynn to experience whatever she was experiencing. Why was this happening? Maybe this woman could lift the veil.

We were upstairs in the barn in what was then Lynn's

psychotherapy room. She wanted me to go first. As I lay on Samantha's massage table, my eyes closed, the psychic began: "I can see in your physical body that your last life was at Auschwitz." Literally worn thin from overworking in Austin, I weighed around 100 pounds. After some silence, she continued, "You were important there. You had a group of women around you, who depended on you to keep their spirits up. You died there. " Oddly, that felt completely obvious; I could easily picture it even though it conflicted with a Steiner teaching about the amount of earth time we take between incarnations.

"You wanted to leave Germany, but your father wouldn't listen to you. He was prominent in the city and didn't believe that your family would be affected. You disagreed but were helpless to do anything. When the Nazis came, your brother tried to fight them and was killed." I imagined it all as if I were watching a film of my past life. But was it true?

"Before that…those women in Auschwitz…knew you from a previous lifetime. Centuries before you were a high Tibetan monk, surrounded by disciples. The Buddha stood in the center. You were a high bodhisattva, one of the highest enlightened beings." She acted humble, honored to be in the presence of someone this evolved. Again, I could picture what she was saying: serene, joyful bodhisattva in a circle of devotees. This launched me. What does anyone do with information like this? I guess some reject it as absolute crap, but I was too vulnerable, too susceptible to suggestion. Instead I tried to integrate this revelation into my present reality.

And then Samantha offered a warning: "The biggest obstacle to your present spiritual development is Rudolf Steiner. You need to give him up in order to evolve."

"That's impossible," I thought, shocked and rattled. I

may have even said it aloud.

"He's not good for you. He's in the way."

This was jarring. It wasn't only that I loved Rudolf Steiner, which I did: my worldview rested on his teachings. My meditative practices were rooted in *How to Know Higher Worlds* and lectures regarding spiritual development. How could Steiner possibly be in the way? He was the way. If she were right, I was in trouble. In my new position, I would publicly be representing Steiner's teachings, introducing them to students becoming Waldorf teachers. If Samantha was wrong about this, though, maybe she was wrong about everything. But it had felt so real. Yet letting go of Steiner – that was impossible!

Samantha sent me off with what she called the rainbow meditation, in which I was to imagine each color in the spectrum, climbing into higher and higher vibrations. She told me to do it as many times a day as possible. Despite the fact that this meditation was antithetical to Rudolf Steiner's indications and I suspected it would lift me out of my body instead of grounding me, I felt compelled to try it. After all I was an esoteric superstar and wanted to actualize that reality in this incarnation. In retrospect, of course, Steiner *was* in the way of this degree of egoism. If anything his teachings inspire humility, revealing how far we have to go to develop ourselves into truly loving human beings.

Samantha told Lynn that Jim was shocked when he died. It happened so fast that he didn't know where he was. It took him time to realize he was dead; and when he did, a band of powerful angels had to hold him tight as he raged. His death created so strong a force that the insane man broke out of the local mental hospital at the same time, desecrated the cross in the Catholic cemetery, and then went after Lynn, trying to kill her. Jim wanted Lynn to die too, to be with him, because he loved her so much and didn't want her to be alone. That was intense for all of us to hear and took months, if not years, for Lynn to process. She finally thought it was horseshit, or so she told me.

I tried to reach Samantha after that first session. I needed more guidance from her, greater understanding, more support. I was already beginning to take flight; I didn't mind. She didn't answer my calls, and when she finally did, she emphatically and rather coldly, I thought, told me that I didn't need her anymore, that if I wanted to get a group together of about 15 people, she might be willing to come to Rockland County. You didn't need to be psychic to know that a community of anthroposophists was not going to be rushing to a meeting with a psychic masseuse from Kingston.

Destabilization 4: Vocational Shift

While I was aflame with the secret thought that I was a powerful bodhisattva, I simultaneously felt totally inadequate to my new responsibilities. The previous directors of teacher education had been my teachers – erudite, wise, men of profound depth, brilliant lecturers – who knew the works of Rudolf Steiner inside and out. I was nothing like them. Others assured me that I didn't need to be like them, including them. Still, not only did I feel completely over my head but worse, that I couldn't show it. I also knew it was true that the only thing I could be was authentic; I could only do the best I could do. The previous director offered to help that first year. He did the interviews that summer and would teach the main course for the teachers. I was grateful for this transition, but I still needed to prepare six new courses and create a part-time program for the following summer. The music teachers, foreign language, and gardening teachers also wanted preparation in their specialty. This was a puzzle on a timeline, needing to be solved relatively quickly, and I had no one to create with. Thinking I was a bodhisattva was not taking me in a productive direction.

At the height of my hypomanic ride, the music teachers were on campus for a one-week course. They were playing music together in the auditorium when, enamored with the inflated dream of who I was, I floated upstairs in that building into the wood-paneled library. I was looking for what Steiner had to say about who would be the next Buddha, the Maitreya Buddha. Of course, I opened a book to a page that addressed just that. Why does that shit happen? Anyway, to my mind it affirmed everything Samantha had said about me. I sat on the stairs as the musicians filed into the foyer below. They were surprised to see me perched there, eyes glistening; they acknowledged me and went on their way. I was to address them later about a future program for music teachers, but I wasn't clear what to say: I felt pressured to be wise. Knowing I had a mere shadow of an idea what their program might be the following summer, I apparently said something about choosing from column A and column B like from a Chinese menu, which I thought was clever and funny. Were these also my disciples? I wondered as we sat together.

The following day the college's music teacher gently confronted me. Felipe asked if we could take a walk; I saw the concern on his face and knew he had something specific on his mind. Had I fucked up already? When we were far enough away from the College with no one around, the coolness of old pines towering above, the softness of their needles carpeting the ground beneath our feet, he turned to me and asked what was going on with me. "What do you mean?" I asked, somewhat confused, my stomach unsettled as if I'd been caught in the act – but of what exactly? What was he seeing?

"What you said yesterday to the music teachers was incredibly disrespectful."

"Really?" I was shocked. What *had* I said? I explained that I had no intention of being disrespectful; it was just that so little was really planned at this point. I asked him what I had said and if he thought we could repair it.

He then looked at me and said, "Sure, Cat, but right now something's off. You need to come back to yourself. Can you do that? We need you to do that." That felt like a cold shower. I thanked him for talking with me, afraid that he had lost respect for me. He was one of my firmest advocates at the College. Something had stepped between me and myself – something I can now name hypomania. Felipe could point to it and ask me to realign with my true being. I didn't have to keep going in the hypomanic cosmic superstar direction; in fact, I mustn't. I needed to turn away from the pictures that Samantha had painted. She had tapped into a powerful force, pulling me away from my more grounded self, already unsettled by leaving Austin and Jim dying. While I felt my reluctance to withdraw from its allure – the pull was powerful – I knew it needed to be over, including the rainbow meditation.

On our way home from work and school that same day, Wil was driving and 14-year-old Morgan was sitting in the backseat. How much would I reveal to them? My gaze drifted out the window when Wil spoke: "Morgan and I have been talking, Cat. You are not yourself. Do you know that?"

"Yeah, Mom, you're flying, saying really crazy things,"

Morgan piped up, leaning in close from the backseat.

"Yes, I know. I'm not sure how to stop it, but what are you seeing? Felipe spoke to me today too. I'm going to try," I promised. They described a little more – speed talking, not listening to anyone else, talking to myself and to the invisible. In my heart of hearts, I began to see and own what they were saying about me. I trusted all of them and knew they weren't making this up. In a full-blown manic episode, as I experienced 13 years later, I wouldn't have been able to find that narrow shore of self-reflection, a place to anchor, from which I could right myself once again.

That night I decided on a plan, a prescription for my mental health and grounding. Every day I would do Steiner's thought exercise, thinking about an object for at least five minutes,[17] and some specific eurythmy – a form of movement, created by Steiner and a young dancer – particularly "I think speech. I speak. I have spoken. I seek myself in the Spirit. I feel myself within myself. I am on the way to the Spirit, to myself."[18] This has gestures that balance above and below; right, left, and center. Miraculously, thankfully, it worked. New responsibilities at work and with dear ones – being the main breadwinner, raising our son with my husband, being his wife, being present for my sister and mother, both recently widowed – all helped me regain my inner balance.

That winter I slid into a mild but lingering depression. There was a lot less sunshine, and it was much colder on many levels than in Austin. Even though I'd grown up in the Northeast, it had been 10 years since I'd faced winter. But it wasn't only the season: the beloved community I'd always experienced in Austin was gone, my mother had a serious back operation, and Lynn was out of her mind with traumatic grief. She was essentially living in her Volvo, driving up and down the east coast from her home in the Mid-Hudson Valley, where she still slept in the bed where Jim had had the brain aneurism, to D.C., where she played house with an old lover who both comforted and belittled her, to her ground floor apartment on West 95th Street, where she saw patients and New York City friends. She visited Kim every one or two weeks and other family less frequently. We talked on the phone. This was not what we'd planned. How like life to behave this way!

In March the administrator approached me, said he thought I was depressed, and suggested that I see one of the local anthroposophical doctors. It helped for him to name what I wasn't able or willing to see. I had seen Dr. Hermes regularly when I was a student at the College; he was originally trained as a psychiatrist and was now a family doctor, practicing complementary anthroposophical medicine. Over the course of a week, his nurse gave me three injections of homeopathic primrose, an early spring flower, and by the third one the depression lifted. Although there was snow on the ground, I had spring inside my soul. I could hardly believe it. Why don't more people who suffer from depression know about this? I was grateful I did and had colleagues who cared about me enough to say something when they saw me suffering.

Reflections

I saw this up-down instability, and still do to some extent, as situational mania and depression. In fact, I didn't think about this hypomanic episode again until 2014, nor had anyone else in my family. "We should have been more responsible," Morgan said. "That episode in 2001 should have been a warning." Besides that not being the concern of a 14-year-old just moving to a new place, the timing wasn't right in any way. I certainly would have dismissed any suggestion that there was something deeper going on or that I might need medication. As a family we had been using homeopathy and herbs to treat most ailments for years; we only took mainstream drugs when absolutely necessary. Mentally there was nothing wrong with me that some select Steiner exercises and homeopathic primrose injections couldn't rebalance. Hadn't I just proved that? In fact, this short up-and-down episode confirmed that I could manage my own moods, even when they got a little more extreme. I chalked this up to practicing the basic exercise of equanimity, one of the foundations for leading a healthy spiritual life.[19]

Therese posited this idea: because of the external pressures and responsibilities in 2001, once made aware of it, I was able to halt a hypomanic process in my psyche, which reemerged unstoppably with greater force in the spring of 2014. We agreed that the mania hadn't been that strong yet: I was able to hear my family and my colleague. I was present enough to acknowledge that they could see more than I could and strong enough to pull me back to myself.

Can the anatomy of this particular hypomanic episode, its destabilizations and traumas, serve as a scaffold for examining the more perilous mania of 2014? To summarize, there was the expected death of my father, sending ripples through the larger family system and creating currents in our destiny; a move away from a beloved community; Jim's sudden death and an attack on my sister's life; a psychic, whose waves rocked an already unsteady boat, resulting in delusional self-aggrandizement; and a change of vocation from a position where I felt increasingly masterful to one where I felt like an insecure novice if not an imposter.

There are two stressors I haven't yet mentioned. The first – I began teaching potential teachers on September 11, 2001. A whole country, perhaps the world, was shaken by the attack on the World Trade Center. "Conspiracy theories" abounded, making it all the more terrifying. The second, more specific to me – I'd been working too hard for 10 years, first to carry a class from third through eighth grade, and then to start and build a new high school. I always had a lot on my mind and took my work extremely seriously. I wasn't sleeping enough. Nothing was wrong physically, or so I thought, except that I'd been eating in a highly controlled way and was distinctly underweight. I'd been told I was allergic to many things and wasn't eating dairy, gluten, sugar, or chicken. I was so thin that one of my past teachers, then a colleague, known for being dependably klutzy in the delicate art of human communication, welcomed me as I was about to start my new job with a hug and the words, "Are you okay? I hope you don't have cancer."

Death and trauma, moving, loss of friendships and community, a psychic, an identity-rattling vocational shift, and physical vulnerability – how were these 2001 realities alike and different from the weather system surrounding the mania of 2014 in my 67th year? What propelled a yet more perilous journey? Were there other powerful aspects as well, not present in 2001 that further tipped the scales of balance and sanity? Probing, piecing it all together is imperative for my healing, examining the pieces, the losses, the forces at work, like a captain once more at the helm after the storm has subsided. And would this exploration ultimately explain anything? If nothing else, it is what I can do to try to understand the mystery of who I am and what life dropped on my doorstep.

6
Anatomy of a Manic Episode

The second episode in 13 years brought not only taxiing down the runway of hypomania, but lifting off into full-blown psychosis: living in a world that others do not see, a world real only to me, that felt truer, in fact, than the illusions to which everyone else consensually agreed. I was undergoing a huge transformation, a breakthrough, an initiation of sorts. I found myself unleashed and ungrounded from the mundane limits of time and space. Everything was achievable, including within my own psyche, where every obstacle to health and well-being conditioned into my personality could be overcome, where every complex could be optimized, where I could be completely reborn into the evolved being I knew myself to be. This time I could hear nothing from those I trusted most: Wil, Morgan, my therapist. They were only trying to control me because I was united with a holy, elevating energy and they weren't, or because they simply couldn't understand what was happening to me as I was living it. As Stanislov and Christina Grof describe it, spiritual emergence became spiritual emergency.[20] I couldn't tell I'd crossed that line, and I didn't care.

In 2000 Dad's death from multiple myeloma was expected and sent a current in motion. He lived with the illness for six years, and since I was in Texas, I wasn't involved in the details, except on our weekly Sunday phone calls when I could hear about the toll it was taking – recurring infections, thrush, shingles. I arrived three days before he died, appreciative of Lynn's acute timing. There was nothing shocking about it. Dad was 82, and I'd known his health was failing. In a different scenario less than a year later, Jim's sudden brain aneurism stunned all of us. Again death showed itself: in 2012 there were two, much closer together, one expected from illness and one a freak accident.

Lynn's Diagnosis

Lynn's diagnosis came in July 2009, her most dreaded month because of Jim's birthday and death day. To our horror, it was stage IV metastatic lung cancer, a death sentence. Once again, she was in shock: in her mind she had always been the one who would outlive us all. After all, she swam a mile a day, and walked faster and farther, leaving the rest of us huffing and puffing to catch up. What was wrong with God's insane universe? First Jim, now this, it couldn't be right.

The previous winter and spring, Lynn had a cough that wouldn't quit. I didn't like the sound of it. I felt that something was wrong, but knowing Lynn didn't like being told what to do about anything, I gently asked a number of times if she'd seen a doctor about it. "No, it's nothing, just a spring cough." By mid-June it started to be debilitating, and the local doctor, looking at an x-ray, identified the problem as pneumonia. It seemed odd that Lynn could suddenly get pneumonia out of the blue. When nothing changed after the antibiotics, the doctor ordered a CT scan, which showed a nasty spiculated tumor, barbed tissue, the sign of cancer.

A PT scan revealed that the cancer, originating in the lung, had metastasized to two lymph nodes, T7 of her spine, and her right hip. A node biopsy at Sloan-Kettering got more specific than the upstate hospital's results: non-small cell adenocarcinoma.

The disease was on both sides of the family. It killed Grandma Ross, my mother's mother, who had died within four months of being diagnosed, and Aunt Doris, my father's sister, who had about a year and suffered a miserable death. Aunt Vera, my father's other sister and her daughter had both had malignant tumors in their lungs, which mercifully were caught early enough to be removed with the affected lobe. Mom was beside herself; Kim was terrified. All of us were weighed down with sadness yet knew we had to remain positive as Lynn walked her path and lived as fully as possible for as long as she had left.

Lynn always loved the 23rd Psalm, and it certainly came in handy at a time like this, especially verse 4: "Yea, though I walk through the valley of the shadow of death, I will fear no evil: for thou art with me; thy rod and thy staff they comfort me."[21] Lynn's Jungian mind wrapped itself around "thy rod and thy staff" and how they could be a comfort. The rod was the trial given her, along with the certainty that she could bear it with dignity and learn as many lessons as she could along the way. The staff, she could dependably lean on as she walked "through the valley of the shadow of death." Lynn had had a lifetime of exercising fearlessness – as she faced the realities of being a single mom with a handicapped child, as she lived with the aftermath of suddenly being widowed after 16 years of marriage. Living with cancer, however, presented the grittiest challenge of her life.

There was loss on so many levels. The two of us had

often fantasized being little old ladies, growing more and more alike, sharing her New York apartment part of the year – going to plays, concerts, museums, and galleries; eating in our favorite restaurants and walking in the parks. The apartment was cozy, and we'd return there with gratitude that we got to live in the best city in the whole world. In the winters we would walk the beach in Puerto Morelos on the Mayan Riviera, swimming when it was warm enough, reading, watching movies on her computer outside on the porch (which we called being at the drive-in), and enjoying everyday in paradise.

With the diagnosis all dreams dissolved, some quickly, others in slow motion as she moved toward her death over the next three-and-a-half years, generous for that killer disease, thanks to a designer drug she took daily. Life moved more and more into the present moment: feeling a breeze on her skin, lying on a couch on the porch in the company of friends and family, watching the birds come and go, especially the beloved pair of cardinals. Every day she spent time in her garden, picking a weed or two until she was exhausted. One day walking with a hand-carved cane, she climbed into the middle of her perennial garden and crouched amongst the zinnias and snow-on-the-mountains so only her head was showing, a warm smile on her face as bright as the sunshine she inhaled.

Joy, humor, and intimacy breathed amid the sadness, pain, and suffering. One stormy autumn night the electricity went out. Lynn was already in the hospital bed in the living room. Wil and I lit candles and pulled up chairs on either side of her. How could we take advantage of this unusual atmosphere? We decided to make up a story, anything that came to mind. After all, we were three creative people – a jazz musician, an English teacher writer, and a Jungian psychologist artist – steeped in play, improvisation, imagery, and archetypes. I wish I could remember the story, something about the heroic adventures of a fox. We took turns, the room soon disappearing in the glow of the warm light. When one person felt she or he had contributed enough, it was the next person's turn. Sometimes it was fun to stop just to see how the next person would continue. It could turn silly in a moment and be rescued in the next by an offering of wise symbolism. The loving connection we wove, as the story unfolded, was magical, candles flickering, story emerging from deep human time.

Lynn let her vulnerability show too, which was unlike her. "Cat, come into bed with me," she'd say. And I'd crawl in under her pink satin quilt as her body got smaller and smaller, weaker and weaker. We'd compare hands, as we had always done, marveling at how alike our small-boned wrists and hands were.

Yet with all of the growing closeness and deepening love, I was acutely aware, as I watched her suffering, of the wall between her pain and my experience of it. While I could empathize, I could not actually feel what she was feeling in the way she was feeling it. We humans only feel our own sensations and emotions. No matter how empathic I am or another person is, we only share external realities – heat, cold, wet, dry, rough, smooth, hard, soft, shapes, and colors – but even then you may experience heat differently than I do, or red as khaki if you're color blind. I know sadness because I've been sad; I know heartbreak because my heart's been broken. If you have a toothache, I can reimagine it because so have I. We depend on these experiences to build bridges to one another. I guess this fundamental separation built into the human condition is a necessary blessing, so we can not only function but also help and love one another.

As the intensity of Lynn's pain increased, out of my love for her, I stretched my empathy as much as I could, using my attention and imagination to stay as connected as possible to her reality. All I could do was open my senses to observe, ask her what she needed, and respond to her requests.

Hope was born out of the prospect of medical breakthroughs, and Lynn was always looking for the latest. She attended a support group with others with cancer once a week at Gilda's Club, which also offered lectures by the City's top oncologists.[22] We attended one especially depressing one by a physician who worked exclusively with lung cancer. His PowerPoint showed the significantly lower amount of funding for research for lung cancer as compared to other cancers. Why? Because most people blamed lung cancer on those who had it: they were smokers and hadn't heeded the surgeon general's warning on the pack. Lynn didn't have the kind of lung cancer smokers get; she was never a smoker. Jim had been, but smoking was banned from the house. An unfinished basement, however, without radon mitigation may have been the cause. Who knows? What does it matter?

Art helped Lynn integrate and mark this life-flipping death sentence. Over two or three days that first weekend after receiving the diagnosis, she created a shield of sorts, a protective totem. It included the spiky gesture of the attacker tumor that held her in its clawing grip, pictures of life traumas that might have contributed to her vulnerability to this disease, and her sources of strength, all engulfed in the protection of the angelic host. Hard-pressed to find paper huge enough to express this trial unto death, she built and pasted together cut oak tag and foam-core in the shape of two angel wings until the shield reached 8 feet tall and 6 feet wide. She painted brushstrokes like feathers on the wings and glued fluffy white feathers in as many places as possible. It was decorated with an eclectic array: a long strand of red-orange beads, hanging two feet down from an upper left spike, approximating where the actual tumor was in her lung; three glued photos – one on the mid-right at Jim's funeral, spikes cut on the top, showing Lynn casting flowers onto the casket; the second on the far right of Lynn at 19, holding Kim as an infant and looking off into an unsettling, unknowable future; the third on the far left, Kim at 5, ornery and headstrong with a jaw bone of a cow pasted nearby on the mid-left; two dental imprints of her own teeth, fixed toward the bottom on each side. She painted a small intricate image of the Sephirot, an esoteric Kabbalistic symbol, her chosen cosmic meditation, and pasted it smack in the center at the heart of the shield. Near the bottom she attached a pair of old plastic reading glasses with an arm missing and two tablespoons that Jim had stolen from the Navy. Last she drew two thin delicate feet just like hers, colored in pink pastel, to dangle from the very bottom. She hung the whole shield in the painting studio downstairs in the barn, so she could see it every time she went into the space. Votive candles with the Virgin of Guadalupe were placed at its foot. At 59 she was determined to transform her cancer journey, using everything she had learned in her full, challenging life.

For over two years after Lynn's death, the shield remained in the same spot. Wil and I saw it every time we entered the downstairs of the building and were unable to even think of moving it. Others commented on the power it held, especially soon after her death. As that energy dissipated, especially after my psychotic episode, we were better able to think about respectfully dismantling it. One day I felt the urge and began; Wil joined in. The plastic and metal went off with the Tuesday morning trash. On Halloween at our friend Esther's house under a full moon by a warbling stream, we reverently burned the flammable parts in a blazing bonfire along with Lynn's journals, offering a cleansing ritual and homage to her as we read random fragments of the writing. Eventually the shield was replaced, for a time anyway, by a group painting that Morgan, Wil, and I did as part of a day we spent with Therese processing how each of us were affected by my manic episode and what we had learned.

※

Retiring after 20 years of working in Waldorf education in August 2011, I was left without the daily insistent demands, except the march of Lynn's illness. As my institutional work life ended, her needs increased. She had a team of friends supporting her, at least nine women, their husbands, and children, friends for a very long time. I became the primary caregiver, aware that if Jim were alive, he would have been the one sitting with her in the waiting rooms of doctors' offices, the chemo room, and the radiation room. He would have been the one accompanying her as she sat with her doctors searching for the best ways through this. I was glad I was finally available to be there for her. She wondered if it were best. Wasn't she strong enough to do most of it by herself? Perhaps, she should spread the tasks amongst her friends, who would certainly be honored to be there with her. But after carefully talking it through, we both felt that I should be the one person who had continuity and with her carried the whole picture.

One Friday night, about a year and a half before her death, we walked briskly as she set the pace down Amsterdam Avenue after services at her synagogue. After a few blocks of silence, she asked, "Why do you want to get close to me now? Isn't it just going to hurt worse?" Her inevitable death was never far from awareness and a backdrop of all her relationships, but tonight it was predominant in her mind. There was an edge of suspicion and mistrust that was part of the warp and woof on which her personality was woven. A survivor, above all, Lynn had been through many men over the years when she was making a home for herself and her disabled daughter. Layers of abandonment spread over the buckling wound of Dad's illness, which began when she was 9. She'd been crying in synagogue that night, not unusual for either of us since it was a place our hearts easily opened, but I could see that she was feeling down, isolated, and had an impulse to push everyone away, even me. After all, no one could really know what she was facing.

The question surprised me, though, and puzzled, I stopped to face her. Quiet for a moment, traffic whizzing by, I held her watery blue eyes in mine. She was so beautiful – cancer, shmancer – elegant, her silver hair pulled back and up, full around her radiant face. However, in this moment her mouth was pinched, revealing what I read as rage at this whole predicament. "Why wouldn't I want to be close to you now? I love you," I said. "I want to be here for you. In fact, I want to get as close to you as I can." "Before you leave the planet" was unnecessary to say aloud.

She seemed relieved on one level, accepting anyway, but still wary on another. Maybe she was just raw, and the closeness hurt. A generous soul, maybe this was about how much harder it would be for me once she was gone. I didn't care about that. I knew the right thing to do now; that's all that mattered to me. I needed to be with her through this as much as she needed someone. If my heart broke, it broke. That was life. Besides, accepting help wasn't a strong suit for Lynn, always the caregiver, and she knew that this was just the beginning of how much she would require as the disease progressed.

I didn't want to think about what that would entail. I was the one who couldn't even give Dad a subcutaneous morphine injection. What would it mean to be by her side as she came closer to dying? I was confident that I would do whatever was necessary or ask for help. Step by step, staying in the present was what was called for. Meanwhile I went with her to most of her doctors' appointments, especially to Dr. Sharp, her beloved oncologist at Weill Cornell. We had already been through another physician at Sloan-Kettering, an elegant Indian who Lynn had rejected after a few months. One sniff of being manipulated by a visiting specialist into doing something she didn't want to, and that was all she needed to fire his ass and find another oncologist. I was there to validate perceptions like these. Did I also see the same thing and feel the same way when the fancy S-K doc brought in an expert to try to convince her to do that treatment? I don't remember how she heard about Dr. Sharp, but he came highly recommended by someone she'd met who shared this miserable diagnosis. Another of her goals was to avoid being ripped off. There were plenty of alternative or complementary medical practitioners making a fortune off of cancer. She needed to use her insurance. Making sure that Kim would be left with enough money to supplement her benefits was always uppermost in her mind.

Together we contemplated treatment options, along with her acupuncturist, her gynecologist, and her homeopath – all close friends. Between sessions or after a day's work, Lynn did the research on side effects of whatever Dr. Sharp suggested; other scientist friends helped too. She was always looking for the latest therapies, anything that would extend her life without decimating her immune system. There was plenty of research to do on that as well. I was often a sounding board before she made final decisions, not the only one to be sure, but a central, ongoing one.

Lynn had a completely holistic approach. First stop was to see Paul Pitchford, a world-renowned nutritionist, who wrote a book called *Healing with Foods*.[23] We traveled north on the Taconic to a small community where he was giving a workshop and seeing nearby clients. From his suggestions she established a diet that made sense to her: mostly macrobiotic with lots of greens, tempeh, sprouted tofu, beans, and grains – quinoa, brown rice, millet; no wheat, dairy, or sugar, except for a little honey or agave for much needed treats. Lynn concocted a great recipe for chocolate pudding, from which we all benefited. She also ate eggs, fish, and some meat but infrequently.

Her Chinese medical doctor added a potion of Chinese herbs. Jeremy, her stepson, Lynn, and I made regular trips to Chinatown to pick up the strange-looking herbs, which needed to be boiled, the earthy smell permeating the apartment for the good part of a day. We often joked about the contents bubbling in the large pot – Styrofoam lifesavers, tree bark, bits of paper. I'm not sure how she drank that pungent brew, except that she knew it was bolstering her immune system.

She had acupuncture once a week; took two homeopathic drugs, one in the morning and one in the evening; and gave herself coffee enemas every morning to keep her liver as clean as possible. Sometimes I was drafted to make the coffee for the enemas: grind the green beans, boil the grounds in water, strain, cool to room temperature. What else? She did tai-chi, meditated, went to synagogue every Friday night and sometimes Saturday morning, especially in the winter, and had meetings with the rabbi from time to time. Since she would only pay for someone insurance would cover and could never find a psychotherapist savvy enough to handle her, she saw a young, inexperienced woman until it got too boring for her. Stretching and walking everyday had always been part of the daily regimen. She did as much as she could to heal, the touchstone being quality of life. And she looked terrific. People were shocked when she told them she had the Big C and a stage IV vicious killer at that.

Part of her vibrancy was also due to the designer drug the Sloan-Kettering doctor had prescribed, called Tarceva® (generically known as erlotinib), which she continued to take every evening before bed after she started seeing Dr. Sharp. Both oncologists were clear that the drug worked for about two to two-and-a-half years, shrinking the tumor and the other affected areas by stopping the growth of the tumor's epithelial or outer cells until the cancer ultimately outsmarted it. In Lynn's case, perhaps because of everything else she was doing to be as healthy as possible, there were few side effects. The Tarceva, in her words, "eliminated the metastases, shrunk my tumor in half, turned my hair dry and kinky, wiped out my nose hairs and gave me zits – a small price to pay...."

By March of 2012, the disease began its final attack. I responded with poetry, secreted in my journal.

>First Day of Spring
>
>i
>
>Yesterday surprises –
>trees in Central Park, flowering
>even a magnolia near Alice.
>"Six weeks early, everyone's saying,"

enjoying global warming.
"Getting a death sentence always
makes the colors brighter,"
Lynn says as we walk
toward the white-pink softness,
as we snap pictures
on our "dumb" flip phones,
searching for sunlight streaming through
the waxy triumphant ones, opening upwards
(how soon they blanket the earth beneath).

Stunned, not by this early spring,
but by what the PT scan said –
that the Tarceva up and quit,
that a superclavicular node's aglow,
that the tumor's larger,
that the cancer's returned to T7 and spread to T6,
that it reclaimed ground in her hip bone,

that the cancer's on the move
like spring this year –
much too soon.

ii
I woke at 3 as if
dumped on the floor
of a concrete room
with gray light
without sound
without life.
Ribs hurt
as if I'd been in that corset all my life –
the one that made Edith Wharton's waist

so thin in the picture of her, hung
outside the New York Society Library,
that we admired as we charged east on 79th,
arm in arm, hopeful, before
hearing the unexpected news.

iii
How is it possible I am feeling nothing?
I easily sober up
and get existential at times
like this. I know my heart
is holding itself together
with ideas of the supersensible.

I am here
for Mom who can cry,
so easily,
always true to the rawness
of her being. I am here
for Kim who wants to kick
God in the balls
for not listening to her prayers
and doing the God-damned
right thing for a change. I am here
for Lynn, whose earth
is crumbling beyond anyone's control
as she finds her next step
on shattered ground –
moving toward some kind of stability
without slipping into the abyss.
I am here for Wil who thinks the PT scan
is a medical conspiracy, a nightmare engineered
for profit. I am here with Morgan,

who tries to hold it all
with love and crystal clear vision.
I am here.

As when I was a child, I felt that I was holding everything together for everyone. Though I was not a child, I had to be strong: I was at the core of Lynn's care and the one family and friends would talk to if they didn't want to disturb her or she was simply exhausted. Her passionate blog gave her a way to process, helped with communication, and gained quite a following. She also shared other cancer stories she was avidly writing, filled with humor and profundity. That day we learned the Tarceva stopped working was the beginning of the end of Lynn's "one wild and precious life" as Mary Oliver wrote.[24] But many procedures and decisions still had to be lived, each one bringing us closer as sister-friends. And even though I didn't see myself as a caregiver, life had somehow prepared me, as it miraculously does.

Curing and Healing

Cancer specialists – whether mainstream or alternative – make a clear distinction between curing and healing. All are adamant: there is no cure for metastasized cancer, in some cases remission, but there is ultimately no cure. The opportunity is to heal, make whole, which optimally can occur on all levels of our being: physical, relational, emotional, psychological, and spiritual. This disease somehow introduces a force of energy within the person to heal, and since each is ultimately a complex individuality, all levels need attention and integration into the core self. Sometimes this leads to sustained life; sometimes it doesn't.

But regardless the person feels more alive and connected in however much time they have here on earth. Each level of the person wants tending, like infants, where needs are not met once and for all but are constantly crying out, expecting nurturing. Lynn knew how to work on herself, and she got busy on every level. Often feeling throughout her life that she lacked self-discipline – something she always envied in me – the cancer gave her an impetus to stay on track.

    I knew I could be part of her healing. I never had any hope that the cancer wouldn't kill her within a relatively short timeframe; and while grounded in that reality, I never crushed her hope as it ebbed and flowed. Lynn was pragmatic and courageous. We faced into many possible life-extending options together. She was strong physically, "healthy, except for a touch of stage IV lung cancer," as she often said. Everyone has complex relationships, and she was no different, especially with Jim's children. She had expectations for how to be treated – as she treated others, communicating, staying in touch, which was too high a standard for two out of the three of them. I know they all loved her in their own way, but two weren't able to be there for her in any way. Lynn was generous and always showed up for friends and family when they needed her. She remains a model for me in this regard, but she also expected others would show up for her when she needed them, and when they didn't, she was hurt and angry.

    Her relationship with Kim was complex as is true for any single mother and daughter, especially a handicapped one: they were deeply entangled in predictably draining interactions. I observed when Lynn talked to her 40-year-old adult daughter as if she were 12, when she screamed at Kim over the phone and ended up hanging up on her, when she wanted to fix anything that went wrong instead of allowing Kim and her aides to solve problems that arose.

Our shaman friend Elizabeth perceived a thick etheric umbilical cord between them. Shamans do that – they can see the invisible energies within and between us – and Elizabeth could see how that umbilical cord was holding back Lynn's healing. We were all in Tulum, Mexico, in August of 2010, a year after her diagnosis, and Lynn was having her first session with Elizabeth. The sky turned indigo tinged with green, and a powerful wind bent palm trees and blew through the little house on the beach, driving the mid-afternoon rain and rattling doors and windows. It was not a short storm, as many in the tropics can be, but accompanied their session as Elizabeth cut the cord between Lynn and Kim. When Elizabeth returned to the States, she did the same with Kim. Some things changed immediately. As Lynn felt freer, I often stepped in to speak to Kim when things were difficult or some drama was brewing, shielding both mother and daughter from falling into old habits. By asking them open, honest questions, a skill developed through my Courage & Renewal work, I could help them both have the space they needed to rebirth their relationship.

Other Adjustments

Cancer demanded that other adjustments be made: everything begs to be healed in both the psyche and the family system. I felt that something was off in our relationship, a dynamic whose roots were planted in 1967, a time of great cultural change. Back in the day, when I was a freshman at Smith and Lynn a junior in high school, she was already a hippie, emulating the Beats, reading Alan

Ginsburg, listening to Bob Dylan, hanging out in Greenwich Village on the weekends or when she cut school. Before I left for college, I was listening to Barbara Streisand and Broadway show tunes.

By the spring of 1967, I started smoking pot, and the uptight me wanted to be released. I modeled myself after Lynn, within reason: my bell-bottoms became faded, my skirts mini with leather boots to the knee, my speech riddled with curse words, her music my music, and her drugs my drugs. I was aligning with the counter-culture instead of with the preppy I was when I had chosen this college. But in my transformation, something subtly shifted in our relationship. I looked to her to set the trend and to get her approval: in effect, she took the role of the older sister. Her more outgoing, tough, and aggressive nature overshadowed my quieter, more receptive one, feeding this reversal. Maybe this dynamic became yet more established because I rejected the family for twelve years in the '70s to mid-'80s, leaving Lynn essentially an only daughter with all the concomitant duties and needs of a single mom with a child with cerebral palsy. Some of this dynamic shifted as we grew into adults, but some of it remained, encrusted below the surface.

"I've been sensing something odd between us," I ventured. "You know, you're not the older sister. I am, and you need me to be right now," I said smiling warmly.

Lynn looked relieved; she simply hadn't thought of it. "That's really true, Cat. Thank you." That's all it took; our relationship changed slightly like having a gentle chiropractic adjustment, and I sensed that she appreciated having an older sister again. Something was healed, allowing her to relax and accept a little more support as she faced into the wind of this trial unto death.

Intimations of Hope

Through a friend from her synagogue, Lynn met a woman whose stage IV lung cancer had been in remission for over five years. This was basically unheard of, yet she insisted that her recovery was due to one peyote meeting, held for her healing. Oh, sure, she'd done chemo and had some brain metastases (mets as they're called) removed with surgery, but she was cancer free and had been since that meeting. She connected Lynn with the man in our area who arranged peyote meetings, and as a first step Lynn and Morgan attended one to see what it felt like to stay up all night in a teepee around a tended fire, eating peyote and sipping peyote tea from time to time, in this highly ritualized Native American Church ceremony.[25] It moved them both. In fact, Morgan stopped drinking after experiencing the testimonial of the person suffering with alcoholism, who was at the center of the circle's prayers that night.

Lynn wanted to be a focus of healing. Although a skeptic in many ways, she believed in the power of prayer and felt held by the many prayers that surrounded her every day from friends and family all over the country, Canada, Mexico, Australia, and who knows where else. Close friends offered their land and home for the ceremony; she invited the friends and relatives she wanted to be present. Some accepted; others couldn't make it for one reason or another.

> We came bearing everything we were,
> Lynn with both lightly held hope
> for a miracle and a healthy burden of doubt.
> Mom with "Oy, another *kakamaymee* idea of my
>   daughter's,
> but I'm here for her. What else can I do?"

Kim with wide, moist eyes.
Some came for Lynn, tucking their skepticism inside
    their love.
Some came fearful of peyote, flooded with stories or
    memories.
Friends came with curiosity for a ceremony they
    wanted
to experience. Strangers came
to surrender to the serendipity of the mystery,
to explore a new frontier.
We were all there together, love teeming.

She was the only reason
I was there: peyote had launched me
into my first manic episode. I had
learned respect for its power.

We were called like
bees to a field of sunflowers,
elephants to help an ailing one,
our ancestors to pray that the gods intercede.
Blessed by the medicine –
fire, air, water, earth and its gifts –
tobacco, cedar, peyote, corn, meat.
We held fast to a pillar of calling
the circle: whoever was there
was meant to be.

Later Lynn would say, it was
like attending her own funeral.

    She always liked big parties. We were instructed to bring pillows and blankets, and a dish either for a ritual light dinner before sunset or for the morning breakfast when we would emerge from the teepee at dawn. In the evening we ate gingerly, not wanting too much in our stomachs but enough to sustain us through a short mid-June night. As the sun set, reddening the hillside that faced the opening of the teepee, we were invited to enter the sacred space. It slowly became apparent how many of us were there as more and more people ducked through the flap, finding a place in the wide circle. In some places there were two and even three concentric circles, accommodating about 60 people in what the shaman later called the "starship."

Mom, almost 90 at the time, was there. I sat next to Lynn through the night, Wil behind me. Morgan was often on the other side of Lynn, sometimes Kim, sometimes Jorge the Shaman. Peyote can make you vomit, which made me cautious. Not that I wanted to eat a lot of it anyway, but I knew I didn't want to vomit since that could easily throw off my electrolytes.

Jorge began by laying out how the evening would move. It was a big circle, and we all needed to be attentive to one another, to Lynn, to why we were there. He entreated us to pass the medicine quickly. We began, and the night moved gently. Time dissolved. Drum – copper with water in it, a skin pulled across it – pulsed through the circle under the skillful touch of Nebi the drummer, binding us together, merging heartbeats, each singer shaking Rattle then passing it on like a torch to the next singer. The music lit a path inviting prayer. Chanting, mostly vowel sounds, the carrier of feeling, bearing our supplication, our yearning for Lynn's peace, her healing, her well-being, her protection. Nebi carried Drum, moving from singer to singer, each urgently, humbly offering spirit prayer, becoming one with Rattle, voice dancing with Drum. We joined in as we could.

"Waytsay nay yo, haya waytsay nay yo" repeated over and over until the whole circle was chanting, finding our way into the sounds.

Some singers were more outward, others more inward, their souls naked in the circle. Sometimes the song invited us more easily to join. Despite one man's agitated squirming and increased groaning as the night progressed, his songs were clear, simple, and easy to follow, inviting us to join through their simplicity. A young woman, who revealed that she was suffering with melanoma, had a celestial voice, enthralling and lifting us to fields of pathos, inroads to the heart broken open, to our selves, to Lynn, to our neighbors, to the Native people, to all those suffering, to the earth itself.

I remembered the kind of clarity that peyote brought, as if focusing a lens and cleansing the psychic atmosphere. Again, the medicine came around. I glanced at my watch; it was midnight. My legs needed stretching. I thought Jorge had said we were stopping midway for a break, and before that leaving space for anyone to speak to Lynn who wished to. Maybe Jorge meant the midpoint between dusk and dawn. I wondered when that would be. The peyote powder, then chips, then tea, repeat.

Morgan looked over his shoulder. "How are you, Mom?" he asked, making eye contact.

"Fine," I said, nodding. He looked relieved as he met the grounded place inside me. I felt Wil's loving strength at my back and turned to acknowledge him. He was right there.

"And you?" I asked Morgan.

"Okay, a little nauseous, but I'm working on it," he whispered as we both returned to the drumming.

Lynn kept turning toward Jorge. She gestured for me to get his attention. When he caught her eye, and the chant and drumming ended, Nebi brought Drum back "home" next to Jorge, who spoke: "Lynn, you wanted to speak?"

"Yes. As I've been praying tonight, I've noticed that what I thought was standing in the way of my healing is not there: it is no longer Jim, my husband who died 11 years ago; it is no longer my attachment to Kim: so much has healed in our relationship."

"I'll say," Kim piped up. A tickle of laughter echoed around the circle.

Lynn breathed, consciously ignoring Kim's interruption. "What is standing in my way," and she began to weep, "is...my lack of faith, faith that I can heal this, that it will go away. I don't want to feel the weight of that. I fall into thinking that if I don't heal the cancer it's because I don't have enough faith in this ceremony, in Peyote, in my ability to heal. Again, it's my fault. I need help. I feel so alone in everything I'm doing - in making herbs, in fixing my food, in doing everything I can to get rid of this." She was sobbing deeply now. "That's what I'm going to pray for...for faith."

We all witnessed her breakthrough with our tears and love. Maybe that faith, I thought, was in surrendering, knowing she would be carried and met by the Divine, to whatever degree she was healed or not, whether she got rid of the cancer or not, and that if not, it wasn't her fault. It was clear, though, that she needed more support and how difficult it was for her to ask for it. Maybe she also needed faith that the people around her would help. We certainly heard that she wasn't tough enough to go it alone, that she needed a lot more than any of us - maybe even than she herself - knew.

The drumming continued like the heartbeat of Mother Earth herself, as did the praying, singing, and chanting, her children riding the wave of the throbbing beat and earnest song. *Watzsay nayo, haya waytzay nayyo.* Then Jorge invited friends and family to speak our hearts to Lynn: what came were sacred outpourings about what each of us loved about her, what she meant to us, what we hoped for her.

At the break Jorge said that he'd never had a meeting with so many people. Then and again as the light of dawn streamed through the opening in the teepee, he spoke about how loved Lynn was and how much support she had. Gathered together in that circle, rows of people, prayed in all four directions for her healing. Jorge spoke wisely, "Not every disease can be cured, but this is not in our control." He continued that she was held in infinite love, that the power of the invisible presences surrounded us, upheld us each and every day, and would take her to the other side when it was her time. The peyote meeting was on June 16, 2012, her wedding anniversary; in six months Lynn would be dead. In the meanwhile we continued to bless every day she was with us.

Caretaking

Before I retired as the Lower School Chair in New York, I had been staying in the City apartment during the week and returning to my home and dear husband in the suburbs on the weekends. I called Lynn "my wife" because she helped me clear my head through many difficult situations at the school. She often made us dinner between sessions and helped me keep my priorities straight. "Give it your full 75%," she used to say, knowing what was expected from the environment in which I worked and what I habitually demanded from myself – more like 125%. She arrived on Tuesday afternoon from the country; I kept the apartment clean – just the way she liked it, bought food, and helped in every way I could to make things easy for her.

Lynn could depend on me; I was ready to help, including having a vibrant picture of her transition to a spiritual world from which we all had come and to which we would return. She was an innate skeptic; I was an innate believer. We'd had many conversations about this difference and were at peace with it. We complemented each other well, "my heart...holding itself together/with ideas of the supersensible," hers forever questioning the existence of a world other than the one we could see and feel. My unbending faith gave her hope.

For a while after the Tarceva stopped working, Dr. Sharp suggested more conventional chemotherapy and radiation. Lynn tried two different chemo cocktails, which made her feel weak and sick, hampering her ability to work as a psychotherapist and enjoy what was left of her life. Any chemo with hair loss as a side effect was out of the question; that's where she drew the line. She knew she was going to die, and it wouldn't be bald. She also did some radiation treatments on a painful hip until her skin was suffering badly, looking as if it were burned. That was that.

The most disturbing development yet was a scan showing brain mets. Dr. Sharp set up an appointment for Lynn to see a neuro-oncologist named Dr. Susan Russo. As always, we waited for quite awhile in an examining room, but being anywhere with Lynn could be hilarious even under the most dreadful circumstances. Anything could be a prop. This time she picked up a plastic spine, which the doctors must have used as a visual aid for patients and med students, and put the top near her mouth as if she were playing a tenor saxophone. I took a picture on my flip phone as I kept checking the hallway to make sure no one was watching. When Susan came in, we liked her immediately. Like Dr. Sharp she was born and raised in Livingston, NJ, so we felt at home with them, being Jersey girls ourselves. We immediately wanted to be friends with her, and she treated us like soul sisters. She suggested a high-tech "Star Wars" procedure, called gamma knife radiation, which targeted the brain mets without killing the cells around them. It could be done at Columbia-Presbyterian, which was convenient. Lynn researched and agreed to the procedure; the alternative was far worse. Hopefully, her brain would then be free of cancer until the lung cancer killed her.

We showed up at the hospital around 7 a.m.; Lynn was terrified but courageous. While we waited, we made fun of the odd headgear a nurse had fitted Lynn with, a chunky metal helmet to hold her head still while she was inside the machine. This ungainly thing wrapped around her neck to the front, where it had a resting place for her chin and two vertical braces on the outside of her eyes with metal posts that screwed superficially into her forehead, nothing permanent, thank goodness, but not exactly comfortable either. I was anxious too: we were both keeping up the other's spirits.

When they called her name, Lynn went into the machine in a dark cave-like place while the doctor administering the procedure sat outside in a little booth. He could see on his screen exactly where the brain mets were. I could hear her voice. At one point she told him she was having trouble breathing; she was having a panic attack. The doctor calmly talked her through mindfulness breathing – "notice your breath, now in, now out, in, out, and again" – until she was calm enough for him to continue. I marveled that mindfulness techniques were finally infiltrating mainstream medicine, just in time to help my precious sister.[26] The Star Wars procedure was successful without side effects; we were all relieved.

Treatment's End

Lynn and I had many conversations – I'm sure she had them with other friends as well – about how long she would continue treatment. Then one day she told me she didn't want me to come to her appointment with Dr. Sharp as we'd planned. I gently asked why, suspecting her agenda.

"Because I have something to say, and I need to be able to be fierce with him."

I wondered how best to respond. "How will my being there stop you from being fierce?"

"I'm not sure, but I think I will feel stronger if I'm alone."

I wasn't buying it. "Listen, Lynn, you can be as fierce as you need to be, with or without me in the room, but I would like at least to be in the waiting room, so you can call me in if you need or want, or have me there when you come out. You don't have to decide whether to have me come in with you until we get there, but I'm coming."

I rarely stood up to Lynn. For me gentle submission to her decisive will was the path I usually took: this was her disease, her body, her precious life. I felt little right to an opinion. I asked questions, the best I could muster, to help her clarify what she really wanted, but I was growing more and more protective as she shored herself up for further acts of bravery. Going by herself to the doctor was unnecessary heroism as far as I was concerned. I pictured the alternative to my going with her: Lynn being half way across the city when she announced a big decision to Dr. Sharp, with or without a certain amount of characteristic bravado, and then speeding up Park Avenue in a taxi alone, crying convulsively, the soft underbelly of her tough nature exposed and aching. I wanted to be there to hold her, if that's what she wanted, or just to be present with her. To my relief, she called the next day to say she wanted me to be in Dr. Sharp's office with her.

First, Lynn asked him some pointed questions: Did he have anything else up his sleeve? He had some ideas about other chemotherapy cocktails that might be better than what she had tried at first. She asked him for the names; she had already researched most of what was offered but asked how much longer they would give her. He couldn't say, a few months. She looked in his eyes, fortified, given his answers, and said that she'd decided to stop treatment, go home, and watch her last autumn from her beloved porch. All of our eyes teared up. Lynn formed strong bonds with people she loved, and Dr. Sharp was surely no exception. All of us struggled to keep it together professionally. He stood up and gave her a big hug. We expressed our appreciation for him and all he had done. After all, she had had almost three good years from diagnosis, a lot more than most people get with stage IV lung cancer.

Home to Die

It's a funny thing, knowing you're going to die soon and still not knowing precisely when. Lynn made it clear to all of us that she would not live incapacitated. Somehow she would figure out a way to die with dignity.

By September, as soon as Lynn moved back home for good, hospice was on board, which was key. Her stepson would live in the apartment in the City; I moved into the big Victorian house, which Lynn had bought in 1981. Off and on since Jim's death, especially after spending holiday time together, we would muse about how much fun it would be for Wil and me to move in with her. But life has its own mocking plans. Hospice arranged for a hospital bed, and we moved Lynn into the living room. From her bed, looking straight ahead into the dining room, she could admire the elegant hand-forged chandelier, which her friend Nathaniel had made; to her right she could see a playful kitchen fixture with pigs and cows that he'd also forged. From there she could hear everyone coming and going through the big kitchen as well as monitor the weather from the bay windows behind her and the ones in the dining room looking out over the vegetable garden, modest this year.

As she had announced to Dr. Sharp, she spent most of the waning daylight hours of September and October on the porch, lying on an old paint-chipped wicker loveseat, softened with foam, from which she could watch the leaves turn gold and the daredevil squirrels chase each other over thinner and thinner branches. Maybe her life was like that too: playfully moving through treacherous twists and turns. She often napped. Visitors came and went. And, as always, wherever Lynn was, there was laughter. "Cooking and clowning, cooking and clowning, that's what I've done all my life," she told me once as she faced false aspects of her own personality, ways she felt she had had to accommodate to be noticed or accepted or loved.

The hospice nurse came every two or three days and more often as Lynn weakened, adjusting medications to make her as comfortable as possible. The nurse also helped me create a chart showing when Lynn took what meds, so no one would be confused. This allowed others to spell me when I needed a break, knowing that she would get what she needed when she needed it. The hospice social worker helped too, offering support to Lynn, Kim, Mom, and me. These were our angels.

Other angels were the eight plus women who were Lynn's close friends and their husbands. So many people cared about her and reached out to help. As the caregiving intensified, she could only eat a small spectrum of foods. Chicken soup was a staple, and there was a rotation of friends who brought mason jars full every two or three days. "Who has won the best chicken soup contest this week?" she'd tease. She definitely had her favorites and encouraged them to step up.

Coffee enemas were the order of the day to keep her system moving and liver cleansed, especially once she began taking opiates. Sometimes I'd help make the mixture for her and set everything up in the bathroom. Hot water bottles were imperative around the clock to ease the bone pain in her hip and ribs.

Lynn also asked me to arrange the visitor schedule and any tasks we needed others to do. My least favorite part of organizing the visitors was sometimes having to say no to people who wanted to see her or who she, for one reason or another, wasn't up to seeing. She was raw, with no tolerance for anything but bald truth: like a woman in labor, being sociable was not on the agenda; only intimate, honest connection was possible. Some of that was rational and some not; some of her decisions I agreed with, and some I did not; sometimes I interjected my opinion, but more often I did not. Lynn knew what she wanted and what she could endure, given the energy she had, regardless of the popularity of her decision. For example, except for Jeremy, her stepson who had stayed connected, she would not allow the other stepchildren to visit. "Too little, too late," she said. "Sorry, I just can't do it. Is this for them or for me?" There was unresolved anger and hurt that weren't helpful at this stage of her life and impossible to reconcile. This was no time to push herself: nurturing was in order, and I saw my role as offering her as much support for what she wanted and needed as possible.

A few friends offered to stay overnight, so I could have a day and night to myself every week, for which I was deeply grateful, although it was always hard to be away. They also provided places for me to stay in their comforting homes those nights. Every caregiver needs such acknowledgement and kind, caring attention.

Tasks and Death Circles

Lynn wanted a "home death," which I had introduced her to and totally supported. Not only would she die at home, but we were also committed to learning how to care for her body after death, so she wouldn't be sent off to a funeral parlor for make-up and embalming. She wanted everything in place while she had the energy to oversee it. Amy, one of Lynn's best friends, and I interviewed two funeral directors. One in town was too smarmy and conservative, cold to the idea that we would tend to the body. Then we found a family-run funeral home that was interested and excited about our approach: they would help by setting up and regularly changing the dry ice needed around the body.

We also shopped for a place for the memorial service large enough for at least 200 people. Two possible churches in town were between pastors and were less than encouraging. Lynn and Amy suggested the chapel of a private school nearby where Jim had worked for many years before meeting Lynn; her stepchildren had grown up there for part of their lives. Although it was not in the village, it was perfect. Not only was the chapel welcoming with a soaring ceiling and windows letting in lots of light, but the chaplain was helpful and supportive. Lynn's lawyer generously offered her home for a reception after the service. Sharyn, another of Lynn's closest friends, and I shopped for coffins. Someone we knew was making them, so we picked one out, the simplest pine box he had. We could all rest, assured that the major details were in place.

In October seven women friends plus Lynn began meeting to plan her care directly after death. Two of us did most of the research; some of us had some previous experience. I had an anthroposophist friend who had been involved in home deaths for years and was extremely helpful. The eight of us met three times. I facilitated the circles, which helped create the quality of space I thought we needed to have.

In the first meeting we used peacemaking circle practices, starting with an articulation of the values we brought to the circle: love, friendship, sisterhood, presence, permanence/impermanence, kindness, generosity, service, spirituality, peace. Based on those values, we articulated this set of guidelines for Lynn's care group:

- Have the space to be authentic
- Honor what is happening moment to moment
- Be free to recognize my limitations
- Take care of myself
- Leave judgment at the door
- Be dependable
- Be willing to sacrifice ("make holy")
- Support each other
- Welcome silence
- Allow the full spectrum of emotion
- Know the gift of this experience

To begin, each of us brought something that represented our relationship with Lynn. I wish I could remember what the others brought; I only remember my own – a photograph taken when I was four and she was two with one of my arms squeezing her tight in a loving, protective, big sister way. I do remember, though, that these symbols of our individual connection to her, when placed in the center of our circle, showed the force of love and the bond of friendship that encompassed all of us. In that first circle we also explored our feelings about caring for Lynn's body after death. Sharyn and I reported on what we had learned about what happens to the body within two hours after death. We used a talking piece, which gave each person a chance to communicate her feelings, thoughts, concerns, and questions and the others the opportunity to listen. We ended in a way I'd been taught by Kay Pranis, grandmother of restorative justice in the United States: "I give you my hand." "My hand in your hand." This is sent around the circle as hands are offered and taken. Then, "this is the way we go forward together."

To open the second meeting each of us brought something Lynn had given her as a gift and placed it in the center. Again, I only remember a few things: a bowl, a painting, a scarf. One of the questions addressed how Lynn's presence in the circle affected everyone, including her. I was concerned that she had been completely drained after our first circle, but she was adamant that she wanted to be included. We got practical: what could affect each person's availability for caring for Lynn's body? A number of the women could be working if she didn't die on the weekend. We got a good sense of who would always be on call: Amy, Sharyn, and me. We had assignments: Sharyn would ask Nathaniel to make tall candleholders for each corner of the casket. Esther would get incense and essential oils. Lynn and I would invite and organize the pallbearers; I would email a list to everyone.

We talked about what we still needed: What to use over the eyes? Should we use a tampon in the vagina? We needed votive holders, a cotton cloth for under the body for washing, a sheet for a shroud, cotton strips for securing the mouth closed, a cotton or quilted blanket to put over the dry ice. Still unresolved was where the body should be for the two or three days prior to the funeral. Lynn and I had pictured the dining room since that was probably one of its functions in the late 19th century, but others raised compelling issues. Some people might be uncomfortable with the body being in the house. Instead it was suggested that the coffin be upstairs in the barn, a larger space with skylights, where Lynn had seen her upstate patients. I was resistant at first, but the wisdom of the group prevailed: more people could fit up there, and the family would have some privacy, even though we had specific visiting hours. It also turned out that neither Mom nor Kim wanted to see Lynn's body. With this decision, the barn needed to be cleaned; everyone pitched in.

By our third circle everything was planned and purchased for some of us to wash, oil, and prepare Lynn's body after her death. We felt secure in what we needed to do. We suspended the talking piece, still honoring our guidelines, and I presented an activity I would offer in a Courage & Renewal retreat, starting with a poem by May Sarton, "Sonnet 2" from *The Autumn Sonnets*.

> If I can let you go as trees let go
> Their leaves, so casually, one by one;
> If I can come to know what they do know,
> That fall is the release, the consummation,
> Then fear of time and the uncertain fruit
> Would not distemper the great lucid skies
> This strangest autumn, mellow and acute.

> If I can take that dark with open eyes
> And call it seasonal, not harsh or strange
> (For love itself may need a time of sleep),
> And, treelike, stand unmoved before the change,
> Lose what I lose to keep what I can keep,
> The strong root still alive under the snow,
> Love will endure—if I can let you go.[27]

We journaled on these prompts:

- How is this autumn for you?
- What do you need to let go of in your life right now? How does Lynn dying fit into this?
- What are the obstacles you experience to letting go? What allows you to let go?

In dyads friends shared what they wished and then came back to the large circle. This was a diverse group of women, Lynn's friends over decades: a physician, a psychotherapist, a TV producer, an acupuncturist, a craftswoman, an actress, and me. While the conversation was confidential, I can say that the heartfelt words spoken were held in a circle of abiding love, honoring Lynn's life and celebrating the rich tapestry of poignant relationships about to undergo massive change. These circles were my offering: friends of Lynn's from different places grew to know each other better, to respect each other more. Some wounds were healed. As a group we bonded – along with two other women friends and the families – for the next month of Lynn's life and through the memorial service and funeral.

The Double

In talking with anthroposophist friends who have spent a lot of time around people dying, I knew that it was common for the doppelgänger or double (in English), as Rudolf Steiner called it, to have a last, often violent hurrah a few days before the person dies. Steiner characterized the double as a being, a second ego that we place outside ourselves, emerging when we seriously practice spiritual exercises, purify our own souls, and live more morally upright lives. This being travels with us from birth until death and can be a constant reminder for us to transform. However, as Steiner teaches in a lecture in St. Gallen, Switzerland, on November 15, 1917, "There is only one thing in human life that they [the doubles] absolutely cannot endure: they cannot endure death. They must, therefore, always leave the human body in which they establish themselves before it succumbs to death."[28] This is how I understood what happened three or four days before Lynn died: she was weak, close to the threshold, and the double announced itself and took control.

While I was expecting something, I wasn't ready for what happened. When the theoretical becomes reality, it is still shocking. Lynn had a serious paranoid episode: she trusted no one, not even Morgan or me. On one level we felt hurt because we were closest to her. We tried appealing to her logic, to no avail. The double was holding the reins, revealing the underbelly of mistrust holed up within her personality. Thankfully, Jake, an old friend and lover, had come to stay that weekend. He had the kind of authority with her that we didn't. Lynn had a weakness for position and prestige, and Jake was erudite and extremely accomplished. She also loved him. He got her to agree to listen to him when he set a boundary, for example, about going outside in the middle of the night since she might break a bone and end up in the hospital, which she didn't want. Thankfully, Lynn agreed, granting him enough control to protect her.

Lynn was sure we were talking about her (at times we were out of concern) and conniving behind her back (consulting with each other for her own good). She was convinced something was wrong with the water supply. While Jake slept, she came down the stairs by herself, weak as she was, and put on her cowboy boots and her lambskin coat over her flannel nightgown. It was freezing outside. She looked as mad as she was. It was well after midnight; she was sitting on the steps of the porch, shouting "Wayne," calling our neighbor, over and over again. The sound of someone in distress crying for help outside woke me. When I realized it was Lynn, I knew I would be no help. I had to trust Jake also. I hoped he was with her. I was furious that we had allowed her to sleep upstairs with him – he had dramatically carried her up the stairs like Rex and Scarlet in *Gone with the Wind* – and yet, how could I deny her these last pleasures of life on earth.

By then Jake stirred and followed her out to the porch. After sitting with her for a while, he patiently convinced her that this wasn't the right time to get Wayne's help, that he was sleeping, and that morning would be better. She should sleep, but that proved difficult. Very early in the morning, she was at it again. "Wayne!" she yelled. Jake had made sure she was wearing better boots, so she wouldn't slip on the ice. When it was a respectable time in the morning, Jake agreed to go with Lynn to see our neighbor, so she could tell him to take care of the water supply, which – being the good-natured, compassionate soul that he is – he assured her he would.

Perhaps, this was one of life's completions: at the end of

her life, I got to experience her in a psychotic state the way she had experienced me in one in 1971. The pain of seeing her lose her mind felt parallel; I was shaken. Guided by the on-call nurse, I found the psychotropic drug she recommended in the packet from hospice, which Lynn finally agreed to take. Within a few hours, the Halderol began bringing her back to herself. The next day, Jake told us that she didn't want to talk with Morgan or me until she shared her experiences with her physician and psychotherapist friends – the professionals again. My buttons were pushed, but I quieted myself: there was nothing personal about this. After talking with Lynn, they spoke with us about including Lynn in any conversation we were having about her, to which we could easily agree.

Because of Lynn's inner strength and knowledge of how to work on herself, with the support of the Halderol, she quickly returned to her core self. We had three more days of clarity and presence, common to the experience of people dying after the double rears its head. During those days, while her body weakened and the pain increased, she worked to forgive as many people in her life as she possibly could. The morphine, which she had started as soon as hospice came on the scene, was supported by fentanyl. She was in a lot of pain. Though she didn't like it to show, she got still and steely, requesting more frequent hot water bottles for comfort and more movies for diversion.

Lynn was ready to leave. She had had a good life; she was not afraid of dying. She just didn't want to be more and more of a burden. She could see our strength waning as we cared for her. She also didn't want to lose basic functioning any more than she already had: she wanted to maintain her dignity. "Why can't I die?" she asked, applying her analytic mind. She called the hospice chaplain to help.

"What is there to let go of?" he asked when she appealed to him. At his suggestion we made a list of the people she needed to forgive, including those she was angry with for abandoning her since her diagnosis. We sat together as she mulled over each relationship in her heart and mind, deciding how she wanted to handle each one. Her goal was to be honest and as forgiving as possible, letting go of these sticky relationships, so she could die in peace. One she forgave in person, two of her stepchildren by writing letters to be mailed after the funeral; still others she had to forgive as much as she could inwardly, acknowledging that her hurt was laced with anger and she was out of strength or will to heal the relationships.

During these precious last few days, her shiny blue eyes drilled deeply into mine, peering out of her skeletal face. "You're going to shatter," she said, as if foretelling something only she could see. Why was she saying this to me? Taken aback, I dismissed her words as a consequence of the morphine and shook off the chill they sent through me. Maybe she had an image of me as glass: she always saw me as more fragile than I was. Maybe these were words chosen from her analytic training as she failed to imagine how I could ever live without her. But I also felt a bit affronted: she was making herself too fundamental to the integrity of my psyche. She was central in my life, of course, but I was my own person; I could live without her! I had very successfully for many years. Anyway, I would have to, wouldn't I? I would have to be there for my mother and for Kim without her.

I expected to be sad, even bereft after she died: she was my sister and best friend, my beauty consultant and chief shopper, my dance partner and confidant, my dream analyst and psychotherapist, my editor. And I was there for her;

we trusted we'd be there for each other. She was the one I could always depend on; I was the same for her. All of that would be gone. But I was certain we could stay connected through the portal of death. I had with my father, at least for a while; I could with her too. Truth be told, I myself could hardly imagine life without her and didn't try. I knew I would grieve as I never had before, but shatter? That made no sense at the time she said it, but when I was in the grips of psychosis, lying on the floor mat of the seclusion room, her words, "You're going to shatter," repeated obsessively through my turbulent mind.

Expected Death

This was the night. She was sure. Early morning would announce the Saint Day of the Virgin of Guadalupe, who Lynn adored, prayed to, and had painted on large canvasses at least three times. We all said good-bye at her bedside, so we could get some sleep. There would be much activity the next day. How soon it came. Morgan and Sharyn stayed with her. While Lynn's breathing got more and more agitated – the death rattle, which Morgan had never heard before – he went downstairs to stoke the wood furnace, throwing around pieces of wood, crying, furious that his aunt, who he loved so much, was dying. By the time he came upstairs, she had breathed her last breath. Sharyn came upstairs to wake me: "We think she's taken her last breath." It was certain – the date and time, 2:12 a.m., December 12, 2012.

Wil got up too, and we all sat together with the body for a few moments. Sharyn called Amy first, who was on her way over; she then called the others in the care circle, so they would know. We had a two-hour window before the body would begin to stiffen. That was plenty of time for us to get everything ready for washing and anointing the body while we waited for Amy to arrive. No one else answered the phone; the three of us turned out to be the perfect number for the task. After all, Lynn was petite. How many of us could work on her at the same time?

We knew what to do. It actually felt uncannily normal as if I'd done this many times before; perhaps, in past lives I had. To warm water we added a little alcohol to close the pores, and lavender and frankincense oil; the two of us washed her gently with sponges. Sharyn gingerly reminded me that I had agreed to plug the vagina and anus. I rolled up a round cotton pad, like a cotton ball only flat, and took a deep breath. Again, this was no more disturbing than if it were on my own body. As we'd prepared, we used tape to make sure her eyes would stay closed and secured her jaw shut with one of her favorite scarves. Sharyn and Amy arranged the shroud and her hair. They would do final touches and make-up later in the morning when the funeral home people moved the body into the casket upstairs in the barn. We weren't opening the room for the wake until that evening. It was going to be a long day.

A hospice nurse came that night to establish that Lynn was dead and get the necessary legal information for the death certificate. Her body was still in the living room on the bed; the mood was peaceful in the house. Morgan had made eggs and toast. Mom had joined us, and we were sitting at the round kitchen table eating and talking in tender voices, holding each other close in the unreality of death. Two days later at the funeral, our dear hospice nurse told me what the night nurse had written in the log: "Lynn Schneider died last night at 2:12 a.m.," the official requirement, and then below that he wrote to his colleagues, "Lynn Schneider is not dead!" And I paraphrase: "I have never seen such a beautifully laid out body and such a serene family surrounding it." I don't need to share the memorial service or burial next to Jim's grave. It happened exactly to her high standards: it couldn't have been more aesthetically beautiful, more filled with accolades for the way she had lived and died, more graced with sublime and generous music from friends and relatives. Love teemed to the rafters of the packed chapel.

And then it was over: Lynn was dead. When Dad died, I came for three days at the end of his life, stayed for four more, and returned to my full life in Austin. This was different. This was my sister, one of the people I felt closest to on the planet, one of the people who knew me and with whose life I was intimately intertwined. This experience stretched me far beyond what I thought my capacities were for caregiving, far beyond what she thought my capacities were too. One day in her last week, as I was helping her wash in the shower chair, she confided, "I never thought you had it in you to be the caregiver you've been." I had never shared such intimacy as she approached death or prepared anyone's body after death. All of this needed deep digestion. Was this, too, part of the vortex of change, challenging the organization of my psyche and ultimately undermining it?

Wil and I moved into Lynn's house during the last month of her life. We had all agreed it was to become Wil and my house. How did that happen? Lynn was lying in her bed in the living room. Wil and I were cooking something in the kitchen. Mom was watching and enjoying being with us. "Why don't we buy this house, and all live together?" she asked, characteristically speaking first and thinking later. Lynn heard her from the bed. "What a great idea!" It was as if she were channeling Lynn's deepest yearnings for closure, ensuring that everyone would be taken care of.

Once it was out of Mom's mouth, she immediately wanted to take it back, but she had released floodwaters that could only flow in one direction. Everyone was excited, especially Kim and Lynn.

Wil began moving stuff from our old house, which we immediately put on the market. Mom then told Wil and me that she wasn't ready to move, she liked her life and independence, and anyway she didn't think parents should live with their children. But it was too late. We were swept into the fast-moving stream. She tried to tell Lynn a number of times, but Lynn wouldn't hear it. As a daughter and social worker, she had told Mom many times that moving before there was a crisis was best, but trying to tell Mom to do anything she didn't want to do was impossible. "I'll move when I get old," she liked to say. Besides she had the wisdom to know, which we did not – one thing at a time. Her daughter was dead. Moving too was out of the question. Enough loss.

Traumatic Surprise Death

Although Lynn had been dying for months, it still was jarring being in her house without her. It felt hollow, eerie, with traces of her everywhere and her nowhere. I was bone tired, drained, and in a dull shock. Wasn't that enough? Evidently not. It was December 21st, the winter solstice, a stormy night – windy and freezing – a week after Lynn's funeral. I was in bed that night of the howling winds while Morgan attended a bachelor party for Jason, Lynn's godson, someone he'd known since he was a little boy but hardly knew at all. I hate the whole notion of bachelors' parties. Young men do stupid things on nights like that.

"I have no idea why I'm going, but Jason invited me,"

Morgan had said beforehand. They were going out for dinner and were supposed to be back by midnight. After all, Jason's wedding was the next day.

It got late; I was having trouble sleeping, listening for Morgan to come in. It was hard not to worry on a night like this, the darkest of the year, the wind crying, windows rattling, house creaking. Wil was in the City playing saxophone. I still wasn't used to being in the house alone. I kept snoozing and waking to sense whether Morgan was home yet. Each time, he wasn't. I knew it was late but wasn't sure how late and didn't want to know. Why wasn't he back? Something was wrong; I could feel it all around me but kept brushing off my worry, so I could get some sleep. Then I heard the door close and his steps, heavy on the stairs. I was relieved he was home, but there was something bristling and foreboding in the energy.

Morgan came into my room and stood stock still in front of my bed. I turned on the light. His face was sadder than I'd ever seen it, drained of blood, exhausted, in shock.

"Something terrible happened. Jason is lost in the Hudson."

"What?" I said. "Sit down. Tell me what happened."

He sat on my bed, and I put my arm around my then 25-year-old. "It's as if the whole night were eerily pointing in this direction." He shook suddenly as if a chill came over him. "We had dinner, six of us, and Jason was talking about his fear of water. Two of the oldest guys, one a triathlete and the other a sailor who'd sailed the Caribbean and up and down the East Coast in all kinds of weather, decided that tonight was the night that Jason should face his greatest fear. So we went to an inlet that they knew on the Hudson; they borrowed a friend's canoe. We built a fire on the shore, and the three of them got in with a small bottle of Jack

Daniels, determined to row to the other side and back."

"Did you drink too?" Morgan had not had any alcohol for over two years.

"Yes," he said, "but only one beer at dinner. I shouldn't have though. Maybe I would have stopped them."

"Oh, you can't blame yourself for this, sweetie. I doubt you could have. Go on."

"So they took off in the canoe. If there'd been room for one more, I would have gotten in, so I could help."

My heart caught. "I'm so glad you didn't!" My eyes filled with tears.

"The other three of us waited and waited. We were getting really worried and called their names. There was no response. We didn't know what to do. We were starting to go for help when some policemen came looking for us. They told us that the canoe had capsized and the triathlete swam for help and reached a house, even in the freezing water. The other two were not found. A search would resume in the morning.

"The triathlete was being taken care of, the guy from Connecticut left, which meant that Jason's childhood friend and I had to go tell his parents. The police would soon follow; we wanted to get there first. I'm sorry. I'm so sorry. This is such a nightmare. I wish the whole thing had never happened. And yet it's so odd how fated it seems, looking back." His voice drifted off. "I'm wiped, Mom. Thanks for being awake. I'll see you in the morning."

Instead of a wedding Jason's bride, parents, and friends were out on the Hudson looking for his and the sailor's bodies. Morgan did not go; he couldn't nor could I. The two bodies wouldn't be found until the spring thaw. When Jason's body was found, I didn't attend the cremation. I couldn't: I didn't really belong. It's important to know where we belong and where we don't.

One gratitude I have for all times is that Morgan didn't step into that canoe.

Aftershocks

The reality of Lynn's death sunk in deeper and twisted. The grief of those who had been her closest friends and had known Jason since he was a baby was too much to bear. The whole community into which I'd moved with anticipation and longing was shaken to its foundation. Relationships cracked; individuals fell apart like great oaks split by lightening and crashing to the ground. I heard a lot through the grapevine, wanting, needing to stay clear. Jason's father attempted suicide but, thankfully, didn't succeed.

An echo of something Lynn said a few days before her death haunted me. Her eyes glassy with painkillers, she turned to me and asked, "Are you coming with me?" She seemed to have an inkling that someone was.

"No," I replied assertively, surprised by the question, "I have many miles to travel before I join you."

A few weeks after the accident, I got a call from Jake, Lynn's friend who had helped so much that distressing weekend with her double. He is also Jason's uncle. I might have called the family to see how they were doing, and he answered the phone. I can't remember now. Anyway, he seemed drunk and laid into me, "I want you to know that you did a terrible job in managing things around your sister's death. You hurt a lot of people." Who? What had I done?

"I was just respecting her wishes," I said. "I did my best." Why did I feel defensive? Attacked, was more like it. Okay, he's made it clear: I'll just stay away. They were Lynn's friends, anyway, not mine.

The weight of loss was everywhere. A book called *Grieving Mindfully* by Sameet Kumar was a companion in my own grinding process, as singular as any two people are, as unique as any relationship. For days, weeks, and months, I woke every morning with a dark weight sitting on my chest. Sorrow loomed large.

∽

Why is death such a destabilizing force? I was once part of a game with about 20 people, led by the founder of Spacial Dynamics®, Jaimen McMillan.[29] As we walked around the room, we each selected two others and had to move equidistantly between them. After about 10 minutes Jaimen told us to freeze and close our eyes. He removed one or two people from the group and then instructed us to resume the game. When I tried, I soon noticed that one of my people was missing, making it impossible for me to move.

Isn't this a metaphor for loss, for the death of a loved one? Lynn was a gravitational center of joy, activity, family, relationship, advice, and intimate confidence. She was a gurgling spring and a nurturing cave. Nothing was impossible to withstand if she were there, lifting the situation into the light of the human comedy. She was the rock and the light, and both were gone. My beliefs told me she might be on another plane, but on this one, I was reeling, holding on to everything I knew that would help me go on despite my loss. And then there were the reverberations, the aftershocks – unexpected, undermining, and ultimately, mysteriously resurrecting.

7
Pressure Cooker

I keep wondering whether the 2014 psychotic break could have been avoided. Reality says it couldn't be: it happened. But why? What tipped psyche's scale? What constellation of life events conspired with my own transformation to undermine me to that extent and to what end? Maybe life was insisting that I thoroughly realign with my core self, becoming more integrated with who I really am.

It is understandable that Lynn's death had a destabilizing impact on me. Jason's death, a little more than a week later – especially with the horrifying thought that Morgan came so close to getting into the canoe that night – put an unexpected spin on my already deep grief. And yet, once again, in fact, death wasn't the only destabilizing factor: moving and loss of community, the role of psychics and shamans, and a major vocational shift played their parts. In 2014 the full-blown dramatic mania emerged as a complex fault line of pressure built and released.

Loss of Community

We moved to a new place, not really new to us, a beautiful village in the Mid-Hudson Valley. I had a lot of hope and even assumed that the relationships with Lynn's friends, begun during her illness, would continue after her death. Finally, I would have a community again as I had in Austin. But everything was different without Lynn. Why wouldn't it be? There were initial, generous invitations: the first Christmas just weeks after her death with Amy and family; New Year's Eve with couples; dinner with two of her friends.

Especially when I was with a friend or two, I felt awkward as if watching myself squirm from a little way off. Who was I? I felt empty, dull, depressed, torn from what used to be my self. How could I be anything else? Lynn's absence was the loudest presence, and I couldn't fill the void. Why did I feel I had to? It was as if a thread in a thoroughly woven garment had been pulled, and that was unraveling the whole. Seeing me, her friends ached for her even more – or so I thought – until it was unbearable. With all but one of her friends and certainly no ill will, the invitations stopped, and I initiated none.

That one friend, Esther, was excited about our being here and about us as individuals and as a couple. She saw something in me that was distinct from my sister, validating that I could be freer because I was no longer in Lynn's large, lovely shadow. Esther herself acknowledged that she could be herself in a different way with me: I was quieter, more reflective. She liked that. I was grateful to be seen and appreciated for who I was. How healing! She became a touchstone for us in our new place. And there soon came another, Ashley, a student of mine from Austin, a writer, who miraculously lived close by. We soon became walking buddies and started sharing writing with one another. In dry times, these two women arrived in the midst of my isolation, disappointment, and confusion, offering a spring of loyal female friendship and nurturing seeds of a community I so desperately wanted.

A memorable thing happened about three months before the mania began. A colleague called me from the Austin school, saying that they were initiating a head of school position and asking if I would consider being an interim head until the end of the school year. I told her I would think about it, thoughts and feelings flooding in on me. I knew I would be walking into a nightmare of school politics similar to what I had just left, with great relief, at the New York City school. This was different, however, in that there would be immediate trust in me there. But did I want to risk failure in a place I had been so successful in the past? I had no idea whether I could help or not. School crises are slippery; I didn't want to be brought down in the midst of it, even as an interim. And then there was the reality: there was no way I could leave Wil, Kim, or my mother and go off on my own for four months. However tempting, I couldn't bury my grief in school business. No, my time in schools was over. I called my colleague and told her; she was disappointed. What surprised me, though, was my sobbing after I hung up. With my heart broken, grieving Lynn's death, I was at last mourning the loss of community and friendship I'd had in Austin, maybe also the loss of energy for my vocation as an educator, facing with clarity that there was no going back.

Moving

3/1/13

stuff...angry this a.m.
faced with more fucking stuff
your stuff everywhere.

> Am I crazy for wanting to be here?
> Does it really make sense?
> Sacrifices for stuff, for location.
> Location. Place.
> I feel out of place – displaced
> Rearranged by your death.
>> I know. It couldn't be
>> helped.

"Why were we here?" was the question riding a merry-go-round through my mind, with little to cling to and no gold ring. After all, Wil had to travel twice as far to his gig three nights a week in New York City. At the time we were paying for a studio apartment, which could barely house both of us when I came in for the weekend. I got incredibly claustrophobic in such a small space and had trouble sleeping, often interrupted when Wil came in at 1 a.m. We lived farther from Mom and just a little closer to Kim. Maybe one gold ring was that the house was accessible for her, where our other house was not. That house didn't even have a bathroom on the main floor. Another plus was that we were maintaining the family home and had enough space for everyone to sleep here on the holidays or for celebrations. Maybe that's why we were here, or maybe we had made a huge mistake in our hasty decision: at the time thinking certainly hadn't played a major role. Yet over and over again, reflecting on how we had decided, it felt like an irresistible wave that had come up behind us and taken us where we had to go for a reason beyond our present understanding or discomfort. Here we were, left spinning without the person who had made this a home. One thing was certain: we weren't going anywhere. We were in it for the ride and would have to see why we were here as life unfolded. We would just have to trust.

The Light Fixtures

There were immediate trials that felt like attacks and further made us question our decision. Nathaniel, Jason's father, a master blacksmith, left a message on the answering machine saying that Lynn had told him that after her death he could take anything from the house that he had made. She'd never told me that, but I wasn't going to argue with someone whose son had just drowned. Dreading the call and what it would mean but determined to stay calm and friendly, I left a message on his answering machine asking exactly which things he wanted. He soon responded. We had to pull the bronze fixture with the pigs and cows that hung in the kitchen and the delicate chandelier from the dining room, both of which Lynn especially loved. I didn't care about the floor lamp; I was glad he was taking it. I was relieved he didn't want the bed in the guestroom although we would have dealt with that too. I reflexively felt invaded and outraged but knew I had to move beyond that and find something positive in all of this.

Thankfully, Mom happened to be visiting that weekend, so we shopped for new light fixtures. I have a hard time shopping by myself. I'm so easily overwhelmed by all the choices that I end up buying something that isn't right. Shopping with Mom, as with Lynn, is like having a lucky charm. As is so often the case with trials, this one too turned out to be a blessing. Changing the lighting was the first major step in making the house our own. Sure, the other fixtures had sentimental value despite the fact that you could hardly see in the kitchen the light was so dim. The dining room chandelier was the tough one: it was so exquisitely crafted.

By the time Nathaniel came to pick up everything, I could have compassion for this man more shrouded in sorrow than any person I had ever known. The pain of losing his son was inconceivable, a love of 26 plus years, the work of his heart that would never return. The least we could do was to return the work of his hands. I thanked him for helping us make the place our own.

Not too soon after a capable electrician hung the practical new ceiling fans in the kitchen and two bedrooms, and an elegant new chandelier in the dining room, I realized that the fixtures Nathaniel had made were the two that Lynn would have seen day after day from her sick bed the last three months of her life. Maybe this was her way of saying, "Enough, get those things out of there." The dead have a strange way of interacting with the living.

The House

Another trial we faced was the legal status of the house itself. In Lynn's will the house was left to Kim, and was to be sold and become a substantial part of her protected trust. Everything in the house was also left to her. Although we had talked with Lynn and she was excited about our buying the house, the will was never changed. She was dying, and we were so consumed with caretaking that it had never crossed any of our minds to adjust the will or put the new agreement in writing while she was still alive.

The understanding was that Wil and I would buy the house at market value when we sold our other house. It looked like we had a buyer, but that ended up falling through. We missed the seasonal selling window: it was winter, and our house wasn't moving. The lawyer and Amy – Lynn's close friend, a trustee of Kim's trust (I was the other), and the executor of the will – began to talk with Wil and me about a six-month grace period after which we needed to start paying rent, or they would have to put our new home on the market. The house could be rented to someone else if we couldn't afford to buy it or pay rent, so Kim wouldn't be losing money – the reality as long as the major asset, the house, was not "liquid." Given our vulnerable states, and assuming we were working with friends, this felt like a bitter cold wind. Wil and I felt betrayed. The lawyer and Amy reiterated that this was not personal but our legal obligation as trustees.

Suddenly the foundation upon which we were building a new life was shaking. Wil had moved everything with great effort out of our other house and gotten it ready for sale. We were already paying utilities on both properties plus a mortgage on the old house. Paying rent was financially impossible. The thought of undoing all we'd done and the rage I felt kept me up at night. It felt grossly unfair, punitive, even cruel to bring this up now while we were adjusting to Lynn being gone. The rawness of grief was drowning my normal capacity for equanimity. As I look back, this was a point when I began feeling the fault lines of my fragility. Was I was losing my sanity? The stress was pressurizing the cracks of my grief.

Thankfully, Amy was sensitive to our predicament and cared more than we initially gave her credit for. She prayed and asked Lynn for help. Before we reached the deadline, she received guidance – whether from Lynn or her own higher wisdom, we'll never know. She called me to come to her house one Sunday morning, saying that she'd figured out a way to resolve the situation. In the will Lynn had left me the New York City apartment, which was worth more than the house but had a large mortgage. When Lynn stopped treatment and moved out of the City, we made an agreement with Jeremy, Lynn's stepson, to live in the apartment and pay the mortgage. But Amy had the brainstorm that, if we all agreed, the lawyer said we could add a codicil to the will that would leave Kim the New York apartment and me the house, literally do a swap. We knew the New York apartment was going to sell for a good price and sooner than our other house would since any time of year was a good time to sell in Manhattan. It was a brilliant solution! The trust would not be dependent on selling our house. It did mean, however, that Jeremy had to move out of the apartment, which was awkward for me and difficult for him since he'd just moved in, but while annoyed, good-natured human that he is, he understood, and it worked out. Bless him. I immediately hired a high-powered New York City realtor, and with Jeremy's help and the realtor's furniture, lamps, and bland generic flower paintings to hang on the walls, we got the apartment ready to sell in a short amount of time. Kim's trust would get the proceeds from the sale, and we would pay the difference into the trust up to the agreed-upon market price for the house once our other house sold. We all agreed, the codicil was signed, and some pressure was relieved.

Besides overseeing the selling of the City apartment, I had a lot to do. "One drawer at a time" was my motto although sometimes it was a shelf or a closet. There was stuff that had been in them for years and years. Much was ready for the garbage. I let a lot go but often felt completely overwhelmed by the large house with many, big and little things. We were also integrating our own furniture, plates, cups, silverware, pots and pans, waffle iron, blender, and juicer.

The feeling returned over and again: while paradoxically

surrounding me everywhere I turned, Lynn was gone. It was emotionally confounding. She was a collector with an eye for beauty: a crystal elephant, rabbit, and turtle from Tiffany's, small enough to hold in the palm of a hand; a small mother-of-pearl bottle delicately painted; a chunky green rock embedded with crystals. When she was alive I often coveted her stuff, the way sisters do: the grey wool jacket, the pink cashmere sweater, the long black wool sarong, the multi-colored silk shawl, the crystals, the shells, and other seemingly endless chachkas. After her death they were little consolation, the spirit of her love drained out of them: there are so few things I've actually kept. Large pieces of furniture that we didn't want needed to be sold and the revenue put into Kim's trust: Craig's List, people coming and going, one thing at a time taken away. Other smaller artifacts or clothes were sold in flea markets, all for Kim's trust. We were clearing out, making space for our energy in this new home. We smudged with cedar upstairs and down.

The house we were selling wasn't. This added a level of financial stress. We actually had a second buyer and an end was in sight until the deal fell through in July of 2013, and we needed to start the whole process over again. We fired our realtor, and I found someone on the Internet who'd been in the business for a long time and had high ratings. She vigorously got on the job, which, in itself, was comforting. Within a few months, we had a real buyer. But that period of waiting and carrying the expenses of two houses increased the pressure, even though we had no mortgage in our new home.

In the spring after Lynn's death, I had lunch with another one of her friends I thought might be someone I could get to know. We had a professional talk about how Courage & Renewal work might be of service in her organization as well as a personal one about how life was going for us in what had been Lynn's home. After hearing my story, her response surprised me: "That's courageous of you." Courageous? I thought. Insane, maybe, but courageous, really? Her friend knew how Lynn had thoroughly embraced her home, how utterly hers it was, especially after 30 plus years of living and eventually dying in it. It would be one thing to put it on the market, empty it, and sell it, allowing all that long-invested energy to dissipate into the cosmos along with her own, but the comment made me see that moving into this homey Victorian house and transforming the energy while living in it was a different prospect altogether – difficult, challenging, and courageous, a concept I was still having trouble getting my mind around.

Change of home, place, and community – this would have been enough.

Retirement and Identity

Like many people who follow their hearts into their work, being a teacher and school leader was intimately woven into my identity. In the Courage & Renewal retreats I attended and facilitated, I reflected on the threads of vocation alongside those of true self, affirming that I was more than what I did in the world.

When it came time for me to walk away from Waldorf education in August of 2011, when I no longer felt it was the right place for me to be, I made sure that I could throw my energy into the next thing. My life would still have meaning. I would still be helping the world. I would just have more time available for Lynn and the rest of my family. I wasn't worried about retiring. In fact, like most people I was really looking forward to it. There were so many things I would finally have time to do: write, work on mediation skills and restorative justice projects, organize and facilitate retreats, play music.

That first year, before I moved in with Lynn in September of 2012, I was busy with these new interests. I still traveled back and forth between our home in Rockland County and the New York apartment, where I helped Lynn by cleaning it and accompanying her to appointments. I did a second mediation apprenticeship and began to mediate some cases as a volunteer; I studied restorative justice and was trained in peacemaking circles and community conferencing. A small group from the peacemaking circle training began to meet regularly to explore the process and see how to use it as a tool for community building. When I didn't need to be in the City, I was back home with Wil.

Mediation became less and less compelling for me. I was more interested in community conferencing, a restorative justice process to hear what happened in a situation from all those who were affected. Those in the circle come up with how to remedy the situation for the greatest good. It's a powerful tool for working with young people who have done something without thinking that has gotten them into serious trouble. Here I could be an advocate for children, for inner city children, which was where I'd begun my career as an English teacher in the Bronx 40 years before. I liked that we were directly diverting children from the school-to-prison pipeline and giving them a way to redeem themselves and learn from their missteps. That had always been my goal with teenagers who made mistakes. This approach was especially critical in the New York City schools, where Black and Hispanic students were too often being treated like criminals.

While the work was extremely gratifying, I also observed

how it deeply affected me. I was inspired and moved when the community conferences allowed teens to speak about what they'd done, look at and listen to those they'd affected, experience remorse, and express heartfelt apologies. Healthy plans were made by the group to support these young people and to attempt to effect deeper systemic change. Those weren't the situations I lost sleep over. It was the students affected by gun and drug violence or ongoing abuse, where there was little hope that things would ever change for them. I was privileged and went home to my comfortable life, but before and after the conferences, I was obsessed with the extremely difficult circumstances of these children. I was grateful, though, that I was doing something to help people.

In September of 2012, when I moved upstate to take care of Lynn, she became my focus until her death four months later. That situation demanded everything I knew about life. I used all my skills: master planning, organization, attention to detail, communication, networking, and presence. Love grew. I became her companion and servant, in a way. She was my boss; I was her outward energy, so she could conserve her own, putting herself first for the first time in her life. She'd ask: "Can you tell Jeremy he can come for a few hours on Saturday?" "Can you ask Evelyn to pick up some cellophane noodles for me?" "Can you go to the library and pick up four or five movies we haven't seen yet?" Knowing who was available, I'd ask her which of them she wanted to be with when I had my time off.

After Lynn's death, it was difficult for me to be in the house alone when Wil left to play music; I wanted to go into the City with him on Thursdays. When the apartment we were renting was no longer available, a generous friend, who wasn't living in her Upper West Side apartment, allowed us to stay there. That was a heavenly time, at least for a while. Besides the peacemaking circle group, this is when I began working with Elizabeth on Hidden Water, the program to bring justice and healing to those who had been sexually abused as children. I did the research to see who else was working on anything similar in New York City, in the United States, or anywhere. I continued the research when I was back upstate. Connections were made. Elizabeth did the research on the legal side and created a business plan. We met every month or two in Tribeca and began to build a picture of how the program could work. We really let it cook slowly. I had some experience and training in restorative justice, limited as those were, and besides being a shaman Elizabeth was a master mediator and mediation trainer, and pushed on the business end to determine how this could be financially viable while remaining responsible to the needs of participants.

Hidden Water was compelling for both of us even though when I mentioned the idea to other people, they blanched and responded with something like "that sounds awfully heavy," looking doubtful or expressing skepticism that anything like that could ever work. I interviewed two people renowned in the restorative justice field who agreed with us that it could be of great service if participants were willing. I was inspired just knowing how much the program was needed, given how many people were scarred by early childhood sexual abuse and how many families destroyed by it. We were certain that if we built it, people who wanted to heal would come. We wouldn't have had the impulse otherwise.

Elizabeth suggested that we try our divergent circle ideas with actors, a way that she liked to work, which I had experienced in her mediation apprenticeship. I wasn't sure how to approach my circle but figured I would by the time it came around. That time never came. I always felt that Elizabeth had much more faith in me than I had in myself. She could see something I couldn't see. Maybe that was because she was also a shaman. I think that was one reason I sometimes felt intimidated about working with her. What did she see in me? Obviously it was something good if she wanted to work with me, but I was always aware of my insecurity in relationship to her or who she thought I was. At one point in my life, I don't think it would have been that way, but it was now. Once Lynn was gone, I also mourned the loss of my vocational identity.

> Grief strips away
> any pretense or façade.
> Pristine painted walls peel
> in its atmosphere.
> Laid bare, layers
> of the untended are revealed.
> Time suddenly slows.
> Pay attention, whispers.

For decades I was used to a certain level of intensity, pressure to multitask, to hold a lot in my head and on my heart. Now, suddenly there was nothing, emptiness, not even keeping track of Lynn's meds or her visitors for the day. I was standing in a void. What was on the horizon besides the project with those affected by childhood abuse, which was intermittent? The City was farther away. I reminded myself that I had left a legacy in the schools where I had worked; that was fulfilling but not sustaining in the present. Schools, children, teachers had been my life for over 20 years, almost 30 counting the teaching before Waldorf.

In the spring after Lynn's death, I got a call from a new Waldorf school forming near where I was living. The woman on the phone wanted to know if I was interested in teaching second grade in the fall. I laughed. The universe was tossing me all kinds of strange questions. I was clear: mentoring, yes; teaching, no, sorry. Maybe if I were asked to teach high school English, I might have said yes, but there were no high schools nearby, and anyway something kept whispering inside that those days were over. I didn't have the forces any longer, or maybe the forces I had were for something else, something yet unknown. My sorrow and unspeakable vulnerability had ripped the scab off a way I had been in the world for a long time.

Two Shamans and a Psychic

Both of the shaman encounters, which happened in 2013, I spoke about earlier, but not fully. I go a bit deeper here.

I had a shaman session with Elizabeth three months after Lynn's death, curious what I could learn in retrospect about our relationship and my future without her. To give a picture of my unrealistic idea of a healthy timeline for healing, I thought three months was a long enough period of time to have a shaman session, something I knew was always powerful. Wasn't there enough intensity already? Perhaps, it was the manic in me that instinctively wanted to turn up the heat on the already simmering caldron. Something in me craved a breakthrough, wanted the heavy grey agony of these days to lift.

I hardly wrote anything down; I can only recount what I remember. We talked about my core traumas: at five a car accident Dad had and a trip I took to Chicago with my grandmother "to take care of her"; at 12 my father's first dive into suicidal depression. Elizabeth blew the five-year-old into my second chakra and the 21-year-old into my third chakra. That's what shamans do. Then she blew a hawk – the bird that connects the earthly and the spiritual worlds – into my throat chakra, and on her table I literally became Hawk Woman, my body a mantle of feathers. I let it happen, noticing my thoughts taking me back to a life when perhaps I had a role as a powerful medicine woman.

Who knows what these things mean? Maybe Elizabeth does, but I am so much warier than I was when this was happening. Could I have conjured up Hawk Woman? But why her? And what about the 12-year-old when, all alone in my bedroom behind a closed door, I learned that Dad wanted to kill himself? Did Elizabeth forget how major that was? I found it interesting that the heart was left free. Maybe that was for the 12-year-old, whose broken heart needed space to awaken and become her own. Maybe Elizabeth sensed its fragility, sanctity, and resilience, and left it space for healing.

Perhaps, this session made me ripe for the psychotherapeutic work on early trauma that I did with Therese nine months later. Maybe revitalizing my generative energy center to the young child and my power center to the newborn adult gave me courage to face and welcome the flood of memories that emerged. The uncanny experience of Hawk Woman couldn't help but be woven into the manic episode with its inflated ideas about starting Hawk Feather Center for Healing and Reconciliation.

The second shaman incident was in the summer after Lynn's death when I needed someone psychically sensitive to evaluate what was going on energetically upstairs in the barn, where Lynn's body had lain. I knew Elizabeth was way too busy to visit and didn't ask; John was my next choice. I'd always really liked him, and as the years went on his life work changed from musician, when he and Wil had been friends, to energy healer: he was a Reiki master and I remembered he was training to be a shaman. This is the part I left out before: I was obsessed with losing Wil, one of the ways that grief was affecting me. Of course, I knew that someday one of us would leave the other. That's how life worked on the earth, but I was already planning how I would deal with that should he die first. Standing with both of them in the kitchen as we chatted, thoughts flitted through my mind that if anything ever happened to Wil and John was alone, I could imagine being with him. I guess Wil has highly attuned radar to thoughts like this, or I was a lot less subtle than I thought.

After John left that day, Wil was fuming but said nothing. It wasn't until the next day that we talked about it. I approached the subject nonchalantly because I really didn't think I'd done anything wrong. I could invite anyone over to our house that I wanted to. After all, I was a free entity, wasn't I? But something was off, and I knew it. He was angry, and he rarely got angry, especially with me. I owned up. I told him what I'd been thinking, as embarrassing as that was, and that he was probably picking up on the energy of my thoughts. He was.

Reflecting back to a little more than a year before the mania began, here was an early sign that something was askew. Thoughts are real, and I had flirted with destroying my marriage in a way that I never had before; and while I felt justified, I knew that I wasn't right, and the whole thing scared me. When John wrote to see how things were going, I said that it was best if we didn't communicate any more.

Lastly, just a few weeks before the kiss of hypomania,

there was the psychic and his seemingly benign card readings and deep interest in me in the restaurant where Kim treated me for my birthday. Why do these people affect me the way they do? None of them made outrageous claims, as did the psychic masseuse in 2001 after Jim's death, yet there was still something in their benign energy that infiltrated my vulnerable psyche, a vibration that subtly rocked a cracked vessel. While the shamans and psychic played a less catalytic role than in 2001; nevertheless, it's interesting that they were there at all.

Vulnerability

During the first year following Lynn's death, I voraciously listened to self-help lectures, experimenting with various techniques to build self-worth, self-acceptance, and self-compassion. I was also committed to grieving consciously. Despite all of it, something was beginning to cave in, something over which I had no control. Thanksgiving was another tip-off. I was determined that it would be as good as it had always been with Lynn, and I didn't want anyone's help. Nothing was working: the turkey wouldn't cook; the vegetables were soggy, so unlike me. The Thanksgiving before, Lynn had been there. It was three months before her death, and she valiantly came to the table for a short time before having to go back to bed. We were all so sad. A year later, as our smaller family sat at the table, that image was still burnt into our minds. Lynn and I had always done the cooking together with me relegated to over-qualified sous chef. Now I was alone, and I felt like a total failure. I had to go upstairs. Wil and Morgan found me crying on the bed and assured me that I didn't have to be Lynn, that they would help, that this was hard for everyone, that we would be okay, that they loved me.

At Christmas I was too sick with the flu to come to the table: fever, coughing, weakness. I had lost weight caring for Lynn. She weighed in the 80s by the time she died; the flu brought me down to around 102. The anorexic part of me enjoyed that I could wear her size 4s. But I was weak on a lot of levels, my immune system decimated, and the flu dragged on. I just couldn't shake it, especially a cough, which interfered with my sleep. Knowing the chest was a place to hold grief did nothing for my healing. My left ear wouldn't unclog: I felt locked inside my head.

Everything was telling me that I needed help, and I finally capitulated. My body was speaking clearly: I could no longer continue trying to be the pillar of the family, acting as if I were as strong as Lynn had been before her illness (even during it), being the one who could handle the grief storm and show the way for others. This was a new phase. I admitted to myself I needed both a chiropractor who could help me get well physically and a psychotherapist who could help me process the unspeakable grief I was bearing along with all our other life changes and stresses. Of course, I had my family for support, but that was not enough. We were all grieving, and I now understand that our whole family system was reeling in the fierce wind of sorrow.

Amy told me about her chiropractor, Dr. Andrew, who turned out to be a bit of a wizard. I used to call him a shaman posing as a chiropractor. He used kinesiology and had gentle ways of treating emotional components and experiences of trauma held in the body. Dr. Andrew was my ideal physical/emotional healer. But I knew that wasn't enough. I didn't want to start shopping for psychotherapists and have to explain my spiritual orientation; I didn't want someone condescending or clueless in the face of my spiritual practice and beliefs. Besides, there was no time to spare. I had recently met a spiritual counselor, who attended one of the retreats I facilitated and who I trusted completely. She recommended Therese, who was both a spiritual counselor and a licensed clinical social worker. Once I started seeing her, I worked with her and Dr. Andrew in tandem: I would talk with Therese and then Dr. Andrew would clear the trauma from my body. I was moving fast, maybe too fast.

Reflections

The core elements of the 2001 episode – death, grief, moving, loss of friendship and community, a psychic, a major vocational shift, and physical and emotional vulnerability – were all there and intensely packed, building toward the 2014 mania. To summarize the specifics – Lynn's death, someone so close to me, who took care of me in her own way over the years, someone I helped take care of through the months when she was at her most vulnerable; the shock of Jason's death and the haunting shadow that Morgan could have stepped into that canoe; a beautiful new home with legal complications, farther away from the few friends I had in Rockland County, City friends, and restorative justice projects; financial pressures in waiting for our old house to sell; unresolved grief from having left Austin 11 years before; the vibrational contribution of two shamans and a psychic; the end of my career as an educator, suddenly an outsider to a community with which I'd identified for over 20 years, and feeling the vacuum while I ever so slowly began to forge a new identity; losing weight, mirroring Lynn in the throes of her cancer, and an incapacitating winter illness after one year without her. Added to this was a new burden of responsibility for Kim and Mom. Isn't all of that enough?

Yes, and I think that something unexpected also played a part – psychotherapy itself. The mysteries of the psyche and the journey it takes to essential, major transformation, especially after a loved one dies, are beyond our control. I found myself on a trip without ever consciously booking a ticket.

8
Psychotherapy Before

> Every time you lose a relationship or are faced with uncertainty,
> you grieve the loss of a predictable and safe world.
> – Sameet Kumar

What is the role that psychotherapy played in helping me through the "loss of a predictable and safe world"? How did it aid me in reconstructing life without my sister and navigating the inevitable relational shifts with her daughter and our mother? Did psychotherapy in some way expedite my journey into madness and promise a hand on the other side? Like a detective I follow my own tracks: significant dreams, journal entries, drawings, and memories of an intimate process between Therese and me in the service of authentic growth. Is health and healing a much more mysterious, precarious reality than we wish to think? R. D. Laing, a Scottish psychiatrist whose work deeply affected me, saw schizophrenia and other mental illnesses as necessary, transformative experiences, potential breakthroughs into a healthier way of being in the world. [30]

While in previous chapters I've presented the outer circumstances leading to the psychotic break, here I want to reveal my inner state even before I began therapy. A journal entry from late February, 2013, almost three months after Lynn's death:

> It was impossible to fall apart
> when I was 12 and Dad was ill
> heart sick with deep depression
> manic-depression thru my adolescence
> and not once falling apart
> but holding it together for Lynn
> for Mom, for Dad.
> Terrified falling apart means
> I'm crazy.
> My friend Linda: "It doesn't mean you're crazy.
> It's a sign of health. You've been holding so much
> together for months." For years and years.
> 40 years...a wilderness of holding it together.
> What does falling apart look like?

Even though that was a little less than a year before I started seeing Therese, the fear of going crazy, haunted by Dad's mental illness, pulses in the words. I was conditioned to try hard to hold it all together; now I was doing it again, this time for Kim, for Mom, for Wil, for Morgan, for me. I was doing fine, most of the time – not counting the crying, normal for grieving, or exerting my control over as many situations as I could. I went head to head with Jason's mother Hannah the day before Kim's birthday celebration, a month after that entry. As I look back, that was a glaring sign that I was a lot less all right than I wanted to be. It was Kim's first birthday without her mother, and I wanted her party to be a small family affair. Heartbroken, battered by grief, having lost one of her closest friends and her son within nine days of one another, Hannah called to say that she wanted to come. I told her that it was too much for me. "It's not about you. It's about Kim. When you were away all those years, I was like a second mother to her. I bet you don't even know that.

How dare you exclude us? I'm coming." We were yelling at each other on the phone, her blinding pain pitted against mine. I knew it was crazy, but I couldn't stop. I was shaking when I pushed the "off" button. The party went fine, but what was going on with me?

It took another nine months before I got myself to Therese's office. Not until the weakness of the flu hit me did it become clear that I had reached bottom. Intensive self-therapy was over; I needed professional help. From January through May 2014 when the mania began, Therese and I met weekly – twice a month face-to-face alternating with twice a month over Skype.

Shifting Relationships

In some ways I'm still coming to terms with Lynn's death. As I look back at journal entries, while some thoughts echo still, I react to words that seem to romanticize, wrapping grief and my relationship with someone no longer here in a bubble of spiritual poesy as I move feelings and beliefs into song lyrics:

> Tu casa es mi casa
> A treasure en mi vida.
> Ahora I breathe in.
> Ahora I breathe out
> And give thanks for the blessings
> All around me.
>
> En tu jardin
> En tu jardines
> That you left here
> When you split

>   and ended this dear life
>   But you're still alive in those
>   who love you
>   Resurrected beaming your sweet might.
>   I have a feeling you weave
>   pictures in my dreams
>   the archetypes, your friends,
>   you bestow
>   signs and guideposts
>   jokes and blessings
>   like roses blooming from my back.
>
>   Maybe you're telling my story
>   as you see it
>   as I twist and wind my
>   pathway until the end
>   when I'll be joining you and
>   we'll be dancing
>   and blessing all on earth
>   and heaven too.

Wherever Lynn is, I am: we're still entwined. Therese and I talk about my relationship with my sister, our unique companionship and the ways I miss her as well as the fact that she often overshadowed me with the power of her personality. This complexity is not in the song. I am slowly adjusting to life without the power of her love, advocacy, and friendship as well as her opinions, approval, or lack thereof. As with most sisters, our relationship was complex. It was easy for us to merge, harder to individuate. Lynn and I often marveled at the power of the two of us together like twins born two years apart, two magnetic poles creating a field that mysteriously completed both of us:

she more extroverted and effervescent, I more introverted and calm. A flamboyant Chilean friend of hers who lived in Mexico where Lynn owned a condo, once offered her an observation: "You are como una cascada, a waterfall flowing into a bubbling stream, and your sister is calm como un lago, a lake."

Therese and I explore finding my identity without Lynn. I had lived for many years outside of her sphere of influence, 10 years in Texas and 10 before that in New York City. But now was now, and everything was different back in the vortex of the family. We spend many sessions talking about my relationship with my mother without Lynn, no longer a threesome. How can I be less combative? What is the aggression I feel? Why am I still blaming her for things she had no control over in the past or for things she did or for who she is? And what about Kim, Lynn's adult daughter with cerebral palsy? What is my right relationship with her? More on this as dreams emerge.

We talk about my shifting relationship with Morgan, 25 when Lynn died, as he continues to solidify his independence. I would have it no other way, but nonetheless, it is an adjustment for any parent. Another loss – I miss the closeness of our little family, which also puts more focus on my relationship with Wil.

I begin to reflect on our 29 years together, a Saturn return – when Saturn comes to the same place in the heavens as when we met in 1985. Individuals have Saturn returns but so do relationships, projects, and institutions. With Saturn, the no-nonsense planet, the ruler of time, inner and outer situations mysteriously manifest, encouraging us to face what we've learned and how it's working for us or not. In my relationship with Wil at the time I didn't want to see how resigned I was. My sleep was interrupted when he came to bed late and then snored, but I didn't want him to feel hurt if I said I wanted to sleep alone. I felt annoyed when he sequestered himself in the studio, yet I didn't want to be a nagging bitch. Why was I the one who made dinner every night unless I specifically asked for help, which I was tired of doing? There were other aspects that I carried as my burden: I did all of the finances, as if he were incapable, which he played into. Then again, when have I ever mowed the lawn? But the finances were something he needed to know about, which he was about to find out when I was hospitalized. There was still a halo around our marriage that was soon to be blasted to smithereens. That's another role of a Saturn return: if there's anything ungrounded going on, there's an energetic movement to get more real, to get healthier in the long run although it may be less than pleasant going through it at the time. Saturn is also the God of the Harvest. While our marriage was verdant with love, joy, music, and mutual respect, there was also a garden ripe for pruning and weeding.

These core relationships were creaking within old constructs, demanding adjustments, and pressurizing my sorrowful soul.

Dreams

In my first session with Therese, I presented two dreams. In the first my mother comes into my room naked and gets into the bed next to mine, which I was in with a lover. I yell, "Get out of here, you fucking bitch. Go into your own bed." That seemed pretty clear – rage! While my mother would never do that – not now, not ever – she could be invasive, and I guess I was a tad angry about it. Anger that I needed to deal with rose raw and close in my subconscious.

The other dream was seminal and a touchstone we returned to many times:

January 7, 2014

Wil and I are on the beach. It's morning and warm. I wonder if I need sunscreen then feel I'm okay without it. I put my feet in the water. Wil's swimming. I see a serpent in the water – a large sea snake; no one else, including Wil, seems to see it. As I try to get his attention, it morphs into a penguin buried in the sand. Wil says, "Look, a penguin – we should help dig it out." Then the creature easily wriggles out itself, only it's not a penguin but a slimy prehistoric, primitive thing that drops slimy shit on the beach and in the water. I'm revulsed.

From feeling relaxed on the beach, except for wondering about protection from the sun, there is a transformation first into fear – a large sea snake, threatening Wil, my love and companion. The sea monster morphs into the unlikely image of a penguin – a fascinating human-looking animal, caught, trapped in sand, hampered by what lies between earth and sea on the shore, between consciousness and the vast sea of the unconscious. The unthreatening animal needs our help and just as quickly doesn't as it shapeshifts into a primitive slime blob that defecates all over the beach and into the water, spoiling any ideas of recreation. Therese pointed out that babies shit all over everything too. "How was your mother with the uncontrollable reality of you as an infant?" she asked. I imagined she wasn't too happy. I'm disgusted by what I can't control, what's messy in the parts of me emerging from the great unconscious, wanting to be seen and integrated, including rage at my mother.

Therese and I began to unpack these complex dialogues in my psyche.

In another dream I see a celestial event in the sky as two clouds collide that only one other person sees too. "If we told the police what happened, they would put us away for being crazy." In February of 2014, was I already sensing insanity coming my way, four months before it happened? Was this a harbinger of the path I would take? What fears were stalking my psyche?

A lot of anxiety dreams – taking care of a dog that's not mine, forgetting about Morgan (he's 4 or 5 in the dream) – waking in a panic. As I review those days, I can see that I had no sense of how steeped in anxiety I was. Therese and I began reflecting on my capacity to discern and work with what I was feeling: Was I excited about something and reading it as anxiety? How could I befriend true anxiety? What did it have to teach me?

Another generative dream was dated January 28, 2014:

> *Sitting in a truck at a train station. The train is there on the track, but the doors are closed. We have to wait for the next train. I'm with Peter and Eric* (two facilitator colleagues). *We go into the station. I try to find out when the next train is leaving for Mexico City. I ask at a concession stand, but they don't have schedules. I go to another desk. They say that I have to go up to the sculpture studio – Peter says he knows the teacher – or down to the ticket office. We're on the 4th floor; the sculpture studio is on the top floor, the 6th.*
>
> *I go downstairs, thinking I'll get the tickets, but I don't know if I should just pay for Eric and Peter and get*

reimbursed – if I have enough money. I go downstairs. I ask at a booth when the train leaves for MX. He tells me. We have time. I don't get a ticket. I'm hungry. I go to a stand where someone has authentic homemade food. He's roasting four big hunks of meat. I ask what kind. "Lamb." He points to two and tells me what the others are – pork, I think. I ask for the breakfast menu; he points around the corner. There's a guy cooking a huge egg dish with layers of stuff. It looks incredible. I wonder if it has wheat; I think it's probably corn and will be all right. I go back to the menu but it's gone. I ask for it again. It's right there.

Therese works with dreams by asking me to choose the most prominent image. This one has so many – food, hunger, money, companionship, needs for direction, the train. The one loudest for me was the train standing in the station with its doors closed while I sat in a truck in the parking lot. Then she poses a series of questions, which come from her work as a SoulCollage® practitioner, to be asked to the image.[31] Most begin with a prompt, which are in capital letters.

> Who are you?
> I AM THE ONE WHO takes you where you need to be.
> I am the one who is waiting.
> I am the one who wants you to get in.
> I am the one waiting for you to ask me
>   to open the door.
> I am the one who has to get moving.
> I am the one standing still.
> I am the one grateful for my power.
> I am the one who has possibilities.

I am the one at a juncture.
I am the one following the track laid by the great
> Unknowable.

What do you have to give me?
MY GIFTS TO YOU ARE patience, satisfaction, strength, power, alacrity, motion, protection.

Is there anything else you want to tell me?
The doors will open when you are ready. I am always at the station here for you. You have the power.

How will I remember?
YOU WILL REMEMBER WHEN you feel your feet with your breath.
You will remember whenever you choose to.

Therese added one question of her own:
> What do you want from me?
> I WANT YOU TO get in.
> I want you to ask for what you need.
> I want you to stop taking the back seat.
> I want you to stand up and shout out.
> I want you to ride when you're ready.
> I want you to listen to your own time, to find
> > your own schedule.

A few months later in April, a month before my break, as the dream and God-knows-what-else ripened in my psyche, lyrics tumbled from my dream notes into a song we called "There's Time." Wil wrote inspired music and recorded it for a project we began about our family. Three months of therapy after the dream, the song shows movement, but none of us could predict just how fast the train would leave the station.

> There's Time
>
> A train stands on the tracks,
> Ready to leave the station,
> Smoking to go but not pulling out,
> Stuck in anger, rage, or frustration.
>
> As it sits there waiting to leave,
> With all of its doors shut tight,
> I'm sure that I've missed it, a ticket I need
> For the next when the time will be right.
>
> <u>Chorus</u>
> And there's time, time, plenty of time,
> Time to watch and time to wait.
> There's time, time, plenty of time,
> Time to live and time to create.
>
> Cause I am the one who is waiting
> The one who needs to be free
> (I am) the one who wants to thrive,
> To be just who I'm meant to be.
>
> The one who's got to get moving,
> And the one who's standing still.
> I am the one chugging with power,
> the one with the faithful will.
> I am the one at a juncture,
> Possibilities ripe to the core.
> I am the one hot on the tracks,

CAT GREENSTREET

Laid by the Miraculous More.

I am the one with the doors shut
That could open for all folks to see
I am the one standing here by the tracks,
The one who yearns to be free.

<u>Chorus (above)</u>

I've been gifted with a long line of patience,
Strength, creativity, power,
Protection, clarity, motion,
And now I'm beginning to flower.

I'm riding my own timetable
When the doors will be open at last
My power claimed within me
My soul freed from the past

I'll remember when I am breathing
I'll remember whenever I choose
I'll remember whenever I need to
I'll remember whenever I muse.

<u>Chorus (above)</u>

<u>Coda</u>
I'm ready to ride this train
To feel its direction and force
To celebrate the gifts of this powerful trip
Free of anger, blame, and remorse,
Full of love and hope from the Source.
Maybe I was pushing myself too hard, expecting my

grieving to be over. While I felt ready to dive back into life, maybe I wasn't really ready at all. Maybe I was. Do we get to decide what the journey is? Not usually. The image of the train resurfaced after the break. "The train had already left the station" became the way Therese and I referred to my inability to hear the ones I loved or my mental health professionals when they said that I needed help.

Drawings

Drawing was a central part of my therapeutic process in those four months before the mania, externalizing what I was thinking, feeling, and doing on a large pad, which offered me an opportunity to step back and observe different aspects of myself.

Life 2014

I am looking at one of these drawings now, called "Life 2014," which schematized the doing part and the relational part. There are three circles: red, blue, and violet. In the red one, labeled "service, work, research, passion, activism," are

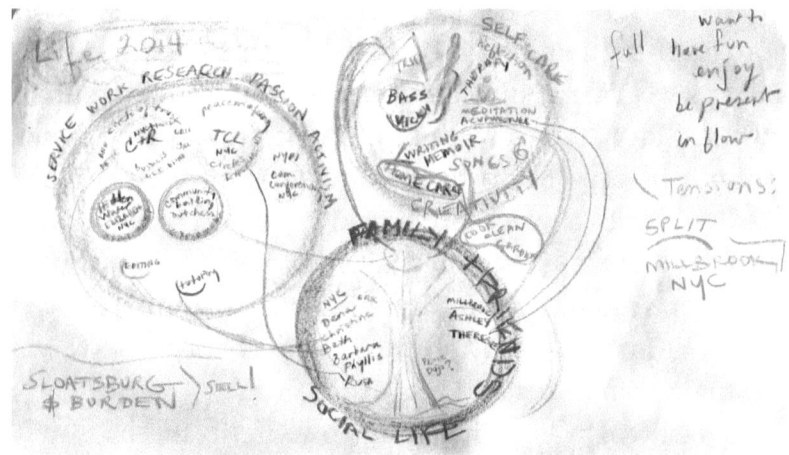

smaller circles – Circles of Trust, Transforming Conflict Lab and peacemaking circles in NYC, Community Conferencing, Hidden Water, and an empty placeholder circle, labeled Community Building in Dutchess County. Nearby were two tentative half circles – marked editing and tutoring. (It's interesting now, as I write this, to notice that Circles of Trust and community building in Dutchess County are the only things that have not fallen away.)[32]

Lines are drawn from the red circle to a large blue one, dubbed "family and friends, social life," in the center of which is a tree with Wil, Morgan, Kim, and Mom written over the branches; on the left side is a list of seven New York City friends, on the right a list of two Village friends. At the top are connecting lines from the blue circle to the violet circle, marked "self-care, creativity." Inside it is a triangle with "Trio" inside, a band I was playing in with Wil and a drummer friend; a picture of a bass guitar, my instrument; the name of my bass student; writing memoir; home care; songs, garden, therapy, meditation, reflection, acupuncture, painting with a question mark. As I look at it now, I'm choking on how much is listed on this page. And wait…it's not done yet.

On the right it says in red "full – want to have fun, enjoy, be present, in flow" – and below that "Tensions: split Millbrook/NYC". Lynn could handle going back and forth between Manhattan and Millbrook; there was no reason I shouldn't be able to do the same. But Lynn was working there two days a week and making a significant part of her income there; she rented a place and later bought an apartment. Again, I wasn't Lynn! On the left in red it says, "House, $ Burden – Sell!" Our old house, not yet sold, was stressing our finances and me.

How hard I was trying to fill my life to the brim with

goodness! While there was an exuberance of activity, from the post-episode perspective there was also a level of desperation to fill the void both of Lynn's exit from earth and my life, and of the end of a 20-year plus career as an educator. I needed everything in this drawing to tell me who I was, so I could tell other people. No blame. We do what we must. There are no shoulds in the grieving process. I feel compassion for my self, determined to survive and construct a new life as I doggedly tried to pick up where I had left off after leaving it all to care for Lynn. I was the same person, still interested in restorative justice, in facilitating circles. I just had farther to travel; Lynn did that commute for years, so there wouldn't be a problem. I had started anew many times before, creating a life both satisfying and helpful to the world. I could do it again. But something was troubling me, which was why I drew the picture in the first place, a feeling that persisted like thick fog after a storm regardless of – or maybe because of – all the activity.

Trauma

In an effort to see the pattern of trauma in my life, I drew little pictures of each unsettling point of pain between birth and 22, at least the ones I remembered. I placed these little scenes within a warm orange egg that blended into a yellow background. Outside the egg at the bottom, I wrote, "All Welcome," affirming that everything within my psyche has its place, the nurturing feminine loving each piece into the wholeness I am. At the top inside the egg, expressing an overarching feeling and title, "Something is terribly wrong...." Outside the egg on the lower left, "trauma" in black; upper left, "my beginning" in turquoise; upper right in a cloud of blue and green squiggly lines, "Smith, dream

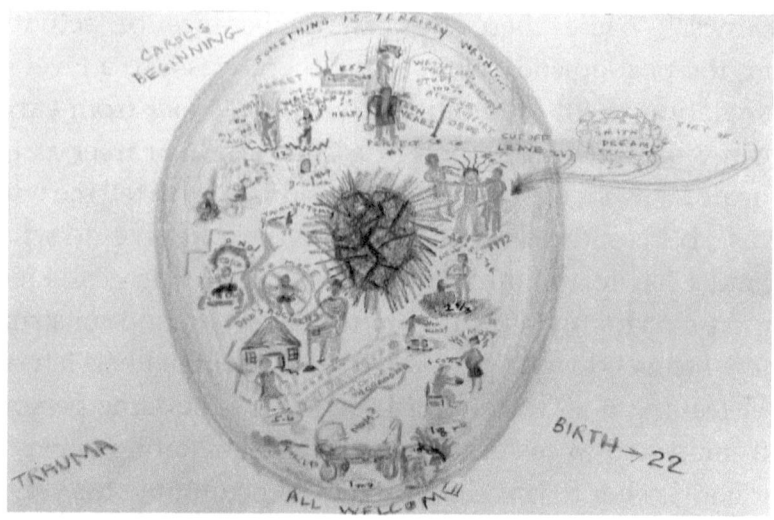

come true...sort of..." pointing to something in the egg, which I'll get to later.

At the bottom of the egg, the traumas begin. First is a pregnant mother next to a curtain set on fire by a lamp underneath it. Mom, in her eighth month, had been cleaning vigorously - the way pregnant women will - when she unthinkingly placed the curtain over the lamp. Before she could detect where the smell was coming from, the curtain was ablaze. Terror must have surged from her through my still developing body. "That was a pre-birth trauma," Therese said. I'd never framed it that way, but of course it was. The next picture was the birth itself, a forceps birth. Was it traumatic to have metal claws around my head with someone pulling, "helping" me leave the womb? I guess. The next trauma came a week or so later when Mom hopped in the car to go shopping while I lay sleeping in the carriage outside our little bungalow in the back of my grandparents' home. After turning the ignition, backing up, and driving the car down the driveway past the carriage to the street, she suddenly realized that her infant was in that carriage. Do newborns sense where their mothers are physically and mentally, and if they've forgotten their existence? I believe they do. Was this the only time that happened? It's the one she remembers, one of those funny stories.

Moving clockwise up the egg, there's a picture of an 18-month-old sitting on a potty. A bubble over the little girl reads, "I can't." Mom, pregnant, stands over the girl with the words saying, "You must." She did not want to have two children in diapers. That wasn't going to happen, and it was up to me to get it together even if it was developmentally unlikely, if not impossible. Is this the seed of never feeling good enough? I feel angry writing this, blame rising in my blood and not wanting my 90-something-year-old mom or me to be dragged back through this litany of blame. But I must continue: it was all part of the process before the mania.

A little girl has three question marks over her head. Her mother holds a baby. "New sister," written above; "2⅓" below. It's always confusing, even for the best-prepared children, when a new being arrives on the scene to usurp the attention of Mom, Dad, aunts, uncles, Grandma, and Grandpa. I don't remember much about that baby until later. All I do remember is feeling confused, abandoned, and alone as she came into our house for the first time.

There's a little drawing of the two of us playing on the floor and Mom hollering, "You kids!" I think the volume of her yelling alone, not to mention the anger behind it, was traumatic for me. Yes, I was and still am a sensitive one, "spiritually sensitive," Therese calls it.

The next image shows a train, under which reads, "Chicago with Grandma," and a little girl, five years old, who was about to enter first grade. It was summer, and we were going to visit my father's sister and family. I was told that Grandma was afraid to take the train by herself and that I would get to go with her, sleep over in the train, and take care of her. It was important that I not look like I was reading because they were buying me the cheaper ticket for under five years old. Was I reading already? Was I not reading yet and had to pretend that I wasn't reading the book I was just looking at? And how could I take care of Grandma? I can't even remember her being with me until we climbed next to each other into a little sleeping compartment. When we couldn't find the water to brush our teeth before going to sleep, I was a little panicked, thirsty too, and too shy to say anything. Was I supposed to fix this somehow, get us out of this predicament? Would she function? Could she? I can't remember who suggested calling the porter. She pushed a button, and a kind man very politely showed us a very nifty little compartment. We laughed, seeing how obvious it was, both relieved. I hardly ever saw my grandmother laugh, so that was reassuring. Maybe she was not as formidable as I thought. Each picture opened up significant memories that Therese and I had a chance to explore, heal, and invite into the wholeness of my psyche.

Continuing clockwise, there is a picture of a girl in a tutu, dancing. It's circled with a slash through it and label over it saying, "No more." This little girl is around six. She loved to dance unselfconsciously, solo for parents, family, and friends in the living room. She begged for dancing lessons, but that was out of the question. No money. No time. No. One Sunday the family went to a bazaar at the Temple. There was entertainment, and one of the numbers was a 12-year-old ballerina, the real deal, wearing the pink tutu and standing on point. I watched, eyes wide, mesmerized; I wanted to be her. My mother's father, Philip, a stocky, gruff man with rough hands and round ruddy face, who rarely spoke directly to me, leaned over to say quietly just to me, "She dances just like you, Carol." His mocking sarcasm sliced through me, before I even had words for that kind of meanness. I ignored him, knowing full well that I would never get to dance like that gifted young ballerina. Determined to have no visible reaction, I channeled seething rage and humiliation into a vow that I would never dance for any of them ever again. And I never did. Thankfully, it didn't stop me from dancing by myself and with friends.

Written in red is a label "Dad's accidents" with a little drawing to the left – a car, a woman lying in the street, and a person saying, "O No!" When I was about 7, my father had driven our babysitter home around midnight. Another car ran a red light and hit my father's car. Mrs. Goldfinger's collarbone was broken; we never saw her again. My father was in the hospital with six broken ribs and a fractured cheekbone. We didn't visit him there; they didn't allow children in hospitals in those days. When he did come home, after almost a week, Mom firmly instructed us not to jump on him as we loved to do. He was bandaged, and it was scary seeing him so fragile. Combined with that memory is one I neglected to draw: Mom asked me to tell our neighbors that my birthday party, scheduled for the day after the accident, was canceled. It's almost unimaginable, but I couldn't have invented the look of compassion on the face of my friend's mother.

Another trauma at five or six: a picture of a little girl on a red bed, a mask over her face, with a figure in black, wielding a knife looming over her. "Tonsillectomy" is written above it. I had to go first because, as I heard mom say to the nurses, "If she hears Lynn screaming, she'll refuse to go." How was that for preparation? My poor mom, she really didn't know what to do, did she? So in I went. Three people – the doctor and two nurses – strapped my arms down, terrifying enough, and brought a mask over my nose and mouth, leaving me no choice but to inhale the sharp, foreign gas, called ether, inciting the panic of not being able to breathe the air I knew. Why were these people smothering me? I seemed to wake almost instantly following that thought but with a terrible sore throat. The only up side was that we could eat as much ice cream as we wanted.

Orange jagged lines separate one trauma and the next. They connect to form a network – as one is sparked, the others animate in response, all traumas psychically linked.

A picture of a girl with a ponytail, wearing a purple shirt, shows her riding a bicycle, and right next to that, the girl all blue, reading a book and wondering, "Am I okay?" A composite memory of growing independence at nine: I was able to ride my bike to my friend Jill's house, even crossing busy Chestnut Street. I could visualize how to get back home, the geography of my neighborhood becoming clear for the first time. I felt alive and grown-up. The next thing I remember is Mom holding my wrist a few times a day, looking worried as she stared at the clock and counted the pulses. She took me to the doctor, a nurse slapping cold gooey stuff on different parts of my arms, legs, and chest as I lay on the table, hooked up to a machine with wires. Even though it looked scary, it didn't hurt, which was a relief.

My mother told me that I might have rheumatic fever, something Dad had as a child. What was that? It sounded bad. They wouldn't know for a week or so. Until then, I was to rest, no school, no bicycling. Mom gave me one of her favorite books, *Death Be Not Proud* by John Gunther, something she had on the shelf that she thought I'd like. She was right: I couldn't put it down. It was about Gunther's handsome, brilliant son who had brain cancer and died at the age of 17. I remember crying in the backyard in the spring sunshine. What kind of book is that to give to an almost 10-year-old? After missing a week of school, I was told that there was nothing wrong with me.

Next, a tombstone and rain falling with "Grandma" written beneath it. I was 11, Lynn nine; Mom's Mom, beloved Grandma Ross, got sick and died at 59 years old. It was my first experience of death. The house filled with family, friends, strangers from the Temple, bearing little stacked deli sandwiches with roast beef, corn beef, and pastrami and alternating cold slaw, which New Jersey Jews call sloppy joes; cakes, babkas, pastries; lasagna – more food than we could ever eat in that week of sitting shiva. Lynn and I found each other in the bathroom and cuddled under the sink, exchanging shy smiles as natural as the sun peaking from behind fast-moving clouds and as awkward as children facing the unfathomable disappearance of a loved one.

"Oh, no!" says the girl in the little picture. "My fault" is written alongside, which is what I thought at the time, oddly the same thought that brought me back into my body: if I were a boy, Daddy would be happy. That's what made sense to my 12-year-old self, ear against the door, hearing that my father wanted to kill himself, the farthest thing from my mind. A drawing of Mom on the phone on the other side of the door. I could help by being incredibly good, perfect in fact, not rocking the boat in any way – the warping logic of a child hanging on for dear life to her sanity, to actual consciousness in that moment of hearing a catastrophic truth. Underneath the drawing is a brown jagged line, broken at the door and "12" circled to indicate the core trauma.

At the top of the egg, drawings depict the teen years. Dad lying on a bed, all blue with red on his head and rays coming out – electroshock therapy. Seeing the effects this had on him is not portrayed but implied and remembered. Over the word "home" is Dad all red, slouching with a cloud over his head and gray rain falling around him. An arrow and the words "Watch over" point there. I have weights hanging from both shoulders, carrying the burden of a father with a mental illness. Early on we were instructed not to talk with anyone, even our best friends, about family matters: "no airing dirty laundry" in public. Under the girl carrying the burden, it says, "Perfect #1, 100% achieve, support. "

Eyes point to "Leave," and at 18 I do. Yellow streams outside the egg, where it says, "Smith dream come true" in a cloud, then the words "sort of…." It was 1966, and finally away from home for the first time, I soon realized how depressed I was. Leaving home triggered a destabilization; although they had their liberating moments, smoking weed and taking psychedelic drugs delivered me to my first acute psychotic break, a manic episode. Red and blue arrows point back inside the egg to me being held by two men in red, 1972, black on my head with wiggly waves of electroshock therapy radiating out. At one point when I was 17, I had stood up to my mother, exclaiming that I would never let her authorize electroshock for Dad again. Ironically, they had to agree that I receive EST at 22. For a long time I felt utterly betrayed. Luckily, lithium worked for Dad, and neither mood swings nor severe depression ever returned.

In the center of the egg is a heart, black with brown cracks within it and rays reaching out in every direction. Is the heart shattered or broken open? At the time I drew this, I thought the latter. Again I hear Lynn's prophesy - "You're going to shatter" - as she looked deep into my eyes, maybe reading my aura, from her sickbed. But I was actively doing the inner work I needed to do, growing stronger and stronger day by day, week by week. I was grateful to be doing this trauma healing with Therese. "You are holding all of that trauma in yourself," she said as she gazed at the drawing. At this point, around two months before the mania began, all seemed constructively contained within that golden egg of my being. I could see it, reflect on it, honor it, and honor my self and my process. Sure, that broken heart had to heal, but it was doing the best it could; time was doing its work. I was actively embracing the trauma of my early life, yet my mysterious soul obviously needed something deeper, a more thorough transformation.

I continued drawing pictures. Energy 1: I'd been doing qigong. A red-orange ball rose from the dantian (core) and warmed the golden heart chakra, the green throat chakra and the mind; the red-orange ball also reached down into the earth, spreading its roots. A ball of gold and orange surrounded the core. Maybe qigong was stirring the energy pot more than I knew; maybe it wasn't. "I am standing in the midst of bliss," the teacher repeated in his classes and on his DVD. Maybe the bliss was a little too much for me; maybe it was just a sound track for what would have happened anyway.

In one drawing labeled "Rebirth," I stand solidly on the earth, dressed in blue boots, blue pants, a red shirt, hair draped around my shoulders, my heart glowing, my dantian strong. Behind me is an egg broken open. Maybe the broken egg was a foreshadowing. I thought the egg symbolized my broken heart birthing a new me, but obviously the solidity I portrayed, felt, and longed for didn't hold or needed deeper integration. The drawing is dated April 25th, 2014.

Therese and I talked about the expectations weighing on me, one huge one being new responsibilities around Kim, Lynn's handicapped daughter. What does that look like with Lynn gone? Was there an expectation from the dead, from Amy, from Mom, from Kim that I step into Lynn's shoes? But how could I? Therese helped me articulate that I could never fill the void for Kim left by her mother's death, nor was it my responsibility to do so. No one could dictate to the living from the other side.

The ensuing sense of relief from that session inspired the next drawing, titled "Release." I'm sitting cross-legged on an orange floor in a yellow room, wearing black shoes, red pants, and a blue shirt. My hands unlock a thick black choker from around my neck. There is a red heart on my chest behind my hands. Red arrows are drawn between the collar on my neck and the floor, where the collar and a key lie. Date, April 27th, one month before full-blown mania. Maybe my psyche wasn't strong enough to contain the release from my self-imposed bondage. Or maybe I had to go through something harrowing, a trial or initiation, a point of no return, before

the ground for authentic integration could be laid.

More Dreams and Journal Entries

As seen in hindsight, dreams and journal entries echoed an encroaching reality of variable warnings that something was rumbling in my soul like a far-off storm. At the end of March, I kept losing or misplacing things – keys, a scarf, an earring. I left my glasses in Whole Foods and had no idea where I had placed them. It was unsettling how many things seemed to disappear although some returned just as mysteriously. Why was I so spacey? More and more I wondered if I was losing it. A dream after my glasses vanished, which, by the way, I found in the trunk of Mom's car:

> *In a large university, there's a performance happening on the big stage. A magician leads it. He's calling people up on the stage. A couple of people signal to me that he wants me to come up. I say – no – it's for children – I'm not a child. Then I see another woman helping the kids and realize that's why he wants me there, to help. I need to go to another level to get there. I have to go down to come up to where the stage is. I go in, and there's a slide down into the gym. I don't have to go the whole way but can take stairs in the middle of the slide. It leads to the library. Someone is giving a talk and will read some excerpts from Dracula....I find the stage and am finding my way to it.*

The learning complex – "large university" suggests a major learning is happening. I assert, "I'm not a child." Good place to start. A magician needs my help; I can do that. But I "have to go to another level to get there." That's interesting. "I have to go down to come up," where this new stage in my life is; I have to slide down to the depths to the gym, where you workout. I can move through the library, a comfortable way through book learning, but I'm repelled by the librarian reading the seminal vampire horror story. I move away from a place, whose story can drain me of life force. Are there other people or situations sucking my lifeblood? In the dream I find the stage and help the children, maybe my inner children, which is reassuring.

I was working hard to heal from my grief as well as resolve deeper issues and integrate old traumas as efficiently as I could. Another dream:

Planning offerings at the college, there may not be space. I'm raising my arm and a colleague says, "You're so thin! Do you have diabetes?" Feeling – oh, no, something's wrong with me!

When I woke, memories of the hypomanic episode of 2001 flooded in, my psyche churning. As Therese once suggested, since the hypomania was curbed in 2001, perhaps, there was much that still needed resolving but couldn't be at the time. In the dream I seem alarmed that there may be something deeply wrong with me. That was at the end of March.

Around that time I woke in the middle of the night feeling like my limbs were out of control. This was not a dream. I was sure I was having a low sodium event since contracting muscles and shaking are symptoms. Wil called 911. In the ER they gave me valium, which resolved whatever was happening. My sodium turned out to be normal, which surprised me. Although the ER doctor didn't say so, the diagnosis must have been an anxiety attack. I ignored this sign of increasing anxiety.

At the same time I was struggling with my relationship

with Kim. I felt stuck with the weight of Lynn's hopes and plans for Kim: her continuing to live independently. I was trying my best to consciously face what was now before me. In early April I tried to take a step back from my involvement with her, and she freaked out. "This is what you signed up for," she shrieked hysterically into the phone, responding out of her own fear of abandonment. I didn't fucking sign up for this, I wanted to scream but fortunately didn't.

> *We're watching from a distance. A woman is lying down. I know she's having a seizure. There are people there to deal with it. I don't have to do anything. I watch as other people take care of her, but I'm shook up. A man is in uniform. He's in charge of blowing the sirens. "When do you do that?" some women ask. They're making fun a little. He says, "When something's happening near the shore. It lets people know there's danger."*

While Kim has 24/7 care, a psychologist, a psychiatrist, a social worker, a physical therapist, an occupational one too, and a job coach, I'm still shaken by how much help she needs. What is my part? What is not? And the shore, again, the place between consciousness and the unconscious, where so much transformation is possible – this time a man will blow a siren when there is danger. Is my psyche preparing, warning me?

Therese was helping me find my right relationship with Kim as her aunt. By late April the tension was mounting, and I write in my journal:

> It's not my job to fix Kim – to grow her up, to do anything I don't want to. I have no responsibility here – I have a relationship, a growing relationship of caring.

> I can expect little from her. Anything that comes from Kim to me is a pure gift. I would like to have a 'normal' relationship that an aunt might have with a niece. I don't really know what that means. She is my only niece. I need to give myself permission to explore what that is, to find what feels right and feels possible.

I was finding my way out of the blackness of grief into a new way of being. I didn't know where I was going, except that I was committed to healing. I was striving intensely – maybe too intensely – the way I'd worked on everything in my adult life: my posture with an Alexander Technique teacher, my vision with a world-renowned specialist, my trauma with Therese and Dr. Andrew, my qi with the qigong master. This was interspersed with listening to online lectures on shamanism, self-acceptance, and neuropsychology. Could I have blown my own mind with self-help overload? I wasn't wearing my glasses at the time, except for driving and facilitating circles when I needed to see clearly so that others wouldn't be harmed. Otherwise, I could see only blurred images. I walked myopically through the fuzzy streets of the City, at home, wherever I was. I was fine in the fog with moments of incredible clarity as I repeated like a mantra the specifics of the visual system taught by my teacher. I was keen on healing my vision and convinced it was actually improving.

As my journal reveals, in mid-April I addressed my myopia with three of the five questions Therese and I used with dream images:

> Who are you? I AM THE ONE WHO doesn't want to see things in focus or too clearly. I am protecting you in the fog of existence.

> What do you have to give me? I GIVE YOU protection from seeing the truth that was too much for you to bear. I give you a place to hide.
> What do you want from me? I WANT YOU TO heal me. I see with courage. I want you to stop straining and relax.

Journal, April 16, 2014, a month before launch:

> I believed the story that I was sickly & weak & fragile. I lived the story. Things happened. I was susceptible to mental instability. I was hospitalized for insanity – a break – drug-infused but not initiated. My shaman says that it was good. My therapist says that it was important.

Therese and I were exploring vocational possibilities: what was it that I wanted to do in this new stage of my life? How did I want to spend my energy? On April 7, I journaled in response to a poem I offered in a monthly friends circle:

> We can create warm currents in which to brood the new age. Let's do it together. We can seek what stirs our blood, what leads our way. We create harbors where conversations can happen, where we can talk about our woundedness and show our scars.

In another entry from early May:

> Where to put my energy? Feeling a need to focus. Seems there's not enough facilitation work – how to create more and serve my need to contribute where there has been harm done? Do I really want that or was that a detour?

My identity seems shaky as I explored, questioning next steps, feeling for the way forward.

On my birthday, May 8, 2014, I lay in bed, the early morning sunlight connecting me to myself at 21 before my 1972 psychotic break. I got up and wrote:

> Being in Apache Canyon, NM – what I loved –
> experiencing the essence of my being for the first time,
> consciously experiencing my multifaceted self. I had
> little context for who I was.

I thought about the struggle of having to leave that place and being faced with where to unfold. It was a time of revolutionary ideals. How would we change the world, on the streets or on a rural commune? I was struggling with my self, yet I was part of a "we" that overshadowed my own budding identity and autonomy. I seemed to have no choice but to be with this group until something snapped.

> When I broke out of all I'd known, trying to live in
> the reality of the seen and unseen messages – I was
> incarcerated and zapped to bring me back to reality – a
> reality that could help me ground myself in the world by
> serving it – editing, teaching, living in community where
> people depended on me to show up... but Spirit was
> banished.

Why did I wake up on my 66th birthday reviewing my first psychotic break? Was this another foreshadowing? Was psyche getting me ready? It didn't feel like it at the time: I felt strong and on a healing path.

I was beginning to take off but still here, in a state of spiritual emergence but not yet an emergency; a poem, dated 5/10/14, was born:

> All threads dropped
>   cut off
>   buried
> are reemerging
>   only this time
> rewoven in a tapestry
>   of miracles.
> Tapestry of tears
>   of melting fears
>   of wounds blowing down
>   at the spring of life everlasting
>   healing times
>   healing times
>
> I'm finding my voice
>   the deep one
>   the one that cracked from the strain
>   the one that so wants to heal
>   and be whole so it can
> play and ray, reaching for star dust.
> Feet, you with me?
> I want you with me, too.

Maybe my feet didn't hear the plea. So many dreams each week, so many images. Less than two weeks before lift-off, Mother's Day at Mom's, I had trouble sleeping, and when I finally did, this disquieting dream came:

A teeny baby is lying on the floor on a blanket. I hover over it. As I touch it, it seems to be dying. I touch its penis, and it falls off. I save the life of the baby and take it to its mother to see if it is dying, if she can save it. She'll know what to do.

This is dire. What has been born is deforming and dying. The creativity of the masculine, that which goes into the world, inexplicably breaks off. It needs the nurturing feminine who may be able to save it.

At that time, my mind was burgeoning, like the plants in the flower garden, one creative idea after the other about what I or we could do: host community concerts in our home, become a board member of a women in jazz organization, found Hawk Feather Center for Healing & Justice and offer healing retreats. I wrote that I yearned to "be in the flow of life - alive to all around me."

While I was documenting in my journal my unhealthy leanings, which I now know as warning signs of budding mania, I wasn't sharing them with Therese or anyone else:

> tendencies – to not be hungry –
> not to eat, to RARIFY
> tensions – to not be able to sleep –
> to be too AWAKE, I need to metabolize more...
> on a journey to an integrated life
> I can feel it becoming clear.

And I was in it all by myself, a definite red flag.

May 15 was the day I was scammed:

> No sleep last night – finally talk with Wil about 'shaman' John incident weeks before. Coyote came to visit me – saw him – realized not a dog, Coyote. Then feel for Coyote's tricks. How to learn to discern while still being open to spirit reality?[33]

May 18, writing verse for songs:

> I'm keeping farmer's hours, waking with the dawn
> and musician's hours,
> deep into the night.
> That's when the music happens
> and the spirits bring their feast...

The spirits were bringing their feast all right, in buckets. The journal trails off into effusive notes, planning the transformation of the world as we know it: healing Waldorf education, healing the county where I live with each village becoming a 21st century reality. The ideas were thinking me, keeping me from sleeping, eating, relating to others, or functioning in any normal way, my mind off on its own intensely compelling journey.

Reflections

Why so much detail? Who needs to read or know all of this? Compared to other people's trauma, I've led a privileged life. And yet I feel compelled to raise the unanswerable questions: would I have had a psychotic break without therapy, or might I have gone nuts sooner without it? I might have gotten increasingly depressed instead of manic. I was in a pretty down place when I started seeing Therese. This review of dreams, drawings, journals, and songs documents the amount of anxiety I was embodying and trying to process.

Forgiving my mother was a major step in starting to live my life in a new way; it was a turning point in our relationship to be sure. We didn't need to agree; we didn't need to argue. I didn't need to shore myself up against her.

In fact, I could soften and just be with her with love and gratitude while still being mindful of my own needs and attending to them. That was not her job or her fault if I didn't do what I needed to do. My ego had been organized for so long around blaming her for various aspects of our lives, including Dad's illness. I had created an identity around that blame, not speaking to either of my parents from when I was 26 to 36. There is still the pain I caused, which we process from time to time; we are healing.

Gratitude and forgiveness began when I had a child as it does with so many of us when we begin our own parenting. When we lived far away in Texas for 10 years, I had no context in which to further heal the relationship with only two visits a year. But now with Dad dead over 15 years and without Lynn as an element in our mother-daughter chemistry, I squarely faced – with self-compassion – the last of my blame-based organization. Something turned when I released needing anything from her. I didn't need her to take care of me; in fact, the opposite was increasingly true. My ego organization had to have been disorganized by this new no-blame way of relating. Everything in my psyche needed to find a new balance. Would everyone experience mania after going through a fundamental change in a core relationship? No, of course not, we are individuals, and I do have a genetic predisposition to bipolar disorder that probably goes back generations.

Doggedly facing old traumas – digging, tapping, claiming – until each was held like a geode broken open, crystalline in the stratum of my psyche. Self-acceptance and self-nurturing began to quell the voices of self-criticism, minimization, and low self-esteem. Therese validated authentic self, pointing out whenever I cast myself in a negative light, teaching me how to acknowledge and reframe. And although I had begun this work myself in the year following Lynn's death, Therese as loving witness was helping me walk a path of wellbeing. Neither of us knew what was ahead.

I first presented to Therese in a knot of grief and depression, and she midwifed my adept emerging. I was ready. She may have sensed that I needed more grounding: we worked on it in almost every session, but we had "time, time, plenty of time." Can anyone, even a psychotherapist, truly know where another person is? Clearly not. I don't think she expected me to stop therapy so abruptly, but I did. I was feeling great! I was done. We'd done our work. She convinced me to have at least one more session. I was a little annoyed.

I wrote her a poem, a summary praising our work together. We were both moved and cried over Skype as I read it to her:

> ....You helped me stand and learn from what's inside me,
> you helped me summon everything I am, all the gifts
> I have and had abandoned, discounted. You saw me,
> you saw them, you pointed to everything you saw. And
> the gifts are weaving their way home into the tapestry
> of my being.
>
> You walked with me across the bridge
> from life woven with my sister, uprooted into
> the fullness of my life in bloom,
> with everyone my sisters and brothers,
> the beloved community I yearned for always here,
> waiting for me through my walk through
> the valley of the shadow.
> Thank you.
> I emerge with tools for most occasions,
> with books and cards and oracles for years,

with me, my body, poetry, and stories. Not fragile,
resilient. I'm here, now, walking, on my way.

You walked me through the passage until I could see
through the trauma
I'm picking up the gifts, they're coming in.
I'm born anew on this 66th birthday.
The weather system clearing, almost passed,
contract signed, closing on the horizon.
Images of new life everywhere,
living now the sweet excitement of life at 21,
my inevitable cracking, a jail break embraced.

I'm here.
And you're here. And we're walking
the labyrinth of life.

Thank you for being who you are.
For your loving, generous, welcoming, nurturing being.
For your wisdom and centered, grounded strength….

I was finally emerging from under the dark cloud of a year and a half of grief. Perhaps, what ignited the fuse was the spark of my beloved community as I joined 150 people at the Global Gathering that May. Even though I loved being there, I had no idea how open and vulnerable I was. I can see now that I needed a stronger vessel to navigate the soul complexity alive in this facilitator community. There was too much fire, positive creative energy, more than my transforming being could actually bear. As the sun shined brightly, I merged with diamonds shimmering on the waters when suddenly a soaring wave came and took me with it.

In a May 4 journal entry, written at the Gathering, whose

theme was roots and leaves, a song began to sing inside me:

> My tree was uprooted
> when she died,
> our roots on earth
> entangled, yours here
> quickly died
> and mine...oh, mine
> you said I would be
> devastated. You warned me.
> I was being strong and
> could not hear.
> I knew that I would live
> whatever happened.
> I never thought
> what you said would be true.
>
> But we don't know until we get there
> what our lives will bring,
> lessons harsh and kind and all between.
> We don't know until we get there
> the gifts it all can sing
> if we live it to the fullest
> one step at a time.

This emergent song foreshadowed something coming. The praise song to Therese was already hypomania beginning to unfurl its ribbons. Even as I probe into its causes, I keep coming back to the questions. Did some greater eruption of psyche need to occur for the pieces to come together into a new, more balanced way of living? Was one missing piece my need to face the reality of the bipolar gene I was sure I'd overcome, a gene now laid bare without the scaffolding of work, with the grieving of Lynn's loss, and with ensuing core relationship adjustments? And what about a neurobiological need for medication? Yes and yes and yes.

As I look back on the terrain a few months before take off, there's something eerily exquisite and faithfully courageous in the psyche's insistence to heal, to be whole, to integrate no matter how treacherous the journey. As R. D. Laing wrote in *The Politics of Experience*, "Madness need not be all breakdown. It may also be break-through. It is potential liberation and renewal as well as enslavement and existential death."[34]

How then did I have the faith, grace, and grit to live through the manic episode, becoming the light, and then "through the valley of the shadow" to the other side?[35] What enabled me to move in the direction of wholeness and renewal instead of floundering in extended madness, fracturing, and death? What in the fabric of my self and my relationships was conducive to reweaving instead of continued unraveling? What and who surrounded me that supported my healing, recovery, and resilience?

Part III
A New Integration of Self

…the given world that we think is there, and the solid ground we are on, is so tentative. And I think a threshold is a line which separates two territories of spirit, and I think that very often how we cross is the key thing…. when we cross a new threshold, that if we cross worthily, what we do is we heal the patterns of repetition that were in us that had us caught somewhere. And in our crossing, then, we cross onto new ground, where we just don't repeat what we've been through in the last place we were. So I think beauty, in that sense, is about an emerging fullness, a greater sense of grace and elegance, a deeper sense of depth, and also a kind of homecoming for the enriched memory of your unfolding life.

– John O'Donohue

9
Recovery and Resilience

> And so there must be in life something like a catastrophic turning point, when the world as we know it ceases to exist. A moment that transforms us into a different person from one heartbeat to the next....
> Or are such moments merely the dramatic conclusions of lengthier processes, conclusions we could have foreseen if we had only read the portents rather than disregarding them?
> Jan-Philipp Sendker

I lived through a "catastrophic turning point," of that I'm certain. It wasn't the first time; of course, I want it to be the last. Flying to the heights of creativity and freedom inevitably meant falling to the depths at the hands of those implementing our societal way of dealing with people experiencing mania. The seclusion room and the wrong psychotropic drug led to a near-death experience when my sodium level plummeted. The final hospital stay was "the dramatic conclusion" of a much lengthier process that perhaps I might have foreseen if I wanted to read the tealeaves. But neither I nor anyone else even knew they were in the cup. By the time they had spilled in my lap, boiling water and all, I refused to read them. I had long before rejected the genetic inheritance of bipolar disorder from my father. Not me, no way. Once I was hospitalized, I was aware the psychotic break was a major turning point; however, I never could have predicted how I would be from that side to this. I guess it is impossible to know from one side of a threshold what life will be on the other side. My intention always was to cross this new threshold "worthily," as John O'Donohue put it, so I would heal deeply "what had me caught somewhere."

It's Good Friday 2016 as I write this. Often on this day, Jesus's words as told in Matthew 27:46 are on my mind: "My God, my God, why have you forsaken me?" This question, crying out through the ages, reveals a Man-God apparently forsaken by his God as he hangs on a cross, the nadir of his "catastrophic turning point." Perhaps, that is the archetype, the stamp on each of our lives. It rings true for me. I felt utterly forsaken that morning in the seclusion room when no words would or could come from my mouth. What if that moment of feeling forsaken *is* the turning point, the eye of the needle, the ineluctable now that must be lived – alone – regardless of belief or faith? As the story goes, the miracle of resurrection can only occur following a journey through the land of the dead; and resurrection itself, as it was for Christ Jesus, is an incremental process.

Part III reveals my journey from the land of the dead as I slowly found my way to a new integration of self, crossing "onto new ground, where we just don't repeat what we've been through in the last place we were." To show shifts that took place within the first two years after the psychotic break, I offer a chronological look, following my experience of what happened when I resumed psychotherapy and reentered my life. Journal entries, essays, and poetry, my own and that of real poets, starting a month after I was released from the private hospital, tell the story of recovery and reweaving. Bathed in questions, the resilience within me gradually, miraculously bubbled, rebirthing me into a new way of being in the world.

Being

I am a verb,
not a noun, a thing.

I am a seeker,
a being,
a this, a that.

I am a person with a
diagnosis, with a psychiatrist
and moods
to be or not to be
stabilized. I am
angry about all of that.

I am a grammarian.
"A verb" is already
a noun. I am
free. That statement is,
or could be,
true.

What is free, besides
an adjective? Really?
I am? Are you?
Who are we
together, apart?

July 26, 2014

10
Psychotherapy and Other Self-Care

...our 'normal' 'adjusted' state is too often the abdication of
ecstasy, the betrayal of our true potentialities....
— R.D. Laing

That was my biggest fear. If I succumbed to a diagnosis of bipolar disorder with a life-long Depakote prescription, would I abdicate ecstasy and betray my "true potentialities"? Therese didn't think so, nor did Dr. Wilson. I wondered.

After a month of hospitalizations, I was back with Therese, a session every other week in her office, every other week on Skype, searching to understand, to assess what this "catastrophic turning point" meant. But why had the psychosis happened at all? Why couldn't I control a manic surge as I had in 2001? And who was I now? I felt fragile, and I was. I weighed under 100 pounds – in "the double-digits" as Dr. Wilson called it. I had finally capitulated and was taking a drug to stabilize my moods; I still inwardly recoiled at the idea of having a diagnosis. I stated my case to both of them: I had had only three manic episodes in 44 years; depressions were non-existent or at least not severe, nothing I couldn't handle. I wasn't on a seesaw of ups and downs like my father. Therese acknowledged that I was indeed atypical but didn't see my argument as a reason to stop taking the medication, as I had hoped.

Dr. Wilson didn't either. I was seeing him once a month, so he could make sure the meds were working, the dosage was correct, and side effects were minimal. He insisted that he didn't care much about labels: he was, though, interested in how I was doing. Was I sleeping? Was I eating? How were my moods? Were there any side effects? I wondered what he could do about them if there were. He reminded me that a significant percentage of people, especially women, had recurrences of mania as they grew older. I didn't want to hear it; I wasn't a percentage. "You don't want to risk going through that again, do you?" he asked. "And what about your family?" That got my attention. In fact, before Morgan went back to his life in the City, he had me sign an agreement that I wouldn't go off my meds without consulting with Wil and him, Therese, and Dr. Wilson. That was fair enough; I signed.

My process in psychotherapy this time around was different: no drawing between sessions, instead journaling and lots of writing, this writing. I shared some with Wil but only now and then when certain sections asked to be read, giving us the opportunity to process parts of the experience and for me to hear his perspective.

"I was terrified that you would never come back. What would I do without you? They wouldn't let me talk with you when you were in the seclusion room. They said it wasn't good for the family to be involved. Even though I disagreed, it didn't matter to them."

There was healing for me in the writing, for us in the conversation. Therese encouraged me to write. There were probably others who could learn from my experience. Dr. Wilson didn't discourage it as long as I wasn't staying up all night writing, and that was certainly not happening.

I went easy on the bodywork, especially at first: no chiropractor, no massage. I began to have acupuncture once a month. I was seeing Dr. Coffino, the nephrologist who helped me stabilize the sodium, and I returned to my original program of drinking 750 ml of water a day, what my system seemed to require. After a few months, he said that no blood pressure medication was needed – something I had wanted to be rid of for a long time – which immediately helped raise my sodium level considerably. As it gradually approached normal, I felt more grounded in my body, sodium being "the salt of the earth." Gaining weight, graduating to the triple digits into the low 100s, helped too. In about nine months after the break, my personal care physician said I should gain five more pounds, which delighted Dr. Wilson, and which I did, giving my body more substance than I'd had in years.

Therese often reminded me that I had had a near-death experience, to be kind to myself, and to accept myself where I was. We worked with grounding visualizations, which set my feet on a solid path. I was on new terrain, slates swept clean, familial and self-expectations altered. Everyone simply wanted me well; and most interestingly, for the first time in my adult life, I wasn't pushing myself to wellness and over-achieving on the path of self-development. I observed that I could only say "yes" to what was a robust "yes" within me; anything short of that was a "no."

All that was well and good, but what about the Depakote? Was it enforcing "the abdication of ecstasy, the betrayal of our true potentialities" as Laing, the renegade Scottish psychiatrist, warned? This question niggled at me and sometimes still does. There is no guarantee, on or off Depakote, that I won't have another psychotic break at some point. It could be in 10 years, who knows? It's more likely that I won't, though, if I stay on the medication. Isn't it worth whatever dampening I might feel to protect my family and friends from a potential repeat under some other set of challenging conditions – another inevitable death of someone dear to me, for example? Anyway, maybe ecstasy is not all it was cranked up to be in the mid-'50s when Laing wrote this. What exactly was causing a feeling of flatness? Was it the drug, or was I exhausted from the harrowing experience I'd had and from which I was slowly recovering?

There certainly has been a clear before and after the psychotic break. What has changed? I am in a quieter time of life. I enjoy space at my desk, in my garden, with my bass, with a friend on the phone, with my husband. Space.

There has been a shift in my relationships. My episode made clear to Kim and Mom that they could not rely on me the way they had on Lynn. I stopped trying to somehow fill her shoes. With Therese's help I could face that my relationships with them were significantly different, and everyone needed time to rebalance. One thing was certain: I could not be Kim's pillar of security. I needed to regain my own equilibrium. Over time we would all have to figure out how best to support Kim.

In a ceremony Therese facilitated for Wil, Morgan, and me, celebrating a year of recovery, Morgan articulated how my episode changed him: "Before it I had you on a pedestal, as if you could do no wrong. I feel like I have a more realistic picture now and feel more like a peer." Isn't it strange how life works? My manic journey was part of Morgan birthing into full adulthood. He was the one we needed to rely on: centered, calm in the storm, he was there for all of us. Clearly, I need to be healthy, so he can live his life in freedom. I am devoted to that.

My relationship with Wil also shifted. I wasn't alone carrying our finances, for example. He could see how important it was that we do that together. In fact, we do more together than ever, even cook dinner. Everyone grew from my changes. Life is like that. We are all connected, and even though I know that in my mind, I'm still surprised when life confirms it.

11
Searching for Clues

August 26, 2014

As I search for clues to why I went mad, convinced that will lead to my recovery, I find this dream from November 17, 2013, a day after my dad's birthday and six months before my own run in with more mental hospitals:

> *Mom, where is Dad? I keep asking, knowing he's been taken by the company he worked for and put in a mental hospital where he's been drugged for years. We have to reach him and find out. Someone he worked with confirms that, yes, they took him away for demanding something or other. We have to do something. I call him and get him on the phone. He is going to come home to visit. Mom doesn't believe me or think it's important. When he's there – I say, see....*

Was this a foreshadowing? "[T]hey took him away for demanding something or other." Was I inwardly demanding something that caused a crack up or crack down? It's eerie. I probably *will* be drugged for years.

These hospitals seem to be a thread in my life. Why? And why as humans are we compelled to ask this question?

From the time the ego begins to find a home in a three-year-old body, as we move from saying, "Me do that," or "Carol wants that" and start saying "I," we start asking why about everything we see. "Why is the sky blue, Mommy?" leads to other questions: "Was I born in your belly?" Maybe asking questions is intrinsic to the "I," seamlessly interwoven into its invisible fiber. Whatever we call that part of ourselves that travels with us through life – the ego, the "I," the inner teacher, the soul, the spirit – it seems to come and go from time to time, smothered by outer noise or the inner noise of other parts of ourselves. I think of the "I" as the witness, the one who observes, lovingly when at its best, merging with the observed into the reality of the wholeness so difficult to experience. The "I" is the one who has seen it all, the one who connects the dots, the one who frames and ponders the deep questions of my soul.

I'm digging into Lawrence Durrell's *Balthazar* for inspiration. Why that particular volume of the *Alexandria Quartet*? It was there on the bookshelf, and I'd never gotten past *Justine* in my desire to read these four brilliant books. When I was nine months pregnant, KPFK in Los Angeles did a three-day reading of the four novels. I listened for hours, drinking in the language, which may have seeped into the soon-to-emerge fetus as Morgan, a writer himself. Durrell inspires me – the voice of his narrator, the use of language, the imagery, the sensitive searching to feel the timeless pulse of what it is to be human. "Each psyche is really an ant-hill of opposing predispositions. Personality as something with fixed attributes is an illusion – but a necessary illusion *if we are to love!*"[36]

And what happens when holding onto "the fixed attributes," "the necessary illusion" becomes impossible or abhorrent? I want to explain everything that happened to me this past May and June. The crickets sound the same; leaves begin to fall in the same way. Yet all seems distinctly new as we move toward autumn this hot August day, Lynn's birthday a week away, the second year she is on the other side of this mystery we call life.

My sister's light and shadow, her brazen panache and gentle understanding, her wide generosity and clawing need for attention were all part of her "ant-hill of opposing predispositions." As Whitman put it in *Leaves of Grass*: "Do I contradict myself? Very well then, I contradict myself, I am large, I contain multitudes."[37] But as Durrell says, "*if we are to love,*" must some of that complex reality of self be sacrificed? It is easy for me to feel the projection of what others think of me: my mother, my niece, my husband, my son, this friend, that one, each projecting his or her concept of my qualities, of who they know to be their daughter, wife, mother, aunt, friend, colleague. What is that urge in each of us to reduce the other and the world to a pinned butterfly in someone's collection – one of the images that arose at the height of the mania as I railed against anyone who said I wasn't being myself? Maybe the need to see each other as a thing instead of an ever-changing being is deep in our cells, so we can go about the business of living. The quantum physicists alongside the timeless sages tell us that everything is always changing, always in flux, and what we see as solid is illusion.

I love that Durrell points to "opposing predispositions," the paradoxes that live in our psyches, as Parker Palmer has so often pointed out, our strengths being the flip side of our limitations. Finding middle ground, the still quiet place where the voice of true being can speak, is the only vantage point from which we can feel true self, the only place from which we can hold the paradoxes of our being and of being itself.

And what does all of this have to do with me now at 66 as I continue to recover from a major psychic earthquake, the aftershocks of which reverberate into all my relationships and all I do? Perhaps, tumultuous waters are still finding their place of inner calm, the earth and water of my body realigning with the air and fire of my soul-spirit. Words, words, words.

12
I Believe

September 30, 2014

A quote from Geri Larkin's *The Chocolate Cake Sutra* came into my email this morning:

> "After all the years of [spiritual] work, ... I've realized only this: that everything and everyone is precious beyond words. Everything and everyone is holy. And the point of our being on this sweet planet is to be of service to all of it. And when we understand this truth in our bones, joy fills our hearts."[38]

I find myself reactive these days as if hopeful quotes like this are offered as punching bags for something unsettled and angry inside me three months after my manic episode. Admittedly, after all my years of spiritual work, I know that what Geri Larkin is saying is true to some extent. I don't think, though, that life is a chocolate cake sutra even though I haven't read her book. I know, it's clear I'm reacting to this and many other quotes and people standing firmly on their spiritual perch. I've fallen off of mine and am not exactly sure where it is anymore. While I know in my head that "everything and everyone is precious beyond words," I wish I could actually feel that viscerally – as joy, as reverence, as a living reality that everyone, including me is precious. I believe that's a practice and not an arrival point. Is Geri Larkin's annoying neighbor – everyone must have one –"precious beyond words"?

For a couple of decades, I was secure on my own spiritual perch – sometimes outwardly and definitely inwardly – cultivating a complex worldview in which I felt spiritually at home and self-assured. From studying Rudolf Steiner, I knew what life was all about, what happened afterwards, and how to stay connected with the so-called dead. The exercises and meditations worked for me, helped keep me centered and focused on my mission in life. Steiner knew about everything, even things we could never confirm with our own every day experience or, at least, I couldn't. I was a believer. Am I still?

I experimented and processed a lot with my father after he died. We healed certain hurts through journaled conversations. But I cannot do that with Lynn. Why not? Maybe because I am too close to her – we are living in her house; I am wearing her clothes and driving her car. Maybe it's because there's not a whole lot to discuss through journaling since we had talked in depth about our relationship before her death, at least some aspects of it. Maybe it's because she's permeating my thoughts and words and actions. Is that true? Who knows? The first year after her death was filled with grieving, including going through every drawer and closet shelf of what had been her home for 30 years. There are still pockets left untouched, boxes of old checks and bank statements in the basement, crates of cloth and God-knows-what-else in the attic. The attic – I can't think too much about the feng-shui of the crap spread out over our heads. I'd like to empty it – throw everything out the window – the way we would have had to if we had sold this house. Well, maybe not out the window. Do I detect anger surfacing again?

I have never been someone who has experienced regret; and if I'm honest with myself, life couldn't have happened any other way. What's done is done. It's a good principle to stand on. I need to replace remorse with an acceptance of what is. This is the starting place. I cannot push away or pretend the mania never happened. It did, and here I am. I've been through something powerful that shook me to my core, beliefs and all. Yet some beliefs remain strongly intact.

I believe in listening to beautiful music; I believe even more in making music – playing bass with Wil in a no-pressure situation, singing with the choir. I believe in slowing down and in meditating, no matter how in and out of awareness my mind is. I believe in reading uplifting books written by people I respect and at the same time paying attention to my own responses. For example, I'm reading Thich Nhat Hanh's *Teachings on Love*; I resonate with the loving kindness meditations and feel the way they slowly seep into my being.[39] I need to have patience before I turn too quickly to offering those mantras for the other. I need to spend time on self-love.

At the same time I know that I will never be a Buddhist monk or a Buddhist for that matter. I crave the experience of sangha – of spiritual community – but not when it's tied to ideology. Perhaps the other Courage & Renewal facilitators are my sangha; perhaps offering Circles of Trust creates the kind of sangha where I feel the most authentic. I have always strongly identified with the opening lines of May Sarton's "Now I Become Myself":

> Now I become myself. It's taken
> Time, many years and places;
>
> I have been dissolved and shaken,
> Worn other people's faces...[40]

I have worn the mask of too many groups in my life – of a hippie, of the psychoanalytic-artistic-commune that became a cult, of the anthroposophists. Adhering to these groups feels too pat now, too tied with a neat bow. I'm finding myself allergic to my old way of belonging. Lynn pushed against my faithfulness to Rudolf Steiner, my north star. Eventually, she surrendered to the fact that my belief was unshakable. My faith helped her when she was ill; now it's been shaken.

I feel different as I continue to recover. I'm not sure what to think of myself any more, what to think of the drug I'm taking. What is blocking access to as much bubbling joy, energy, and enthusiasm as I remember regularly experiencing? Is it the Depakote? Is it my own recovery from a psychophysical nightmare, moving from blissful contact with the spiritual into a kind of hell as I had more and more trouble grounding in normal earth life? Is it both? It's impossible to know, so I lean into my gratitude that I am here and intact after all of that. I have my heart; I have my emotions; I have my mind; I have my life; I have my love; I have family and friends who care about me. I have seeds of new friendships. What a miracle!

I believe in friendship and loyalty. I believe in showing up although I am not doing it very well for others right now. I have to put myself first. The last words in Geri Larkin's quote hound me: "And the point of our being on this sweet planet is to be of service to all of it. And when we understand this truth in our bones, joy fills our hearts." I am moving slowly toward authentically discerning what I can and can't do for others right now. There is no way I can be of service although I want to be; I also don't want to be subsumed in serving others as another mask to wear. Maybe the problem for me with the quote is that it's *"the point of our being"*: it may be *a* point of our being here.

I believe in the Christ mystery, which to me is that each of us can experience a growing capacity to love in full freedom, both as an individual and in our connection with other human and non-human beings. I do believe that I am loved: that the Christ Being loves me and is available to me.

And the dead…sometimes they're still too close – or not close enough. I'm still sorting that out.

13
Pilgrimage

2 Noviembre 2014
Puerto Morelos, MX

On this autumn day – quite different in New York, I'm sure – I look out at the choppy wavelets on the Caribbean. It's a cloudy day on the cool side, high 70s, and I am at the kitchen table in what was Lynn's apartment. The palm trees are swaying as Wil practices nearby.

For some reason I'm thinking about how many years I've wanted to walk the Camino de Santiago in Spain, envying those I knew or even didn't know who'd made the journey. Lynn thought it an exercise in self-punishment as did Wil. I didn't get why they didn't understand the draw. Why self-punishing? Difficult, yes, but I didn't understand why neither of them could have an inkling of enthusiasm toward the idea. I just read a friend's description of her pilgrimage from the Cathedral of Santiago to the Camino Finisterra, where pilgrims on the Camino often continue, the road that takes them out to the edge of a precipice with the roaring Atlantic crashing below.

I'm quite sure I'm never going to walk El Camino. I've faced that reality. Everything about my physical condition is too delicate – low sodium issues and all, especially after my own journey this spring, which was not without its wild imaginings about who might walk the Camino with me – George, whose mother walked it in her 60s after his father died, or Stephan or both. Maybe my life has been mi solamente camino, my only way, my pilgrimage.

Every day, step by step, the road meets me. I walk it, lately not so sure if I am lost or on some kind of path, frightened or realistic, courageous or damaged by mental illness. I can't discern from in here. It takes interaction, so if I ever get to walk any other camino than the one that is mi vida solo, it will have to be with other people. That's the biggest problem right now: besides Wil my friends are far away – two hours away at best. Esther is a friend, but she is extremely busy. Our couples circle is a breeding ground for friendship. Patience, patience, and a lot of loneliness in between. Activity – there are things to do – to keep busy – but it's the people and engagement that matter most to me, that fill my heart.

Mi camino has a familiar terrain: at certain times I get big surprises – hit upside the head by a tidal wave in the storm of life. That happened in my childhood when I was awakened at 12 to the terrifying reality that my father wanted to kill himself. I was alone, behind a door: my initial wound, not the first trauma but a centerpiece around which all the other traumas vortex. Life was different from that moment when I had to adjust. It remains a signpost on mi camino. We all have them, don't we?

I don't know how to articulate what exactly overtook me and everyone in my orbit in mid-May through June of this year. The docs call it mania. It's neatly labeled, but no one really understands it. I don't either, and I was in it. I know it was a culmination and a dead end, a beginning on a road with psychic landmines, something I thought I knew that was something else completely, something no one but I was living, yet I didn't know what was going on. I was killing body and soul: not sleeping, not eating, crazed yet enamored with the machinations of my mind gone wild. All my energy was consumed with breaking boundaries inside and out that were constraining me, challenging my tendency to contract, repelling others' opinions and projections of who I was.

I was mourning, but I was doing so much better or thought so. Then like an earthquake, the mania unexpectedly rocked our world, changing everything. And what has been the effect of those six weeks on my own life?

The Way became what was put in front of me as alternatives: I could go with the police, screaming naked or put some clothes on. The look on my mother's face would have broken my heart if it hadn't already been shattered and my feelings masked by enthusiasm on steroids. Morgan fighting me on the stairs to protect my dignity. The police, beside themselves with embarrassment, doing their duty.

The Way became which psychiatrist we would choose. The Way became facing the dire situation I was in. Everything was about me and my care. I could do nothing for myself. I couldn't cook, wash dishes, weed, do anything normal at all. I could spin convoluted ideas about how to transform our village into a 21st century prototype; money was no object. I could float around the farmers' market and connect with everyone, seeing and feeling a love for each individual far beyond my usual capacity or more introverted nature. I don't feel much of that outgoing energy at all now. Maybe it was all spent. I've always been more self-conscious and reserved; Lynn was the outgoing one. (Who am I without her?)

So why do people travel thousands of miles, spend money, wear out hiking boots, endure bleeding blisters, and choose to suffer on the Camino de Santiago when Life is the Way, the ultimate teacher? Is it because millions have walked it before them and millions will after them? Is it because hundreds are walking with them – you see them and talk to them and have experiences that are karmic and cosmic because you are all suffering the same and individual adversity, sharing the same and individual hopes and dreams, having your own insights and breakthroughs and helping others to have theirs by your presence and through sharing your own? Is it because everyone is determined to complete what they set out to complete, and the presence of the others is what gives them strength? There's a community on El Camino so hard to find in our world today. At least I'm having trouble recovering a feeling of community. It's elusive – now I feel it, now I don't.

14
Cynicism and Rebirth

November 4, 2014
Puerto Morelos, MX

I find myself responding with indifference, at best, but more often with skepticism, even cynicism, to books on self-development, truths I myself espoused and offered to others for so many years, truths I still hold with some shard of my heart. I brought two books with me on our vacation this time. I just finished Lawrence Durrell's *Balthazar* – a lush world of place and complex relationships created in his poetic prose, where I could rest as I heal. I wish I had *Mountolive*, the third in the *Alexandria Quartet*, but I don't. The other book is Elizabeth Lesser's *Broken Open: How Difficult Times Can Help Us Grow*.[41] I got it, based on an interview Tami Simon did with her, but I'm having trouble getting through the preface, no reflection on Lesser herself. This is clearly about me.

What am I looking for in a book like this? The truth in the title is self-evident to me. I certainly didn't bring it in order to reflect on my own impatience with hearing her version of "how difficult times can help us grow." But I don't want to hear what she has to say. How many times had I been through difficult times and grown? I was still in a difficult time and clear that it was much easier to talk about than to be in, so could she just shut up please? I close the book. No advice will help. Does knowing that difficult times can help us grow matter? But I did know, and times are still difficult. I know about hearts broken open. I've led retreats about that, and yet my knowing seems to have lost power in the reality of the crash in the rearview mirror.

Maybe my heart was more than broken open, which sounds gentle in comparison. My heart, as Lynn had predicted, shattered and in the aftermath, my "I" organization with it. Rebuilding a life, recovering – that's the business now, Therese keeps reminding me. Healing happens in its own time. Lynn saw the threads woven intimately between us, perhaps, due to her analytic training and nature, honed over 30 plus years of working as a psychotherapist. As she was getting ready to leave the planet, perhaps she saw her own threads loosening and knew what was woven so finely between us would indeed unravel. "You will shatter." I keep searching for metaphors to describe what has been happening in me and to me since her death almost two years ago.

As I walk along the Caribbean on a clear but windy, warm November morning, I think of her. She seems to be everywhere. I can't escape her or how much I miss her. The pain drives me into the back bedroom, where it's dark and quiet, in contrast to the bright sunlit beach. Overcome with tears, I'm determined to move this feeling through and out of me, to explore it through movement, a method Therese taught me in our last session. I go with the sound, a sobbing, that becomes the feeling of longing with so much tenderness, the sound continuing, projecting into a feeling around my heart of a birthing, an infant wanting to be swaddled, to be held, and gently released. I put it down tenderly on the bed and stroke it then cannot help but pick it up once again, rocking it in my arms until I return it to the foot of the bed with a soft kiss, feeling cleansed…for the moment.

The next morning the breeze is kinder, and after a late breakfast I head for the beach by myself. The last time we were here, Kate was with us for four days. It helps me to have another friend here, a girlfriend. It was always Lynn, Wil, and I. That works better for me since Wil needs his time alone to practice. I need alone time too, but I'm only content for a while, and then I'm not. On the beach alone, I head for the water to take a dip. It takes a lot for me to get myself into the water, but I'm determined. The first plunge is exhilarating; as always, I wonder why it takes me so long. But after taking a few strokes, thinking of Lynn and her long swims, I watch the seagulls overhead and the children playing along the edge, and walk back onto the shore. Too much seaweed on the bottom, something nipping at my toes. It was in the heat of the day, too, and I didn't want to burn.

I wrap my body in a towel and walk down the beach, feet splashing along the way. Is there anything better? I sigh, feeling the deep blue of the sky and the rippling water lapping at my feet. Everything is exactly as it should be. I have been pushing my recovery, wanting to feel better than I do, to be back in the swing of things. What swing? I was a school leader in a hot seat of an independent school on the Upper East Side of Manhattan, and then I wasn't. Certainly I don't want to be back in that swing. For years I wanted to have time to offer more retreats, but once I retired, my sister was dying of lung cancer. I walked beside her and was there for her as I had never been able to, nor had she needed me to, before. That swing is also gone, completely vanished.

As I walk along the edge, where sea meets sand, I realize that everything that has manifested is exactly what I can handle right now. I am still re-stabilizing after the manic journey and near-death experience. So much of that cannot be shared, like so much of our lives. It is part of me though; there's no denying it, and there's no going back to life before it. I'm still integrating the reality that it happened at all and that I have a psychiatric label that those around me believe. Do I believe it? I haven't decided whether I do or not. Yet this warm autumn day along the welcoming Caribbean shore, I know that everything is as it should be. That is a moment of grace, and I cherish it.

And what to do with the cynicism? I think I'll make it my practice to let it be as I read Elizabeth Lesser's book; I'll give the book a chance anyway. It's just odd to me to even have these feelings toward ideas that I also hold as truths. Who is living in this psyche of mine? Maybe these skeptical parts of me also want a voice. What exactly are they whispering? What do they want to tell me? I am not that cynical feeling: I am. And who is that baby, emerging from my sounding the pain within me, the baby who evoked such tenderness?

15
Prelude to Mania

November 6, 2014
Puerto Morelos, MX

Each day different. This morning, a decision to go with the tug of the wild woman. Well, not so wild really, but for me now, yes: to wade into the sea before breakfast after an unusually long walk on the beach, heading north away from town. The wind is mild today with just a hint of the distant cold north in it. No fighting the elements – today it's summery.

I was reading Lesser's *Broken Open* on the beach trying to hang in with it. It must have something to teach me after all.

> When you exercise the last of the human freedoms – when you choose to learn and to grow from the weight of the world – you are putting your soul in charge of your life. You are choosing not the attitude of your smaller and more fearful self but rather the attitude of your soul, which is hopeful, expansive, and eternal.[42]

And suddenly I'm snagged as if on a tripwire, anger rising. But that was exactly what I *was* doing – choosing "to learn and to grow from the weight of the world," heavy with the loss of my sister, committed to mourning as fully as anyone possibly could, always the over-achiever, the grief clinging to me and weighing me down. A year and half after her death, I was feeling impatient. Couldn't this pain be over? I wanted to emerge from it into the part of myself more "hopeful, expansive, and eternal." I was ready.

I also wanted to learn from the weight of other people's wounded world: working on Community Conferences to help youth who got themselves arrested for the first time, with the Transforming Conflict Lab to develop ways to bring people with different views together in peacemaking circles, and with Elizabeth the Shaman on Hidden Water, the project to offer a circle process to adults within a family who had experienced childhood sexual abuse and wanted to bring healing and justice to rebalance the family system. Isn't that weighty enough? And where did my years of work as a Courage & Renewal facilitator fit into this picture?

In the meantime I had been to a Center for Courage & Renewal Global Gathering. I came with the question, how could this trustworthy, safe process be applied to hotter, more difficult, potentially confrontational circles, for example, around race and class? After many individual and small group conversations, by the end of the Gathering, I was convinced that, indeed, this process was one that could handle anything. I was high on it and our mission as an organization: I felt more alive than I had since Lynn's illness and death.[43]

When I met Parker by chance at the soup station in the dining room, he asked me how I was. I responded, "All right," the time and place making it awkward to reveal anything real about how much pain I had been in for months. I assumed he'd heard about my sister's death, but I wasn't sure. "We need you well," was his response. Could he see how not well I was? I like to believe he could, but I don't know. Everything was thick with meaning for me at the Gathering, every meeting, every kindness, every intimacy, and there were many. I felt excited, inspired to apply the Circle of Trust® approach in challenging situations.

What is alive in this for me now? Why am I going over it yet again? I'm trying to find the place where the thread snapped, where I snapped. I know the circle space with the dead had a lot to do with it. Why do I keep trying to follow the thread to where I launched? Is it because I think it could have been avoided? Do I think I could have prevented it if I were just aware enough? Maybe. Probably. Well, I couldn't have. I'm convinced of that now. So can I nurture what has been born from the detour – no, let's say from my journey, my way, perhaps, of making a seismic shift in my life? Can I move these tears into self-compassion? That's my task right now, today.

Bird's Nest

Wonder! A bird's nest resting atop
the grace of the low Japanese maple,
the one under which I always see grandchildren
    playing.
Imagine, not to see it
until today when Wil pointed to it
as we raked.

A mud nest, adobe-like, held
together with wild sticks, thin as straw, and delicate red
    leaves,
the nest dutifully rounded with beak and tongue;
dropped inside, a sweet cushion of faded red filigree.
If I were an egg or baby bird, I would have felt ah,
welcome, home.

Now abandoned, eggs hatched,
young birds strong enough to beat the oncoming
    storm, or not,
the nest remains, a reminder of nature's way of
    nurturing,
a gift for us who remain through the winter.

And for me a reminder that maybe that's what I'm
    doing:
sculpting a space, where a new life can nestle
until ready to be born.

November 26, 2014

16
Mood Stabilizer

November 30, 2014

It's a well-known fact that many manic-depressives play Russian roulette with their meds. In Kay Redfield Jamison's memoir, *An Unquiet Mind*, she talks about her own experiments with and without lithium, her prescribed drug. Mine, right now, is divalproex sodium or Depakote. In one chapter she's on sabbatical in England and consults with her two psychiatrists; the three of them agree to lower her dosage. She comes alive as if a veil is lifted, her senses – previously dulled by the amount of that particular salt – now cleansed. Lithium was also what my father needed to stabilize his moods. It worked from 1970 until his death in 2000. He never missed a day, never questioned the dosage or whether or not to take his pill.

I judged my father during his years on lithium; I still do. His moods were flat; there was a distance between him and the world, definitely between him and me. But he was never again lost in the depths of depression or swinging into hypomania or worse and back. Mom and he embraced lithium as the miracle drug it is for some. It gave him a life and them a good life together. Jamison had mood swings as serious as my father's; hers started even earlier. Dad's began when he was 42 in 1960, Kay's when she was in her 20s when many have their first occurrences, including me. But I always characterized my 1971 psychotic episode as basically drug-induced, especially since it never returned or only once reared its head in any kind of significant way when I was 53. I knew I had the bipolar gene but was confident that with many years of self-development work, I had forged tools for maintaining my equilibrium. I actually did manage any ups and downs myself until the spring of 2014 when I couldn't. A vortex was unleashed, lifting me far off the ground, spinning me away from any center I had held. The mania had me: I was it; we merged.

I agreed with Dr. Wilson not to talk about stopping my meds for six months to a year. A little shy of that, I want to talk about it, and we've begun. Is the Depakote keeping me from being more engaged in life than I am right now, or is it helping me adjust to a balanced lifestyle for someone "retired" in her mid-60s?

What have I committed to in the last five months? Healing, listening to who I am now, and being true to that. That's huge. That's what Therese has been validating. "What you are doing has enormous value. Honor it; meditate on it," she said in my last session. I still cry easily. Perhaps, the mania unhinged the armor protecting me, holding me together through the many years of my life as a school leader. What do I mean by armor? The armoring was in layers: first that I did not have a mental illness. Why would I think I did? I did have occasional depressions, which were all situational from one point of view: during my first year of college, after leaving Ann Arbor in 1969 at 21 with no idea what I was doing with my life, after an abortion in 1986 when I wanted nothing more than to have a child. Were there no depressions during my time in "the Group," a therapeutic-artistic-political community in New York City, where I spent 12 years from ages 23 - 35? There I medicated with extreme work and play. School, Group responsibilities, and work took literally 20 hours of the day. Group life included therapy two or three times a week and a lot of pleasurable activities: playing bass, doing lights or sound, props or assistant stage managing for our theater productions, not to mention relationships with both men and women, and plenty of times for the wild woman to shake it out, aided by alcohol when needed. There was always therapy for processing this mood or that. Sure, sometimes I was happier than others, but that's true for everyone, right?

On a trip to Northern Europe in January 1984 with three other women, I fell into a deep depression with Berlin the nadir. Everywhere I looked I wondered how people felt about the Holocaust. Old ones had been alive then. Were they still Nazis? Some young ones looked like they could be in the SS now. Others I met were dear people. At the time I was in denial about my identity as a Jew: I felt no connection. Since I was rejecting my family, a Group requirement, I ignored my Jewish heritage as well.

I never imagined that anything would come up for me in Germany and was surprised when it did, and with a vengeance, an unavoidable undertow pulling me powerfully into the darkness of what had been launched there – the hatred and annihilation that had destroyed so many of my gene pool as well as Roma, homosexuals, disabled people, Communists, and others. While I didn't want to face that reality, it faced me nonetheless. Some of my paternal grandmother's sisters had been killed in the Holocaust. My other grandparents never spoke about relatives of theirs. Maybe they had all left by then. It didn't matter. A gene is a gene.

I ended up changing my ticket to return earlier, which I couldn't have done without my therapist telling me to do it and one of my traveling companions walking me to the ticket office and literally functioning in my stead. I was close to catatonic. Yet as soon as I was on the train leaving Berlin, the depression lifted like a dense fog clearing when climbing out of a deep valley.

Does it matter whether I went undiagnosed for years? The structure and rhythm of heavily rule-based environments – the Group and then the Waldorf school movement – gave me stability. Both of these communities agreed with my conviction that drugs were not the answer, that they only masked the true being of the person, robbing the ego forces needed for self-development and authentic growth. Diagnoses and drugs were part of the general conspiracy to make people bland, unimaginative, and easily controlled. I was also incredibly busy and later had my students and my family to be well for, not to mention a school community depending on me.

Now all of that is behind me. There are no community mandates, explicit or implicit, except to take my meds, an agreement with my family community. I still wonder if the Depakote is affecting my ability to commit to anything. And there I am, back in the loop. I am committed to my healing, which includes writing like this, reading, seeing my therapist every week on screen or in her office. I'm committed to playing the piano and the bass again and enjoying doing that with Wil. I'm committed to mentoring a new teacher as long as the school is paying me.

I'm absolutely committed to facilitating retreats, but I am unable to be a driving force behind much of anything right now. I can't initiate things, do things I know I could do, for example, get a brochure together and send it to principals and heads of schools around here. I don't feel it. The insight I had walking on the beach, feet splashing in the Caribbean, comes to mind: whatever is happening right now is exactly what needs to be happening and exactly what I can handle. Acceptance, self-acceptance, self-love, and faith. I am enough just as I am.

17
Moving Forward

Imagine. Something yearns in us to come round right. Something creaky, rusty, heavy, almost calcified within us tries - in spite of us and all of our fears and self-deceptions - to turn and turn and creak and turn again and come round a little truer.
— Victoria Safford

January 3, 2015

Snow falls, the kind more like rain, flakes streaming quickly and close together. What are the next steps in unfolding a story of reclaiming my life on new ground? Threads circle round with invitations from a school to mentor and from a friend to co-facilitate and participate in a retreat. My heart says, yes, I am ready. I feel an inner pyramid – four sides to the base, triangles rising from each of the four sides, an image of stability. Breathing within this new, evolving, sacred place, I am quietly active – being, contemplating, gently doing.

How can I describe "losing it"? What exactly was lost? I was on a trajectory of rapid growth, living in what felt like a blessing, a reality more and more inhabited by spirits, speaking with me. This blessing looked evil to Wil, my husband, the one I love and trust with all my heart: to him it looked like black magic. I didn't understand. He couldn't sleep, with me standing in front of the window deep into the night, conversing with the spirits in the garden. Was I being seduced by the dark side? One thing about 21st century psychiatry is that it doesn't moralize about mental illness: it doesn't equate a diagnosis with being under the influence of evil forces, although some approaches to treatment do feel like medieval punishment. And yet from another viewpoint, even if evil did infiltrate my weak, disorganized psyche, it did not have the last word. How far I am from the power of those forces now, whatever they were!

The snow falls more softly, a little more slowly. Playing in the snow, a dog romps outside the yellow house behind ours. Knowing me, I won't get out in it.

January 12, 2015

A fellow facilitator-friend invited me to participate in a Circle of Trust with seven other women, seekers after what is "wild and precious" inside. While I was a bit nervous, I knew it would be a small group. As we introduced ourselves, I wondered whether to share the road I'd been traveling. As a guest facilitator, while not compelled, I decided to take the plunge, to set a tone of honesty and vulnerability. It took courage to say, "In the spring I had a manic episode. I have been recovering since then."

I wondered what they thought and, more importantly, what they felt. My imagination ran the gamut. A glimmer of recognition made me think that one or two had been on the fringe in their own lives or in a loved one's. It would be different if I had said that I had a period of clinical depression. Heads would nod, everyone knowing what it meant to be depressed. But the word "mania" stirs a soundless in-breath, a dark terror of the wildness hidden within the psyche. Did some wish they had the courage to let go so fully, to erupt out of their old ways? Did others grip just a bit tighter to insure that nothing like that would ever happen to them? Still others, so far from the edge, might feel quite sure that it never would.

The mania I experienced didn't call for courage. Maybe that came before and after. No, I felt swept away in a tidal wave of my evolving psyche, a response to the earthquake that had rocked my life from 2009 when Lynn was first diagnosed. Was that where it had begun? Perhaps the first step was earlier when I left my beloved community in Austin to move closer to family. Maybe it all began in 1960 when I learned that Dad was threatening to kill himself. Who can say where this journey began? Does it matter? All I know is that what happened as the lilacs, tulips, and wisteria blossomed, so did I, only my opening was an unexpected liftoff into another reality. It was stimulating and enjoyable until it became terrifying as it faithfully collided with the lives of those I love, those who care most about me. They named what I was experiencing a psychotic manic episode. I called it a journey, a breakthrough. We argued; we were both right.

18
Why Have You Forsaken Me?

May 2015

Since September I've been attending a church I can walk to in my new hometown. I joined the choir, practice every Thursday night, and sing every Sunday morning. I was looking for pillars in my week, something to give some shape to it. But why church? And why this one? It is a federated church of Quaker, Methodist, and Reformed Church of America. The Courage & Renewal facilitating I do is infused with Quaker energy and some principles and practices since Parker Palmer, its founder, is a Quaker. Silence is welcome; people only speak to improve it. Clearness Committee, an over 400-year-old Quaker questions-only discernment practice, is integral to the retreat experience.[44] I couldn't find much silence in what I'll call my church, but that was okay. The tradition was in its roots or at least in a branch that at some point had been grafted with the other two. In Austin our family had been members of a dynamic United Methodist Church, so I had a feeling of being home. I'd never heard of the Reformed Church of America, but that didn't seem to matter. Most importantly, there was something about the people that I admired and could be with, their welcoming warmth and ability to be inviting without being suffocating. There was gratitude for whatever I wanted to contribute.

When I joined, the pastor I'd really liked the previous spring decided to leave. There was a lot of backstory to that, but the church moved forward with a mixture of grace and what looked like avoidance to a newcomer like me. They hired an interim pastor for a year to see how he'd do. Pastor Thom seemed like a natural fit; somehow he galvanized the congregation with his positive energy. At the end of April, during Eastertide, he spoke about the many bad things that happen to people in the course of their lives. We all knew what he was talking about: many in the house were cancer survivors; others had lost their husbands, wives, or, in my case, my sister to cancer and my sanity to mania; there was a teenager who had been in a devastating accident, who was paralyzed and could not speak, whose rumbles and grunts punctuated the sermons in what seemed like perfect places. Oh, yes, suffering had visited these congregants and was, we all knew, inevitably on the prowl for most of humanity. Pastor Thom is a bear of man, a friendly bear, who comes down into the midst of the people to give his sermon. In his resonant, downhome, comforting Western Michigan twang, he concluded with an approximation of these words: "In my 55 years of living, I don't think that God protects us from bad things happening, but he does promise to be with us."

That is the essence of Easter, of Christianity itself. As the story goes, the Christ – a shining, much beloved god – went through a courageous transformation, becoming a human being, suffering in a way we find viscerally horrifying, and resurrecting after three days with this promise: "...I am with you always, even unto the end of the world," as Matthew ends his Gospel (28:30). Christ Jesus had lived as a man and walked among those alive at that place in time for three years, teaching his disciples in ways difficult for them (and us) to comprehend, healing the sick, restoring sight to the blind, raising the dead, and confronting the Jewish establishment every step of the way.

Jesus of Nazareth, who became Christ Jesus when baptized by John in the Jordan, was the center of a mystical transformation that ultimately allowed us human beings to experience divinity within. We, in turn, get to walk in the pathway he forged, undergoing our own mystical transformations as individuals on the earth: companionship, celebration, excommunication, suffering, crucifixion, death, and resurrection. Not in the specific way Jesus did, of course, but his life gives us a way to understand our own human experience. I am walking that road. Many are and know they are, whether they relate to Christianity or not.

This God will not protect us from the lessons of life; in fact, suffering and its miraculous redemption are the key. The deed of Christ-Jesus – his teaching, the crucifixion, the resurrection – certainly didn't create a paradise on earth. We all know that, and for many that is why they cannot abide God or religion. He left his disciples and us with one commandment, "to love one another as I have loved you." (John 13:34-35) That's been the challenge for two millennia and counting, and as I look around the world, we're not doing too well. Let me speak for myself. My circle of loving is usually quite limited, but I'm open to learning. In this story the Cosmos offered no quick fix when the Christ was sent to help humanity. His call to each of us was and is to learn to love each other, those we easily love and those we really don't like very much at all, even our enemies.

Whatever path an individual chooses in the smorgasbord of 21st century spirituality, for me to be truly spiritual that commandment to "love one another" must be at its core. Loving oneself also needs to be included in this, not in a narcissistic way, but in creating a loving center from which to love the world. Part of this is the experience that "where two or three are gathered together in my name, there am I in the midst of them." (Matt. 18:20) To me "in my name" means in the name of love, openheartedness, and forgiveness for each other and our lower, habitual selves.

※

It was understandable that the feeling of being forsaken would occur in the seclusion room; however, what came as a surprise was feeling a disconnection from Spirit in the first months of my recovery. Even in the hospital the spiritual world was close, woven into my identity. I'd been a meditant for years and almost always felt that Spirit was accessible, even through Lynn's process of dying and throughout my grieving. This connection peaked and warped during my manic episode, where my life was driven by the words inside me that were, to my mind, from the Spirit.

Spirit is tricky. After all I went through and in my first few months on Depakote, however, it was as if I were left quite alone on the shore. I didn't even feel the kind of devotion that had become so integrated with who I knew myself to be. Instead, like my reaction to Elizabeth Lesser's book, I was more apt to experience cynicism at worst and impatience at best while reading books or listening to podcasts by spiritual teachers. What was happening? Lynn was the doubter; I was the believer. How had so much changed? What was my relationship to Spirit now? Maybe Spirit was giving me lots of space after flowing through me like a gushing spring river after snowmelt.

"Maybe it's a spiritual maturing," Therese suggested, one of the positive outcomes of the psychotic episode. Perhaps. I am definitely less interested in imagining spiritual worlds or being clairvoyant, less drawn to shamanism. Spiritual ambition, pushing myself on the path of self-development, has vanished; ambition in everyway has evaporated. Is it my age, being in my mid-60s? Somehow the psychotic episode was mysteriously part of my transition to a new way of approaching life. I'm still in that transition.

I must acknowledge the grace woven through all the flying high and crashing suffering I experienced. Here I am, after all. I had to rebuild slowly from the leveled ground, new ground somehow, to regain a relationship with my whole self, including the Spirit. I have been able to do nothing but follow my heart, despite nudging self-judgment. All recovery is from within and voluntary: a humble daily meditation practice, which I strive to keep simple; the church choir and church most Sunday mornings, which has brought a kind of social stability and community regardless of its limitations. Because I believe in the power of commitment, I recently joined the church to see what that would bring into my life. Will these relationships grow? Before sleeping I review the day, then list gratitudes and prayers in my journal, which often reads with the repetition of a 12-year-old's diary.

Faith is not abstract. I had to begin, so I did what I knew would help, even when I didn't feel like it: having a meditation time, taking a walk down a dirt road or around the village, cooking something I'd concocted, playing the bass or piano, writing, being in the moment, and noticing what nourishes me. I had faith that in time I would heal spiritually as well as physically and psychologically. Even when I felt abandoned by what I had recently known or thought I'd known, I remembered many times when the Spirit had shone clearly in my life, when miracles abounded. That's faith renewing itself. Yet faith itself is a great mystery: why do I have it – most of the time – when so many don't?

After my last hospital stay, weak and exhausted, I had to rest and intentionally take the first step toward some kind of spiritual practice. Maybe my faith, intention, and disciplined follow-through built resurrection soil or grew in it or both.

Over time the feeling of the Christ, the Universal Human Spirit, is growing in and with me through these humble practices and daily commitments. I also see this Universal Human Spirit, whatever the name, alive in the world if and when I'm awake to it – in the play of light before sunset, the squirrels spiraling one another around a tree trunk, the red bud with its branches ripe with pink blossoms, the crabapple rolling with puffy pink flowers, the magnolia's sweet drooping waxy pink purple petals, the daffodils' trumpets bowing in the breeze, the surprise red tulip hidden between the shrubs and the house, the in-breath miracle of seeds pushing through the soil, the full moon rising, the soft night breeze caressing us under the starry sky.

It is said that after the crucifixion, Christ Jesus went down into the Underworld and freed all the suffering souls. That's what he did on the Saturday after Good Friday – Holy Saturday some call it – even though for the Jews it was the Sabbath. Can you imagine being in the land of the Shades and suddenly the Light of the World descends to free you by connecting you to those you love who still remain on Earth? The picture warms and inspires me. And the next day, beyond human understanding, Christ Jesus himself is raised from the dead, the stone rolled from the mouth of the tomb where the body had been.

We are free in our spiritual life. Everything is available in the 21st century for the seeker of the spirit. How-to books abound, podcasts plentiful, choice unlimited at least for those of us in the "free" world. This is the nature of the time in which we live. We're free to take this step or that one, or to not take one at all: atheist, agnostic, pantheist, any or all of the world religions, undeclared spiritual, dipping into whatever draws you to create your own relationship with what is felt as divine. Rest assured that no God will come knocking at our door or blaze at us through a bush, although I do entertain that angels clothed as humans, more often than we suspect, may walk among us. I wonder at the beauty of the natural world, which can mysteriously restore us with ferocious faithfulness.

I was glad to hear Pastor Thom say that "God can't protect us from bad things happening...." because it's true. That He will be with us always resounds with the mystery of the Resurrection itself. If it weren't for those perennials in the garden and spring returning after over six feet of snow for most of the winter, it would be hard to imagine at all. Aren't we fortunate to be part of this glorious Earth under, and within, an inscrutable Heaven?

The impulse for this essay started because something felt unsaid in Pastor Thom's sermon about God not protecting us but being with us through our difficulties. For a while I wondered where God had gone; many folks wonder if God exists at all. If Christ Jesus never doubted the existence of the Father, why did he call out from the cross, where he hung between thieves: "My God, my God, why hast Thou forsaken me?"

There have been many sermons and much commentary on this. Here's mine. After all he'd preached, did Christ Jesus doubt the Father, or was he anguished at how alone he felt in that moment? "That's what makes us love him," my friend said on our walk down a country road. That's what makes Jesus someone we can relate to because we doubt all the time; we feel forsaken and abandoned. Jesus had to experience those emotions as well to live the full range of the human being, including going through death alone. How could he know faith if he were never forsaken? For in feeling a void of connection to Spirit, faith is the only way: faith in what we hear when we listen inside ourselves, faith in the great emptiness and eventually in its message of loving peace. In times of forsakenness, we have to find faith somewhere inside or outside of us, or fake it and just go through the motions until a living, inexplicable reality sidles close at an unexpected time, the reality that we, in fact, too are spiritual beings, unforgotten by the wholeness of which we are a part. Besides, we mustn't forget that we don't know how God responded to Jesus after he cried out, do we? That was a private, intimate live encounter.

In a recent sermon Pastor Thom warned about relying on our smarts, on our heads in relationship to our faith – in essence, that we're too smart for our own goodness. I took that to heart. I love being smart; I was raised that way and rewarded for it. I know a lot of this essay is pretty darn heady too. I love thinking about the images, the stories of Moses, of the prophets, of the Buddha, of Mohammed, of Christ Jesus. I like stories and writing about them. I was an English major after all. I am forgiven. What I know, now, is that giving my life energy to the activities that nourish me also nourishes the world. That is an act of faith, and mysteriously, doing what I love creates my place in the cosmos.

CAT GREENSTREET

Mysteriously Over

A current of mind – like wind or water –
a force, impossible
to stop, smooth for a time
but then whipped up, begins anew.

Twisting, it must run its course:
moving dust, mud, living and dead –
on, in, under, for, from, until

it rests, mysteriously spent,
changing all in its wake,
leaving nothing the same.

January 9, 2016

19
Community and Other Nourishment

"What about group therapy, Mom?" Morgan asked soon after my release from the private hospital. I felt the advice of his psychologist friends or friends who'd suffered psychotic breaks standing behind the question. I had no intention of doing that. I could barely process my own story; I knew hearing others' was not my way to integrate my own. Besides I couldn't be sure that the therapist facilitator would insure safety in that circle. Nope, that wasn't for me, and I was way beyond "shoulds."

As I look back, though, there were ways I built community that supported me in my recovery process: choir, a peer learning circle (PLC), and a group that I'd formed that we called the Circlers. There were also daily, weekly, and monthly practices that nourished me in a time of gestation.

Choir

When I first heard the church choir, I was hypomanic. It was the time between the County Hospital and the Private Hospital, and I was certain I was improving. That service had a lot of green lights for me: for one, the pastor at the time mentioned Parker Palmer in her sermon. My intensely twinkling eyes were affirming every word she said, and after the service I told her about my work as a Courage & Renewal facilitator. She was really excited about my coming to the church. A small choir sang so harmoniously and in tune that immediately following the service I boldly approached the members and said that I wanted to join. Welcoming, they said they'd love to have me in September when they started again after summer break.

The timing turned out to be fortuitous. I did join them in September, having had a few months to begin to restore my strength, build my body weight, and reorient to a new ground of being. I was challenged to sing a new part: I'd always sung soprano, but my voice had dropped, and the soprano part was too high. Singing harmony was difficult at first. What note was I supposed to sing? One of the women, who turned out to have been a patient of Lynn's, took me under her very experienced wing, and slowly my confidence grew.

The choir was important to my healing. First, it was rhythmic, literally and figuratively: every Thursday night we rehearsed, and every Sunday morning we rehearsed and sang for the worship service. Second, singing with a group was healing in itself and the music uplifting. I literally breathed beauty in and out every week. The choir and church became pillars in my week, around which I began to restructure my life. At first I felt socially alien: none of these people would ordinarily be my friends. Yet miraculously, over the months and years I began to feel a strong affection and sense of belonging, even when my alto singing buddy moved away. People are glad to see me; I am glad to be with them. We care about one another. Now I extend the hospitality I received: that's how we are. Also a festival choir that performs twice a year was formed, through which not only do we sing wonderful music but in which I met a couple, who have become dear friends.

Peer Learning Circle

Following the May Global Gathering, small peer learning groups were offered to support our development as facilitators. A group of five equally experienced facilitators, including me, had already begun forming at the Gathering. We committed to meeting on the phone for two hours once a month during which we would bring questions about our work and ask specifically for what we needed: open-honest questions, resources, or learning stories.

That fall we had our first call. Would I tell them what had happened to me over the spring and summer or not? To be as fully present as possible – one of our Touchstones for creating a Circle of Trust – I felt I had to.[45] I trusted there would be no fixing, saving, advising, or correcting – another of the Touchstones. Without being able to see my colleagues' eyes or body language, hearing only their silence at first, I felt anxious about how they were responding. Was their silence shock, discomfort, or judgment? I was nervous about whether sharing had been the right choice. Then a few gentle words were spoken, acknowledging how much I'd been through and how courageous it was for me to have shared what I did.

Over the years that we have met, I have come to deeply appreciate this group's embodiment of faithfulness, by which I mean, that each of us is faithful to the essence of each other's true being. I never felt that any of them treated me as if I were fragile or crazy. I always felt there was encouragement to grow, our purpose for meeting. Perhaps, my offering of truth helped set a direction of being vulnerable in our work together and in the issues we bring, knowing that we will be met with gentleness that has grown to become a bond of dependable trust, mutual respect, and love. How blessed I am to be part of this group!

The Circlers

In the summer of 2013, I began talking to Jay, who made and sold nondairy ice cream, in the local farmers market. We had a connection since he and his wife Judy had been acquaintances of Lynn's. I was airing my idea of a monthly potluck and circle in which we could build community. Jay's an incredibly enthusiastic human being and was all for it. He would talk to Judy. I knew that Wil would want to be part of this too. The following week Jay told me that Judy was interested. When could we start? In the fall of 2013, the five of us, two couples and my friend Ashley, sat in a circle upstairs in the barn. I was using the peacemaking circle practice of sending a talking piece from person to person around the circle. When you held the talking piece, it was your turn to talk and others' turn to listen. I can't remember if we created our own guidelines or I offered the Touchstones. I was experimenting with what form was best for this purpose. I was also aware that Ashley might feel awkward with these people old enough to be her parents. In fact, soon after that first circle she told me it wasn't for her.

Judy had an idea and asked a yoga instructor she knew if she and her husband would want to join us. They were excited about it and had some friends, who lived across the river, who also might be interested. Life being what it was, it took until September 2014 for us to meet again with this new group. In the interim I had had a manic episode. Could I even facilitate? My "holding" forces were thin and out of practice. After all, I'd only been out of the hospitals a little over two months. But I yearned to return to this part of my life. This time I had left the restorative justice work behind. I was clear that I wanted to focus on the Circle of Trust approach with Touchstones as guidelines for being together.

Some of these potential new friends were not without skepticism. What were all these rules? What was all this control? We couldn't just talk whenever we wanted to? I wondered whether I was holding things too tightly for this group of free spirits. Yet I trusted the process from which I had learned so much. I knew it would give us an experience of being together that wasn't social in the ordinary ways we already knew. It would allow us to go deeper into our selves and with one another as we grew as friends and as a caring community.

This group still meets monthly as I write; another close friend has joined us. (The couple from across the river hardly ever comes: proximity is an important element.) From the beginning I was completely transparent about my psychotic break. Again, I was met only with compassion, support, and faithfulness. As these friends began to value the principles and practices of a Circle of Trust, the original resistance faded. We all do our work in this circle as we grow together invisibly, humbly sharing our lives, and nurturing each other as we continue to learn to ask open, honest questions and create sacred space.

Other Practices

Besides morning meditation, before bed each night, I reviewed my day and then wrote gratitudes and prayers in my journal. While often repetitive, it was a way to digest the day, be grateful, and send my concerns, worries, and well-wishes to a higher power. Here are some examples:

January 27, 2015
<u>Gratitude</u>
- Wil ~ that he didn't get badly hurt [in an accident in the City] (still seems a little confused ~ rest deeply ~ help with his head and neck), for his love
- Therese
- Cocoon of this room
- Life's wisdom ~ the hidden wholeness of inside and out

<u>Prayers</u>
- for Morgan in last few days in Accra ~ his safety & protection ~ for his health, strength, & well-being
- for Wil's healing, strength, well-being & safety & protection in ice and snow
- for Mom ~ for an easing of her anxiety & aggravation – she is sensing her death or wishing it – I can't tell which – help her in her unease
- for Kim ~ may she be happy & fulfilled – may she continue losing weight & get the physical therapy she needs!
- for me – for my safety – protection on the roads tomorrow. May I be helpful to the teachers I'm mentoring.
- for the world ~ for the homeless in the cold ~ for those caught in war zones ~ for those in the path of terrorists ~ may grace be there too – may there be a turning in individuals toward the Spirit.

March 4, 2015
Gratitude
- Intimacy with Wil
- Playing music together, the bass
- My healing from a cold. Reminder: not to try to do too much
- Center for Courage & Renewal
- Judy's generosity and encouragement
- Morgan, Mom
- Thich Nhat Hanh's progress from stroke

Prayers
- for Kim's well-being, fulfillment, strengthening, health, joy; for our finding right relationship
- Blessings for Mom, Morgan, Wil, and me for health, well-being, healing, joy, fulfillment, safety, and protection
- for the impulse of love to become more and more visible in the world even as it continues to destabilize.

You get the idea. It was a bit obsessive, but it was soothing to end my day this way. By September I said my prayers silently and only wrote down gratitudes.

September 23, 2015
Gratitude
- Healing Habit of the Heart circle went well – 15 people![46]
- Wil so supportive...
- the day ~ the beauty
- the village beginning to feel like my town – astonishing
- Grace of Spirit in & through life

Life is certainly packed with danger and impending loss as well as beauty and grace, which can too easily remain invisible when ignored. Both my practice of gratitude, as I reviewed each day's gifts, and of prayer, as I articulated the yearning of my heart to ease my own and others' suffering, comforted and stabilized my new way of living.

Who needed group therapy when life was so rich?

20
After the Storm

When you pass through the waters, I will be with you; and when you pass through the rivers, they will not sweep over you. When you walk through the fire, you will not be burned; the flames will not set you ablaze.

Isaiah 43:2

February 25, 2016

We had a harrowing rainstorm last night with violent winds that shook our two-story house. Could the house blow down? Was this a tornado? I wondered, listening breathlessly as I lay in bed. Thankfully, after one especially forceful gust, nothing as severe followed.

This morning, looking at the sturdy, long-living maple outside my bedroom window, I asked it a simple question: "How do you interact with such a violent storm?" As I listened, I couldn't help noticing how alive the tree looked today, the moss a spring green carpet hugging its otherwise bare branches. It always amazes me that answers steeped in wisdom arise from sincere questions asked to the mineral or plant worlds. "With the integrity of my whole life…the strength of my limbs, my trunk, and especially my roots," said the maple. Now, I admit, it becomes difficult to know what are my thoughts and what the tree's. The tree and I need not rely on faith to know the roots are there. For me, it's knowledge of plants and verification of its roots bulging above the soil, but the tree doesn't know as I do. It doesn't need to: it is the wholeness of itself. Maybe that's how I too went through my own violent storm – with the integrity of my whole being – regardless of how vulnerable I was, how difficult the trial, and what the psychiatrists name it.

Debbie Hampton's website, www.thebestbrainpossible.com, says that

> Studies have shown that some trauma survivors report positive changes and enhanced personal development, called post-traumatic growth (PTG). PTG refers to any beneficial change resulting from a major life crisis or traumatic event, but people most commonly experience a positive shift by having a renewed appreciation for life; adopting a new world view with new possibilities for themselves; feeling more personal strength; feeling more satisfied spiritually, and/or their relationships improve.[47]

I resonate with this in relation to my own recovery. I have definitely experienced post-traumatic growth since my own personal storm. I wonder about the gift and mystery of resilience, "the integrity of my whole life," that allowed me to move through that tempest and into a new, more integrated place. One essential truth is that it has been a gradual movement from rock bottom to the ongoing present, continually being true to my self, my responses, feelings, thoughts, and energy toward or away from whatever presents itself to me.

I've always loved this quote from the Grail legend of *Parzival* as told by Wolfgang von Eschenbach, which offers an image that promises something similar:

> The sword will withstand the first blow unscathed; at the second it will shatter. If you then take it back to the spring, it will become whole again from the flow of the water. You must have the water at the source.... If the pieces are not lost and you fit them together properly, as soon as the spring water wets them, the sword will become whole again, the joining and edges stronger than before.[48]

The 2001 hypomanic episode left the sword of my ego unscathed, pieces put together flawlessly or so it seemed. Under a changed constellation of circumstances – Lynn's death, my retirement, our move – the second blow shattered it. I am still returning to the spring of my nature, asking the right questions with Therese's help and the support of my loving family and community. I am continually testing to be sure that I have tapped "the water at the source," making sure I am not leaving pieces behind, working to embrace them with the hope that in this process of life I have "become whole again...stronger than before."

21
Questions and Hope

> Whether life is worth living depends for me on whether there is love in life.
>
> — R. D. Laing

February 2016

In 1968, as I began to grow in a political revolutionary direction, a copy of R.D. Laing's *Politics of Experience* was put into my hands by another hippie in the commune where I lived. I was interested because I had grown up with my dad's manic-depression. Before, during, and after my own psychotic breaks in 1971 and 2014, Laing's ideas were present in my mind. He was a radical Scottish psychiatrist who saw schizophrenia and other mental illnesses as transformative experiences, potential breakthroughs into a healthier way of being in the world. His thoughts buoyed me during my own tempests. On the other side, there was the potential for better access to inner resources, greater resilience, and a healthier ego organization. Laing believed that even with shattering there could be the promise of wholeness "stronger than before" in von Eschenbach's words. Could a psychotic break be a kind of shamanic journey out of which one can emerge with greater wisdom and stability? Did Therese and

I together walk up to the gateway of such a journey that ultimately I could only walk alone?

The work I had done in psychotherapy four months before the psychotic break disarmed an ego structure no longer serving me, especially in relationship to family dynamics, without a new one to fit altered circumstances. New wine was beginning to flow but without a new wine skin fully formed. There was another big change in the family system: Morgan was becoming more and more independent, so my identity as a mother was also shifting. Lynn's illness had drawn him close, and after her death and Jason's drowning that cold winter night, Morgan needed to get on with his own life.

Therese recently shared an image from family systems therapy that compares the family to a mobile. If the wind blows too strongly on one of the components, the whole structure is rocked. If one person is ill or dies, if one of us grows up and leaves home, beginning to create his own mobile, the balance of the whole is affected. When Lynn died, the mobile was thrown into a tailspin; the dynamics needed to find a new equilibrium, and we really didn't consciously face that. Instead I tried hard to fill the gap as best I could, but that adaptation wasn't sustainable. That's not how balance is recreated. Life has to show the new way, and we moved forward doing our best. Then unexpectedly I soared to heaven and crashed to hell, trembling through the eye of the needle and back, the mobile once again seriously sent to wobbling.

After Lynn's death a flow toward something unknown was set in motion. Was part of my manic journey facing the reality that I had a gene loose, my father's, passed through his mother, a depressive bed-ridden for much of her life? While I can accept that genes are a factor, do I have to accept a diagnosis of bipolar disorder? Dad's regular wrecking-ball ups and downs were not situational like my ups and mild downs. Perhaps, if he'd become a gym teacher and fulfilled himself vocationally, he never would have been depressed. Maybe that was at the bottom of it, but we can never know. Once he made the decision at 40 to stay in the sporting goods business instead of following his heart and returning to school, his moods swung like a pendulum, regardless of anything else happening in our lives.

I wonder, though, if Dad's initial depression was situational. My grandmother, Mom's mom, died nine months before that one that set the mood swings in motion. I often wondered how her death affected him, seeing Mom bereft and more vulnerable than he'd ever known her to be. Perhaps, that frightened him. Dad was bullied at the store; maybe Grandma had been a buffer between him and Grandpa or the other employee who picked on him for being short and not as mechanically inclined as they were. I can imagine her saying, "Stop it, Phil. Stop picking on Hy." My dad was anything but macho; oh, he loved sports and could shoot the shit with the guys, but he was kind, good-natured, a jokester, non-confrontational. If Grandma did have those conversations with Grandpa, her loss could have contributed to his first clinical depression. And yet, don't other people go through difficult, intense times without crashing into depression like Dad or flaming into mania like me? I'm obviously still wrestling with it all.

Different from 2001, in 2014 there was no demanding job or family financial responsibility or a growing 14-year-old to anchor me, to make certain I could find my mooring. While I wanted to facilitate restorative justice circles, these were not essential to the sustenance of my family as was my position in 2001. If I had lost my job then, I would have put our family in jeopardy: we were paying a mortgage; we were paying Morgan's tuition; we would be in a geographical place we had no need to be. I would have destroyed everything. With Jim dead, my mother and sister also needed me to be sane. In 2014 my family needed me to be healthy, of course, as we all want our loved ones to be, but Morgan was an adult out in the world, Wil was the major breadwinner, and I was collecting social security. I had lost my ballast.

I count my blessings that I returned from the psychosis. Wil wasn't sure at one point although I never doubted that I would, maybe because I'd come through it before. Many don't recover, though. What is the source of my resilience? When do I stop wondering whether I am truly recovered? When do Wil and Morgan and others in my family, even Therese, stop worrying about me? Is it worry or caring and accepting a new reality? I remind myself that recovering is a journey, accompanied by many conflicting feelings from anger and cynicism, like I'd never known, to relief and deep gratitude for being reborn.

Walking today on a cold February day almost two years since the manic episode, I ponder the strange world of emotions. I felt a bit depressed this morning because I've taken on some temporary responsibilities for arranging Kim's care. Luckily, a call with a friend helped, an attentive, warm, sympathetic listener, a sister in a sense. "You are an only child now," Therese said to me recently. My sisters have to come from elsewhere. Doing what needed to be done for Kim this afternoon, at least for now – one step at a time – I walk with a sense of fulfillment: something I was seeing as a burden flipped into a heartwarming feeling because I could help. Three hawks circle overhead, flapping, gliding, blessing from above. "We have your back," the spirits in my mind say, the ones on the other side of light and air, water and earth.

Funny about the movement of emotions – dread so close to satisfaction, tears to laughter, blame to forgiveness, depression to mania. They live in a circle, one beside the other yet look dualistic when we view them as polarities. If we can observe them with the all-inclusive oneness of "I am," holding that tension, they can flow within us, teachers, pointing the way, enlightening our choices, not made when we're caught in any one emotion but when in the quiet of the mind we behold the whole in freedom and self-compassion. I needed my friend, my mother, Wil, and my own determination to accept what I'd said yes to around Kim's care. I needed love from others and myself to move through this day. May it be so tomorrow.

22
Spring

April 19, 2016

The energy of spring, uplifting and somewhat overwhelming, wants to run away with me, but my feet are planted. I'm in my body. I notice and am a bit surprised at the comfort I'm feeling in my own skin. As the temperatures get friendlier, the weather of my life feels more hospitable too.

The birds are busy building nests on our front and back porches. Wil and I are spending whatever time we can in the garden while we hang on to the artistic work that feeds us. All is well.

Recovery continues, resilience is alive and hopefully will be a companion through the rest of my life. There will be losses; there will be celebrations. That's life, isn't it?

23
Evolution

July 2, 2016

A nudging voice speaks, wondering if there was something I could have done to avoid the manic episode, if there was something I did wrong. What if I had more community around me? Would it have happened then? What if Lynn hadn't died? What if…ad infinitum?

This line of thought whirls me into the spiral of my own being. How am I now? How am I different? I'm better. I'm calmer. I no longer deny that the genetic is real. I wrestle less often with anxiety, which demanded a lot of attention and energy.

Lynn's death left me without her persona to merge with, without her being to balance my own. I have to be in myself in a different way. We were too entwined. No blame. We were like twins so many said over the years. As children we felt it and always wanted to dress alike. Mom made us Mickey Mouse Club skirts that we wore together with our plastic mouse ears. What could be better than to be with someone you loved so much and felt so close with – a playmate, a friend?

When I broke contact with my family for 10 years, I balanced and defined my being by subsuming myself in a politically radical therapeutic community and theater company. My identity was inextricably connected to the Group. I was young and vulnerable when I first arrived, having found my way there after my first psychotic mania and hospitalization. More than a decade later, reconnected to family but living far away, my identity was interwoven with the worldview of anthroposophy and Waldorf education, my work.

Back in Lynn's sphere, she called me on my Christ complex as I sacrificed everything to teaching and schools at the expense of self and family. She challenged my conviction that because I saw my work as a spiritual deed, it could justifiably be all-consuming. I rejected her diagnosis. After all, the future of humanity was at stake. Now I see I was susceptible, again, clinging to a solid life raft that served many others as well as me.

In my evolution Parker Palmer has balanced Rudolf Steiner. There's been a shift from a focus on spiritual worlds to a greater trust in my inner teacher, which freed me from straining everything through an anthroposophical sieve. Now life has slowed down. I am in a quiet place. I am taking my meds and don't feel hampered by them. I wait for life to show the way. I am not passive, though. I am alive, attuned to "now" as best I can. And now, into the garden.

24
Down to the Marrow

August 2016

I continue to monitor my blood every one to three months because of the low sodium condition. Dr. Coffino has definitely helped me get it stabilized through salt tabs and water restriction. We're experimenting with whether the 750 ml a day might be expanded to 850. After two months my sodium began sinking, not to dangerous levels, but I didn't like the direction. It's summer, and I wonder whether all the juice in the fruits is adding at least an additional 100 ml. It's become a way of life for me to watch my fluid intake this carefully. We will try 800 ml and see how that goes.

The other thing, though, that has shown up repeatedly on these regular blood tests, when they include a CBC (complete blood count), is a high platelet count. Platelets are the colorless cells in the blood that are involved in clotting. The normal platelet count range, depending on the lab, is approximately 150 to 450 (thousand/mcL). Mine is up to 542, a condition called thrombocytosis. Looking at my last group of blood labs, Dr. Coffino suggested I see a hematologist. Another doctor, I inwardly sighed. He was wondering if there was some anemia, one of the possible causes. Initial tests by my primary care doctor came up negative; she made no suggestion about exploring the matter further. In fact, no one seemed that concerned about the elevation, except Dr. Coffino, who made me more attentive to it. A high platelet count can cause blood clots, strokes, heart attacks I read on the Internet, source of all medical knowledge. I certainly didn't want any of those, thank you very much.

I scoured the possible hematologists in my insurance plan, finding things I didn't like about each of them, and then decided to ask my personal care physician for a recommendation. She suggested Dr. Updike, so I scheduled an appointment. Wanting to be prepared for the visit, I got curious about when this had all started. A high platelet count was something new, after all. As I combed through the copies of the lab tests I'd had, the first indication of a high platelet count was in the private mental hospital. Aha!

What to me was a major discovery held little interest for Dr. Updike. He sent me down to the lab, where the technician took five vials of blood, which would tell him exactly what he needed to know. Besides what did it matter when it began? It was here now, so let's treat it.

He called me last week. There is a genetic mutation of JAK2, which according to the NIH Genetics Home Reference, "provides instructions for making a protein that promotes the growth and division (proliferation) of cells.... The JAK2 protein is especially important for controlling the production of blood cells from hematopoietic stem cells. These stem cells are located within the bone marrow and have the potential to develop into red blood cells, white blood cells, and platelets."[49] In my case, explained Dr. Updike at a New York clip, I have a genetic mutation of JAK2, switching something on in the bone marrow that makes the platelets proliferate too rapidly. Those are the facts. There's nothing to do, Dr. Updike reassured, when the count is in the 500s, just take a low-dose aspirin once a day, and call me in the morning. No, he didn't say the second part of that, but he did say to take the aspirin daily, have a blood test, and see him every three months instead of every six. I don't want to know what can happen if it gets worse. I want it to get better or go away altogether. If JAK2 could switch on, couldn't it just as quickly switch off?

In the private hospital, something switched on affecting the very marrow of my bones, causing a new condition that I now have to monitor, a condition that if it worsened could kill or incapacitate me. The mysterious fact is that in the seclusion room, where I lay on a mattress on the floor without a pillow, hips aching, ribs hurting, heart breaking, something moved that protein to alter the biochemistry of my bone marrow. Who knows why? My mind goes to the moment I awoke in that room yet again, having had very little real food, unable to keep track of my water intake, feeling like I was dying from loneliness, rage, and abandonment. "This is rock bottom; I have never felt this much despair ever before in my life." I didn't know if they'd ever let me out. Nothing I was doing was helping me connect with Wil or Morgan, to see the faces of those who loved me. I even wondered if they'd forgotten me. Why weren't they freeing me from this hell-hole?

Usually platelets are sent to the site of damaged tissue, so they can clot the blood, preventing an injured person from bleeding to death. Maybe in the trauma of the mania and its treatment, JAK2 was getting distress signals and sent an urgent message to the marrow to make more platelets. Something bad was happening. Everyone get on it! Sodium was down for the count; something had to come up to try to help. Go platelets!

Could returning psychically to the origin help? Could healing the trauma of the seclusion room have any impact on something as deep as the bone marrow? Could this ever be reversed if deep levels of stress were released? There was no harm in trying.

And what of the metaphor? My transformation since Lynn's death, culminating in the manic episode, has affected me down to the very marrow of my bones. The genetic mutation may indeed be giving the direction for how I will ultimately leave this planet, or not. That's not mine to know. In the meantime, I'll take my baby aspirin once a day.

25
The Seclusion Room

August 17, 2016

"I have an intuition. May I?" I nod, and Therese pulls up her rounded wicker chair and places her bare feet on top of my bare feet.

"How does that feel?"

"Oppressive," I say without hesitation. I might have been more polite in other circumstances. Maybe we're beyond that in our relationship. We've been through a lot. I trust her intimately. We'd already agreed that one "resource" for me in this exploration of the trauma of the seclusion room would be the space we were in and our relationship, her eyes seeing me and mine seeing her.[50]

She pulls back. "I want to move away immediately, but I also want to go slowly." She does move back. "Let's start with that feeling, oppressive." She asks, "Where is it in your body? What does it feel like?"

"My eyes are filling with tears, my throat is bottled up, and my head feels pressed in a vice."

"Go to that place where you feel your core," she says. I had described a place I was recently led to, a place in the Appalachian forest of Northeast Pennsylvania. I was on retreat, and we were given the better part of an afternoon to find and be in "our" place. After a little searching I found an opening in the woods with a number of flat stone outcrops on which I could sit and eat my lunch. From a tree above, a caterpillar dropped on a thread, slowly finding his way along it, descending until he could go no farther, at which point he turned and started climbing back up the thin filament again. My spot also had an uprooted tree, whose roots were worn by rain and sun, covered now with moss and lichen – nature's sculpture. I felt free there, I told Therese, both centered and free. And yet it was right on a trail; one of the others on the retreat walked through, smiling. We were encouraged to let each other be, and I was grateful for that. Light streamed through the trees, glistening on leaves, trembling in the gentle summer wind. I was there, that refuge inside me.

"Now I want to come close again. I think we can use my feet on yours, which you felt as oppressive, as a gateway. Can we try that?" I nodded. She took another chair, a wooden one with a small pillow on it, and moved in close. She touched my toes with hers then once again slowly brought her foot over mine, making more contact.

I started to feel oppressed again, going deeper into the bodily sensations. First came tears then terror. "I feel it in my breathing, deeper, faster," I said.

"I want you to take the terror in your arms as if it were an infant and carry it into the place in the woods, your place, the place you were led to. Feel the terror and the feeling of being in that place, centered, surrounded by nature."

Something shifted. "I am held by Nature. I feel at one with it; I am part of it."

"Yes, feel yourself and the terror held by the Great Mother."

"When I was in the seclusion room, I would feel most

connected to my core when I sensed nature, at sunset and sunrise." I had never before shared this with Therese. "The room was painted a pale blue that changed as the light changed."

"Prisoners of war talk about times like this when something in nature, a tree, a sunset, would help them feel their humanity." We sat in silence, her feet moving gently over mine. She took my hands. "Open your eyes and look at me." I looked into her eyes for a few moments, connecting. "How is the terror now?" she asked.

I closed my eyes again. "I feel centered, more light in my heart." Our hands released.

"It's really painful not to be seen," she said. Tears came to my eyes; I nodded. Silence. "Be with this light in your heart, and let's go back into the seclusion room again. Okay?" I agreed. "See if you can stay centered amidst the psychosis, which masked your core then. Imagine people coming in and out of the room, and actually seeing you for who you are." I did. I could hold my core self, shining, as Therese came to visit, as aides came to bring food.

"How is the oppressiveness now? Let's check in with your head."

"There's no pressure. There's no plug in my throat."

"I'm going to slowly take my feet off of yours. Now how do you feel?"

My eyes closed. "I feel bubbly, effervescent through my chest." I began to imagine walking out of the seclusion room and told her that.

"I was picturing the same thing. Do it!" she said. I got up and walked out the door then sat down again. She suggested that I might want to walk a little more. Every door I walked through was a gateway out of that space, that trauma. Freedom and strength streamed from my head through my core to my feet. I felt triumphant without any edge of anger.

"Let's check in with your body. Are there any residual feelings of fight, freeze, or flight?"

I had enough for one day. My thoughts went to what I had done in the past, not what I was feeling in my body in that moment. But I trusted the thought: "In the seclusion room, I tried all of the above. I first tried fighting, cursing at everyone. When that got me nowhere, I froze, trying to be a very good girl, hoping that would get me out. Lastly, I tried flight. I had gone to the bathroom and thought that they were waiting for me to take charge. I demanded that they release me since I had signed myself in. But that didn't work either."

"Are any of these still living in your body?" Therese persisted.

"Maybe, we'll know as life unfolds. I feel like I've been through a lot today," I said, exhausted yet exhilarated. "I need a lavender bath." We agreed that I should focus on relaxing, writing, gardening, the bath, not getting lost in tasks.

Her feet on mine. Our eyes meeting. My special place in the forest, bathed in dappled sunshine, cradling terror like an infant.

"It's powerful," Therese said, "to invite even the most dreaded feelings into a place of caring attention, isn't it?" I nodded and smiled and, as always, thanked her.

CAT GREENSTREET

Hurdles

Dr. Wilson says life is like running a track
and jumping hurdles,
to be able
to spring over them, land on your feet,
and keep sprinting.

I can run with the metaphor –
sometimes slamming against,
bruising or breaking a leg,
stopped in my tracks,
carried off, cared for by others,
by me, slowly recovering.

Maybe they should be called hurtles,
no, not like turtles, although they'd be
easier to fly over.

I say life is like swimming
and being caught in a whirlpool
or a gentler eddy
or a rip or a tangle of clawing seaweed
or a school of angel fish
or a gang of piranha.

We're in another current now,
swimming into more than we can know:
Mom's in the hospital,
diagnosed with a liver infection.
She's 93.

MANIA MYSTERIES: A GRIEF JOURNEY

We don't yet know how long
she will still be here with us
on our exquisite, troubled planet.
New needs all
of a sudden.

The children parent
the mother. Paddling
into new territory.
Another hurtle, Dr. Wilson.

The feelings haven't yet landed.

March 30, 2017

Epilogue
The Loom of Resilience

> And so now, sharp tang
> of other waters known, I am afloat, skin-
> chilled, core-warm, aware of what lurks
> and grateful to trust and delight
> in our improbable buoyancy.
> – Elizabeth Bradfield

What is resilience? What allowed me to return from the heights of mania and the depths of the seclusion room, not only intact but with the pain and grief of the previous years more integrated with my essence? The root of the word is from Latin resilire, "to rebound, recoil," from re- "back" + salire "to jump, leap." The roots of words are akin to the roots of life itself: "In the beginning was the Word."[51] Resilience, a bouncing back like a coiled spring, like nature's spring from the seeming death of winter. In my own life this is not the first time I've experienced a dead end with seemingly little hope or joy; yet from each of these times, a new journey begins with all its difficulties, challenges, learning, and gifts.

Within our spiritual and, therefore, biological birthright lives the force I know as resilience: with time as an ally, jumping back into life, rebounding from what was suffered and endured. This grace is part of the irrepressible blessing of our life as human beings, spiritual beings here on earth. In the depths of my traumatic journey, following the unbridled mania and the repressive hospital experiences – when all was mostly dark, dull, and seemingly lost – it began to be clear that life and the divine had, in reality, never abandoned me, even when I felt thoroughly betrayed. Instead they silently waited until I could open to their quiet, faithful welcoming of my renewed being until I was once again ready to be in relationship. All that pain birthed a more integrated self: that fact still astounds me as nothing short of a miracle. Woven on the loom of resilience are hope and faith. As Brené Brown, the research professor and writer, reported in *The Gifts of Imperfection*, "Without exception, spirituality – the belief in connection, a power greater than self, and interconnections grounded in love and compassion – emerged as a component of resilience...."[52]

Small, significant experiences of the power of perseverance, courage, and faith have stuck with me over time. In 1985 I moved from New York City to Los Angeles. It wasn't planned. I was ejected from a psychotherapeutic cult I'd been part of for 12 years. Why and how that happened is subject for another book, perhaps, yet more difficult to write. What's relevant here is that in one of a handful of independent decisions I had made over the prior few years, I took the big leap to move to the other coast. Relieved to be out of the Group, it didn't take long for me to find a small group of friends: we danced in clubs, walked our dogs, hiked.

One typically radiant southern California spring day, a group of us went hiking in the mountains. Maybe it was the Westridge Trailhead; I'm not sure where we were. I knew a few of the others besides my new boyfriend Gordon and my roommate Susan. I had a dog for the first time in my life, Maggie, a black lab mix a little over a year old and a true companion. Maggie had never been in those mountains before either; she'd never been hiking before. She was keeping up and enjoying herself until we reached a small pond with a felled log across it. I was a little unsure of my own footing but made it across with a hand at the end from Gordon. The dogs would have to wade across; this was a first for Maggie. She wasn't too sure about this. I knew labs loved the water, and I coaxed her in. She started gingerly then slid, her expression quickly changing from genuine alarm to pure delight as she realized she could swim. She had that inbuilt capacity as we have inbuilt resilience. But that's not the whole story.

Once we reached the top of the trail, we rested in a glen enclosed by tall trees, whose dappled shade sheltered us from the heat of the afternoon sun. We lazily ate the lunch we had brought. I was annoyed by Gordon's flirting with one of the other women and got tired of waiting for everyone to finish. I wanted to be alone and said that we'd meet them back at the parking lot. I was certain I knew the way, just reversing our steps, so Maggie and I set off down the trail.

I jaunted, wanting to be the first down the mountain. I was exhilarated by the outdoors, by Maggie's swim, by the biting air and brilliant sunshine. We flew down the trail and out of the shady woods. Mountains and valleys, greenish brown and gnarly, spread out in the distance. But suddenly I realized I'd lost the trail! I tried going back but couldn't find it. I called out, "Hello," two, three times, as loud as I could, hoping my friends were close by. "Hello" changed to "Help," even louder, but I heard nothing but silence in response.

We would have to go straight down to the road, which I could see clearly below. I wondered how far away it was and how long it would take to get there. I took one step and then another, but I couldn't get a firm footing and found myself sliding, the gravelly earth giving way under my feet. What if I broke a leg? What if Maggie did? She was crying, her feet hot and maybe even cut from the burning, pebbly ground. I sat down to stop us. Then I stood and once again yelled for help at the top of my voice. Silence, an intermittent birdcall, a vulture circling ominously above in the steady blue. What if we burn up? I had a hat but not very much water left. What if the sun sets? How much time do we have left? I sat again, Maggie lying on my empty backpack to cool her paws. She stopped crying, but I started. I didn't know what to do. I was starting to panic when a voice from deep inside took charge: crying is not going to help. I was listening. Of course, that was true, and then, as if instinctively, I prayed, something I hadn't done in years. Needless to say, praying was not encouraged in a therapeutic cult. But Lord knows I needed help, and I asked for it: "Please God help Maggie and me down the mountain before the sun sets. Please help us find the parking lot with our friends. Please, somehow, show me how to help us."

Maggie was panting; I gave her some water in my palm. More comfortable now that her paws were off the hot gravel, she waited calmly for me to act. I was the human after all. Suddenly I had an idea. If I secured the cotton shirt, now tied around my waist, to the top strap of the backpack, I could make a kind of sled for Maggie to sit on. I could go down the mountain on my butt and control our speed with my hands and feet, as she followed in back of me. And that's what we did, slowly and steadily as I watched the sun dropping toward the horizon, my hands suffering little cuts from the tiny pebbles but nothing serious, my eyes on the road below. Were the others already at the parking lot? Were they looking for us? Did they realize we were lost? All we could do was to keep going. (If this had happened in the age of cell phones and there had been service in those hills, this whole life lesson would sadly have been missed.)

I could see the road approaching. But there was a band of white in the way. What was it? We continued sliding down until I stopped us just short of a field of hard, icy snow, glistening in the late afternoon sunshine. Snow, still here in the mountains in April! We had no choice but to go over it, though cautiously since it looked slippery. As soon as we hit the snowfield, we whipped over hills of ice on a mild rollercoaster ride, Maggie's ears blowing in the wind, me laughing with joy as we gathered speed. I have so much fear, I thought. What a ride! I couldn't control us and didn't want to. This was too much fun. I could see the end of the snow-ice coming to meet us, and we landed in a heap on dry earth, both intact. We were close to the road now, stood, and carefully scurried down. Within minutes someone stopped and gave us a ride back to the parking area, where my friends greeted us with great relief. My heart filled with gratitude for the lesson: for prayer that centered me, for the divine mystery, for the crazy ways life works.

We live the metaphors. We are brought to our knees – or in this story on my butt – until we experience the Truth that deep within our cells, within our most intimate being, resilience lives, hope lives. As we acknowledge our connection to the sacred within and around us, we find help and guidance, a reality that loves all things, including us. I am not forgotten. I am loved. Acknowledging and nurturing our intrinsic part of the wholeness furthers our capacity for resilience, for living well through life's inevitable "hurtles."

MANIA MYSTERIES: A GRIEF JOURNEY

Mania brought me to a new integration of self that I don't think I would have achieved otherwise. And I mean *me* with my individual particularities. I don't recommend mania as a path of self-development. Some of us, though, are donned with it: we carry the gene. How we wear its mantle makes all the difference. How our health and mental health caregivers and institutions see this experience matters. Could there be ways of caring that are less traumatizing? I say yes. There have to be. How our families and friends see us and help carry us means everything: not being judged, being treated with dignity while being protected, being seen for who we are intrinsically while witnessing the transformative power of the psychic storm and its aftermath. These are the blessings on the other side for me.

I hear many stories of people who are bipolar who cannot find their way through. It pains me: hospital experiences in which the individual is not seen, that remain primitive in many ways; drugs that don't work, that dull and destroy life force and the ability to think straight, to work right, to love right. I am not against psychotropic drugs any more, although I hope that better meds and treatment will be developed that give more people support and room for a fully lived life. I feel blessed that for now this drug is working for me. I still wonder if it must be forever, or is taking it the safer path, which may be enough reason to continue.

I am attentive to my relationship to the physical: to sleeping, eating, and exercise, making sure I keep my body as healthy as I can. Regardless, death will always be a destabilizer and community a support through the unraveling that death demands. So I will continue to build community in the organic ways that I am: intimacy and honesty in my primary relationships, circles of friends for fun and trusted sharing, Circles of Trust that feed my core self and offer times for discernment to others as well, church, choir, grief circles. I'm devoted to creating "islands of sanity" as Margaret Wheatley calls the kind of spaces and relationships we now need to foster. [53]

There will always be changes. Life is change: waves, some high, some low, some so big you have to hold your breath and go under until you can resurface, hoping there isn't another right behind, hoping someone is right there with you. Sometimes life's waves are gentle, the salt buoying us up. I'm clear we don't control any of it. I can, at least sometimes, control how I swim in it, and I know that I won't be alone in it, that I am part of the huge ocean of life. It is not an adversary even when darkness seems to reign. From the day alone along the shore of the Caribbean under blue benevolent skies and soaring gulls, I have walked blessed with a deeper acceptance of my pace, my path, my new way of being in the world.

"I am afloat," as the poet says. I'm in the flow of my life – "skin-chilled," awake; "core-warm," alive; "aware of what lurks" – in this tricky, intense time on our planet, burgeoning with needs and ripe with the potential for resiliency and love.

Notes

[1] William McDonald, M.D. and Laura Fochtmann, M.D., "What is Electroconvulsive therapy (ECT)?" American Psychiatric Association," January 2016, www.psychiatry.org/patients-families/ect.

[2] Eric Partridge, *Origins: A Short Etymological Dictionary of Modern English* (New York: Random House Value Publishing, 1988), 404. See the third definition of "mind": "Closely akin to Gr *menos* is Gr *mania*, madness, whence, via L, the E word. Whereas the derivative Gr adj *maniakos* becomes LL *maniacus*, whence MF-F *maniaque*, whence E *maniac*, the derivative adj *manikos* imm becomes *manic*...." It is interesting that buried more deeply in the etymology is this spiritual connection, perhaps to the ancient Greek mysteries: "6. Akin to Gr *mainesthai* and *mania* are Gr *mantis*, seer, and *manteia*, oracle, divination...."

[3] Robert Peng, *Qigong Ecstasy,* DVD (Boulder, CO: SoundsTrue.com, 2014). See www.robertpeng.com for more information.

[4] See www.couragerenewal.org. The Center for Courage & Renewal and its facilitators offer retreats, workshops, and other programs "to create a more just, compassionate and healthy world by nurturing personal and professional integrity and the courage to act on it."

[5] In 2013 Elizabeth Clemants and I co-founded Hidden Water. See www.hiddenwaternyc.com for more information about programs offered.

[6] See www.waldorfeducation.org/waldorf_education/lower_school. Waldorf education is a developmentally based and artistically infused worldwide school movement, initiated by Rudolf Steiner (1861-1925), the Austrian philosopher, esotericist, social reformer, and architect.

⁷ Therese Bimka is a spiritual counselor and psychotherapist. She is also the Director of the Interspiritual Counseling Program at One Spirit Learning Alliance. For more information about her diverse background and contact information, see www.theresebimka.com. The quote is from an email correspondence between us, which I use with her permission

⁸ This is from an email correspondence with Kate Musgrove, which I use with her permission.

⁹ This is from an email correspondence with Rona Gonzalez, which I use with her permission.

¹⁰ Laura Stokowski, RN, MS, "Alternatives to Restraint and Seclusion in Mental Health Settings: Questions and Answers From Psychiatric Nurse Experts," Medscape, May 03, 2007, www.medscape.com/viewarticle/555686.

¹¹ Rudolf Steiner, *Gospel of St. Mark*, Lecture 9, trans. Conrad Mainzer, ed. Stewart C. Easton (Great Barrington, MA: Steiner Books, 1990), 172. Steiner often lectured and wrote about "the turning point of time" or "cosmic evolution," a change for all humanity regardless of religion, race, and ethnicity, corresponding to the incarnation of the Christ being. This turning point in human evolution brought us from total separation from the spiritual world and connected us to a renewing impulse to rejoin with spirit consciously, leading to humanity's redeemed evolution. The above lecture is one source of further understanding.

¹² Steve Bressert, Ph.D., "Hypomanic Episode Symptoms," PsychCentral®, 2018, psychcentral.com/disorders/hypomanic-episode-symptoms/.

¹³ John Colapinto, "Lighting the Brain: Karl Deisseroth and the optogenetics breakthrough," *The New Yorker,* May 18, 2015, 83.

¹⁴ Colapinto, "Lighting the Brain," 83.

[15] Lynn Schneider, excerpt from an unpublished manuscript, *Close to the Bone*, which Lynn entrusted to me before her death in December 2012.

[16] Rudolf Steiner, *How to Know Higher Worlds: A Modern Path of Initiation*, trans. Christopher Banford (Hudson, NY: Anthroposophic Press, 1994). Anthoposophists are adherents of anthroposophy or spiritual science, the philosophy founded mostly by Steiner that attests to the human capacity to develop organs of perception into the spiritual world as clear and precise as science achieves in the physical world.

[17] Rudolf Steiner, *How to Know Higher Worlds*, 120. The "practice of the control of thoughts" is the first in a series of what are often called the six basic exercises.

[18] Cynthia Hoven, "Freebies," Eurythmy Online, 2014, www.eurythmyonline.com/freebies/. Eurythmy, one of the creative contributions of Rudolf Steiner, is an art of mindful movement. "I think speech" was one of the first exercises created for eurythmists.

[19] Rudolf Steiner, *How to Know Higher Worlds*, 122. In this version of these exercises, equanimity is the sixth.

[20] Stanislav Grof and Christina Grof, "Spiritual Emergency: Understanding Evolutionary Crisis," *Spiritual Emergency: When Personal Transformation Becomes a Crisis*, ed. Stanislav Grof, M.D. and Christina Grof (New York: Jeremy P. Tarcher/Putnam, 1989) 1-26.

[21] Psalm 23:4, *The Holy Bible*, King James Version (New York: American Bible Society: 1999).

[22] See www.gildasclubnyc.org for more information about the programs at Gilda's Club for those with cancer and their loved ones.

[23] Paul Pitchford, *Healing with Foods: Asian Traditions and Modern Nutrition* (Berkeley, CA: North Atlantic Books, 1993, 1996, 2002.)

[24] Mary Oliver, "The Summer's Day," *House of Light* (Boston: Beacon Press, 1990) 60.

[25] See www.nativeamericanchurches/the-sacrament-peyote-ceremony/ for more information about the peyote ceremony of the Native American Church.

[26] See www.umassmed.edu/cfm/ for more information about the work of Jon Kabat-Zinn, who created the Stress Reduction Clinic and the Center for Mindfulness in Medicine, Health Care, and Society at the University of Massachusetts Medical School.

[27] May Sarton, "Autumn Sonnets, #2," *May Sarton: Collected Poems, 1930-1973* (New York: W. W. Norton & Co., 1974) 385.

[28] Rudolf Steiner, *The Electric Doppelgänger: the Mystery of the Double in the Age of the Internet*, trans. Simon Luke Breslaw, ed. Andreas Neider (Forest Row, Sussex: Rudolf Steiner Press, 2016) 37.

[29] See www.spacialdynamics.com for more information about Spacial Dynamics. This form of movement was created by Jaimen McMillan and the Spacial Dynamics Institute and is inspired by anthroposophy and the work of Rudolf Steiner.

[30] R. D. (Ronald David) Laing, *Self and Others* (New York: Pantheon Books, 1969) 60.

[31] Seena B. Frost, *SoulCollage® Evolving: An Intuitive Collage Process for Self-Discovery and Community* (Santa Cruz, CA: Hanford Mead Publishers, Inc., 2010) and www.soulcollage.com/about-soulcollage. SoulCollage® is a creative collage process in which each person makes a deck of cards, each card representing a facet of their own personality or soul.

[32] See www.couragerenewal.org. The Circle of Trust® approach, according to the Center for Courage & Renewal website, "is distinguished by principles and practices intended to create a process of shared exploration—in retreats, programs and other settings—where people can find safe space to nurture personal and professional integrity and the courage to act on it."

[33] See www.warpaths2peacepipes.com/native-american-symbols/coyote-symbol.htm. The Indians of the Southwest, including the Navajo and the Zuni, experienced Coyote as a holy creator being who often played the trickster. Myths explaining why the world is riddled with mistakes show Coyote so engulfed in his own mischief and trickery that he would even trick himself. Coyote is also associated with spiritual healing. Wily and hard to discern, Coyote the trickster has a paradoxical nature, playful and unflinchingly unveiling the truth behind illusion in indirect and sometimes harrowing ways.

[34] R.D. (Ronald David) Laing, *Politics of Experience* (New York: Pantheon, 1983) 133.

[35] Psalm 23:4, *The Holy Bible,* King James Version (New York: American Bible Society: 1999).

[36] Lawrence Durrell, *Balthazar (Alexandria Quartet)* (New York: Penguin Books USA, 1991) 15.

[37] Walt Whitman, *Leaves of Grass: The Original 1885 Edition* (Nashville, TN: Sam Torode Book Arts, 2009) 63.

[38] Geri Larkin, Introduction to *The Chocolate Cake Sutra: Ingredients for a Sweet Life* (New York: HarperOne™, 2008) 5.

[39] Thich Nhat Hanh, *Teachings on Love* (Berkeley, CA: Parallax Press, 2007).

[40] May Sarton, "Now I Become Myself," *May Sarton: Collected Poems, 1930-1973* (New York: W. W. Norton & Co., 1974) 156.

[41] Elizabeth Lesser, *Broken Open: How Difficult Times Can Help Us Grow* (New York: Villard Books, 2005).

[42] Elizabeth Lesser, *Broken Open*, 63.

[43] See www.couragerenewal.org/about/mission. The mission of the Center for Courage & Renewal "is to create a more just, compassionate and healthy world by nurturing personal and professional integrity and the courage to act on it."

[44] See www.couragerenewal.org/clearnesscommittee/.

[45] See www.couragerenewal.org/touchstones/ for a list of the clear practices that facilitators of Courage & Renewal programs use "to help define clear boundaries for the circle of trust," the kind of practices "that help create safe space for the soul. They derive from the principles and practices of the Circle of Trust approach."

[46] See www.couragerenewal.org/democracy/ and Parker J. Palmer, *Healing the Heart of Democracy: The Courage to Create a Politics Worthy of the Human Spirit* (San Francisco: Jossey-Bass, 2011) 43-46. I offered a series of Healing the Heart of Democracy® circles in our local library; these were based on five habits of the heart that Parker J. Palmer explores in his inspiring 2011 book on our role as citizens.

[47] Debbie Hampton, "What Doesn't Kill You Makes You Stronger," The Best Brain Possible: Information and Inspiration for Anyone with a Brain, September 12, 2014, www.thebestbrainpossible.com/what-doesnt-kill-you-makes-you-stronger/.

[48] Wolfram von Eschenbach, *Parzival*, trans. Meredith Mustard and Charles E. Passage (New York: Vintage Books, 1961) 138.

[49] "JAK2 gene," NIH U.S. National Library of Medicine, Genetics Home Reference, 2018, ghr.nlm.nih.gov/gene/JAK2.

[50] "Somatic Experiencing (SE)," GoodTherapy.org®, www.goodtherapy.org/learn-about-therapy/types/somatic-experiencing. Also see the official website of Somatic Experiencing® at www.traumahealing.org. Therese was integrating SE™ into her practice. This approach was developed by Peter A. Levine, Ph.D. to help people address and process trauma effectively.

[51] John 1:1, *The Holy Bible,* King James Version (New York: American Bible Society: 1999).

[52] Brené Brown, *The Gifts of Imperfection* (Center City, MN: Hazelden, 2010) 64.

[53] Margaret J. Wheatley, *Who Do We Choose to Be? Facing Reality, Claiming Leadership, Restoring Sanity* (Oakland, CA: Berrett-Koehler Publishers, 2017) 4. Also see lecture during Meaning conference 2017, https://www.youtube.com/watch?v=LtaYNxp56gs.

Quote Sources

Prologue
Sendker, Jan-Philipp. *A Well-Tempered Heart.* Translated by Kevin Wiliarty. New York: Other Press, 2013, 36.

Part I: Mania
Gateley, Edwina. "Week 5." *A Mystical Heart: 52 Weeks in the Presence of God.* New York: The Crossroad Publishing Company, 1998, 22.

Chapter 4: Following the Tracks
Nepo, Mark. *The Book of Awakening.* Newburyport, MA: Red Wheel Weiser, LLC; 2000, 26.

Part II: Perspective
Réa, Rashani and Francis Weller. "Darkness and Duende" by Francis Weller. *The Threshold Between Loss and Revelation.* Na'alehu, HI: Sacred Spiral Press, 2017.

Chapter 8: Psychotherapy Before
Kumar, Sameet. *Grieving Mindfully: A Compassionate and Spiritual Guide to Coping with Loss.* Oakland, CA: New Harbinger Publications, 2005, 7.

Part III: A New Integration of Self
O'Donohue, John. "The Inner Landscape of Beauty." Interview by Krista Tippett. *On Being,* August 5, 2015. onbeing.org/programs/john-odonohue-the-inner-landscape-of-beauty/.

Chapter 9: Recovery and Resilience
Sendker, Jan-Philipp. *The Art of Hearing Heartbeats.* Translated by Kevin Wiliarty. New York: Other Press, 2006, 24.

Chapter 10: Psychotherapy and Other Self-Care
Laing, R.D. (Ronald David). Preface to the Pelican Edition (1965) to *The Divided Self: An Existential Study in Sanity and Madness.* London: Penguin Books, 1990, 12.

Chapter 17: Moving Forward
Safford, Victoria. *Walking Toward Morning: Meditations.* Boston: Skinner House Books, 2003, 12.

Chapter 20: After the Storm
The Holy Bible, New International Version. Grand Rapids: Zondervan House, 1984.

Chapter 21: Questions and Hope
Laing, R.D. (Ronald David) and Bob Mullan. Preface to *Mad to Be Normal: Conversations with R.D. Laing.* London: Free Association Books, 1995, vii.

Epilogue: The Loom of Resilience
Bradfield, Elizabeth. From "Learning to Swim." *Poem-a-Day*, The Academy of American Poets, June 12, 2017. https://www.poets.org/poetsorg/poem/learn-swim.

To Go Deeper

Parker J. Palmer and the Center for Courage & Renewal

Palmer, Parker J. *On the Brink of Everything*. Oakland, CA: Berrett-Koehler Publishers, 2018.
- . *The Courage to Teach*. 20th anniv. ed. San Francisco: Jossey-Bass, 2017.
- . *Healing the Heart of Democracy*. San Francisco: Jossey-Bass, 2011.
- . *The Promise of Paradox*. San Francisco: Jossey-Bass, 2010.
- . *A Hidden Wholeness*. San Francisco: Jossey-Bass, 2009.
- . *Let Your Life Speak*. San Francisco: Jossey-Bass, 2000.
- . *The Promise of Paradox*. San Francisco: Jossey-Bass, 2010.
- . *The Active Life*. San Francisco: Jossey-Bass, 1999.
- . *To Know as We Are Known*. New York: HarperCollins Publishers, 1993.
- . *The Company of Strangers*. New York: Crossroad, 1981.

Palmer, Parker J., Arthur Zajonc, and Megan Scribner. *The Heart of Higher Education*. San Francisco: Jossey-Bass, 2010.

Center for Courage & Renewal and Shelly L. Francis. *The Courage Way*. Oakland, CA: Berrett-Koehler Publishers, 2018.

For inspiration from Courage & Renewal facilitators, also see:
Kirkridge Fellows. *Thin Places: Seeding the Courage to Live in a Divided World*. Ed. Sally Z. Hare and Megan LeBoutillier. Pawley's Island, SC: Prose Press, 2014.

The Writers Circle of Trust. *Let the Beauty We Love Be What We Do: Stories of Living Divided No More*. Ed. Sally Z. Hare and Megan LeBoutillier. Pawley's Island, SC: Prose Press, 2014.

The Grief Process

Cacciatore, Joanne. *Bearing the Unbearable: Love, Loss, and the Heartbreaking Path of Grief*. Somerville, MA: Wisdom Publications, 2017.

Jamison, Kay Redfield. *Nothing Was the Same*. New York: Vintage Books, 2011.

Kumar, Sameet. *Grieving Mindfully: A Compassionate and Spiritual Guide to Coping with Loss*. Oakland, CA: New Harbinger Publications, 2005.

Réa, Rashani and Francis Weller. *The Threshold Between Loss and Revelation*. Na'alehu, HI: Sacred Spiral Press, 2017.

Richardson, Jan. *The Cure for Sorrow: A Book of Blessings for Times of Grief*. Orlando, FL: Wanton Gospeller Press, 2016.

Weller, Francis. *The Wild Edge of Sorrow: Rituals of Renewal and the Sacred Work of Grief*. Berkeley: North Atlantic Books, 2013.

Mania and Bipolar Disorder

Jamison, Kay Redfield. *Robert Lowell, Setting the River on Fire: A Study of Genius, Mania, and Character*. New York: Vintage Books, 2017.

–. *An Unquiet Mind: A Memoir of Moods and Madness.* New York: Vintage Books, 1996.

– *Touched with Fire: Manic Depressive Illness and the Artistic Temperament.* New York: Free Press Paperbacks, 1993.

Restorative Justice, including Peacemaking Circles and Other Circle Forms

Baldwin, Christina and Ann Linnea. *The Circle Way: A Leader in Every Chair.* Oakland, CA: Berrett-Koehler Publishers, 2010.

Baldwin, Christina. *Calling the Circle: The First and Future Culture.* New York: Bantam New Age Books, 1998.

Ball, Jennifer, Wayne Caldwell, and Kay Pranis. *Doing Democracy with Circles: Engaging Communities in Public Planning.* St. Paul: Living Justice Press, 2010.

Boyes-Watson, Carolyn. *Peacemaking Circles & Urban Youth.* St. Paul: Living Justice Press, 2008.

Boyes-Watson, Carolyn and Kay Pranis. *Heart of Hope: A Guide for Using Peacemaking Circles to Develop Emotional Literacy, Promote Healing & Build Healthy Relationships.* St. Paul: Living Justice Press, 2010.

Brown, Juanita with David Isaacs and the World Café Community. *The World Café: Shaping Our Futures Through Conversations That Matter.* Oakland, CA: Berrett-Koehler Publishers, 2005.

Pranis, Kay. *The Little Book of Circle Processes: A New/Old Approach to Peacemaking*. Intercourse, PA: Good Books, 2005.

Pranis, Kay, Mark Wedge, and Barry Stuart. *Peacemaking Circles: From Conflict to Community*. St. Paul: Living Justice Press, 2003.

Zehr, Howard. *The Little Book of Restorative Justice*. Intercourse, PA: Good Books, 2002.

See https://www.communityconferencing.org/ for information about Community Conferencing Center in Baltimore, Maryland.

Anthroposophy

Lipson, Michael. *Stairway of Surprise: Six Steps to a Creative Life*. Hudson, NY: Anthroposophic Press, 2002.
— . *Group Meditation*. Great Barrington, MA: SteinerBooks, 2011.

Schaefer, Signe. *Why On Earth?: Biography and the Practice of Human Becoming*. Great Barrington, MA: SteinerBooks, 2013.

Steiner, Rudolf. *Anthroposophy in Everyday Life*. Hudson, NY: Anthroposophic Press, 1995.
— . *How to Know Higher Worlds: A Modern Path of Initiation*. Trans. Christopher Bamford. Hudson, NY: Anthroposophic Press, 1994.
— . *Intuitive Thinking as a Spiritual Path: A Philosophy of Freedom*. Trans. Michael Lipson. Hudson, NY: Anthroposophic Press, 1995.
— . *An Outline of Esoteric Science*. Trans. Catherine E.

Creeger. Hudson, NY: Anthroposophic Press, 1997.
– . *The Philosophy of Freedom: the Basis for a Modern World Conception.* Trans. Michael Wilson. Great Barrington, MA: SteinerBooks, 2011.
– . *Start Now! A Book of Soul and Spiritual Exercises.* Ed. Christopher Bamford. Great Barrington, MA: SteinerBooks, 2002.
– . *Staying Connected: How to Continue Your Relationship with Those Who Have Died.* Hudson, NY: Anthroposophic Press, 1999.
– . *Theosophy: An Introduction to the Spiritual Processes in Human Life and in the Cosmos.* Trans. Catherine E. Creeger. Hudson, NY: Anthroposophic Press, 1994.

Waldorf Education

Pedagogical Section Council. *The Seven Core Principles of Waldorf Education.* Ed. Elan Leibner. Chatham, NY: Waldorf Publications, 2017.

Petrasch, Jack. *Understanding Waldorf Education: Teaching from the Inside Out.* Beltsville, MD: Gryphon House, 2002, 2009.

Steiner, Rudolf . *Balance in Teaching.* Trans. Rene M. Querido. Great Barrington, MA: SteinerBooks, 2007.
– . *The Child's Changing Consciousness.* Trans. Roland Everett. Hudson, NY: Anthroposophic Press, 1996.
– . *The Education of the Child.* Trans. Robert F. Lathe, Nancy Parsons Whittaker, George Adams, and Mary Adams. Hudson, NY: Anthroposophic Press, 1996.
– . *The Kingdom of Childhood.* Trans. Helen Fox. Hudson, NY: Anthroposophic Press, 1995.

Gratitudes

Out of the pain and confusion of loss came a psychic experience that shocked my family, friends, and most of all me. It took me on a journey that I neither wanted nor could avoid. I first want to thank Ina and Ronnie Denburg, Rona Gonzalez, and Kate Musgrove, who took time from their busy lives to be with me when we needed them; also Eric Baylin and Diane Berke, who with understanding and grace stepped in to facilitate when I couldn't.

In the wake of the mania and hospitalizations, as I recovered on many levels, I wrote. I have always been a writer, journaling as a way to process my life and its lessons. So, of course, I began writing to understand what I'd been through and to externalize the images haunting me. Satisfaction, integration, and insight came through the act of writing. For this I am grateful.

As the months went on, Therese Bimka, my psychotherapist, repeatedly suggested I was writing a book, often stating that my experience could be helpful to others. I thank her for seeing the potential without ever having read a word. Her encouragement over the four years in which I was in therapy with her will always be deeply appreciated. I also can't thank her enough for being with me before, during, and after the psychotic break – without judgment, with my well being always uppermost, offering the great gift of dependably seeing the highest in me. I am also grateful to my two expert, compassionate physicians, true healers, one who first met me in the heights and the other in the depths: Dr. Kenneth Wilson and Dr. Alan Coffino. They continue to help me maintain biochemical balance.

I am grateful to the friends who over the four years of my writing this book either read sections or listened with enthusiasm to my ideas and process, tending its gestation along with me: Therese Balagna, Matthew Burns, Walter Brett, Jenna Dalton, Joan Franklin, Liz Faulkner, Rev. Thom Feit, Rona Gonzalez, Dena Malon, Ashley Mayne, Kate Musgrove, Gigi Oppenheimer, Christine Shakespeare, Judy and Jay Spica, Kathleen and Charles Wellcome. I want to especially thank Deborah Falk, the first person to read the entire manuscript. Maria Forrest, the first "stranger" to read the book, offered a most-needed perspective at just the right time.

The love of my life, Wil Greenstreet, has been an incredible support as this book came to birth. He has read it many times and helped with editing and proofreading. Morgan Greenstreet offered helpful editing suggestions.

Sally Hare, Caroline Fairless, and Carol Kortsch, all fellow Courage & Renewal facilitators, were encouraging and helpful in my decision to publish with Prose Press. Gratitude for all the help offered by Bob O'Brien with the publishing process. I was truly moved by David Lorenz Winston's generosity when he offered his exquisite photograph for the cover as a gift.

Last but certainly not least, I am unendingly grateful to my mother Shirlee Schneider, whose faithful love has always awed me, and to Wil and Morgan, who were there with and for me during one of the most harrowing experiences of my life, and whose love endures.

About the Author

Cat Greenstreet, M.Ed. has been facilitating Courage & Renewal® retreats, using the Circle of Trust® approach, for teachers, clergy, healthcare professionals, and others since 2006. She was an educator for 30 years and devoted the last 20 of those to Waldorf education. She previously taught English and writing in high school and colleges throughout the New York metropolitan area, and worked in business as a technical writer.

Cat also studied mediation and restorative justice circle practices, especially Peacemaking Circles with Kay Pranis. With Elizabeth Clemants, a shaman and mediator, Cat co-founded Hidden Water, a restorative justice program designed to help individuals heal from the devastating impact of child sexual abuse within a family system. A thread through all of Cat's work has been creating spaces in which people of all ages can be in touch with their core selves, heal, and realize their full potential. Besides writing, Cat's other creative outlets are gardening, singing in a choir, knitting hats for friends and the homeless, and playing the electric bass. She lives in the Mid-Hudson Valley with her husband Wil.

CAT GREENSTREET

Continuation of the copyright page:

"Learning to Swim" by Elizabeth Bradfield. Copyright © 2017. Used by permission of Elizabeth Bradfield.

Excerpt from *The Gifts of Imperfection* by Brené Brown. Copyright © 2010. Used by permission of Brené Brown.

Excerpt from May 18, 2015, *The New Yorker*, page 83 by John Colapinto. Used by permission of John Colapinto/The New Yorker © Conde Nast.

Excerpt from "Week 5" from *A Mystical Heart: 52 Weeks in the Presence of God* by Edwina Gateley. Copyright © 1998. Used by permission of Edwina Gateley.

Excerpt from "Preface" from *Mad to Be Normal: Conversations with R.D. Laing* by R.D. Laing and Bob Mullan. Copyright © 1995. Used by permission of Free Association Books.

The Chocolate Cake Sutra by Geri Larkin. Copyright © 2008. Used by permission of HarperCollins Publishers.

The Book of Awakening © 2000 by Mark Nepo. Used with permission from Red Wheel Weiser, LLC, Newburyport, MA www.redwheelweiser.com.

Excerpt from *Walking Toward Morning: Meditations* by Victoria Safford. Copyright © 2003. Used by permission of Victoria Safford.

Excerpt from "The Autumn Sonnets, #2" and "Now I Become Myself." Copyright © 1972 by May Sarton, from COLLECTED POEMS 1930-1993 by May Sarton. Used by permission of W. W. Norton & Company, Inc.

"The Autumn Sonnets #2" and "Now I Become Myself" by May Sarton (Copyright © May Sarton). Reproduced by permission of A.M. Heath & Co Ltd.

Excerpt on page 36 from *A Well-tempered Heart* by Jan-Philipp Sendker, translated from the German by Kevin Wiliarty. Translation copyright © 2013. Reprinted by permission of Other Press, LLC.

Excerpt on page 24 from *The Art of Hearing Heartbeats* by Jan-Philipp Sendker, translated from the German by Kevin Wiliarty. Translation copyright © 2006. Reprinted by permission of Other Press, LLC.

Excerpt from "Darkness and Duende" by Francis Weller from *The Threshold Between Loss and* Revelation by Rashani Réa and Francis Weller. Copyright © 2017. Used by permission of Francis Weller.

www.ingramcontent.com/pod-product-compliance
Lightning Source LLC
Chambersburg PA
CBHW021139080526
44588CB00008B/122